Theological Method

A GUIDE FOR THE PERPLEXED

Theological Method

PAUL L. ALLEN

t&t clark

Published by T&T Clark International

A Continuum Imprint

The Tower Building	80 Maiden Lane
11 York Road	Suite 704
London	New York
SE1 7NX	NY 10038

www.continuumbooks.com

British Library Cataloguing-in-Publication Data
A catalogue record for this book is available from the British Library

ISBN: HB: 978-0-5670-1947-9
PB: 978-0-5671-1908-7

Typeset by Deanta Global Publishing Services, Chennai, India
Printed and bound in India

CONTENTS

ACKNOWLEDGEMENTS

First, I want to thank T&T Clark, especially Tom Kraft, whose patience and forbearance has been a source of great serenity and confidence. I want also to thank Kathryn Sawyer, who helped me at the beginning stages of research for the first part of the book. Her timely management of library resources and her deft touch with respect to annotations on certain material were crucial in the early stages.

I want to extend a heartfelt thanks to the friars and staff of Blackfriars Hall, especially Regent Fr. Richard Finn, O.P. and Vice Regent Fr. Richard Conrad, O.P., each of whose gift of hospitality was a treat. Thanks to various other members of the Dominican Priory of the Holy Ghost in Oxford, for their beautiful liturgies and the friendships that we sustained over a few months while my family and I were in Oxford and while I ensconced myself in the library. Thanks, too, must go to the staff at the Faculty of Theology Library and the Bodleian Library. Heartfelt thanks are also due to David Graham, Provost of Concordia University, who approved the six-month sabbatical during which much of the research and writing of this book took place. I remain very grateful for the support made available during the time spent in Oxford.

I want to thank very much the following persons whose various comments aided the book's emergence in vital ways: Daniel J. R. Kirk, Mark Scott, Matthew Anderson and Jason Zuidema. Thanks are also due to members of the 2011 Method Seminar for their comments on a draft of Chapter Seven. Needless to say, any errors of thinking that are reflected in this text are mine alone.

Most of all, I am grateful to my wife Monica and our two children, Jeremy and Sarah, whose patience, joy and sense of what is important are my guides. This book is dedicated to them.

PREFACE

This book was generated by two causes, as Aristotle might say – a primary and a secondary. Directly, I chanced upon T&T Clark's search for titles in their *Guide for the Perplexed* series while browsing Ben Myers's indispensable and winsome 'Faith & Theology' blog in 2008. This coincided with some substantial misgivings I had been having at that time over how to structure the graduate course in theological method that I taught every other year through my department. It struck me then that students studying theological method are in need of material that brings together three things. First, a reflection on the important methodical developments in the history of theology is required. Second, a substantial yet not overwhelming presentation of philosophical *topoi* relevant to the study of theology is needed, a kind of reading and discussion of theological *prolegomena*. And, third, students of theological method need to read a great book, or at least part thereof, dealing with theological method which can transform their own thinking onto a radically new horizon of understanding.

My problem at that time was that the students were getting the third element by reading Lonergan's *Method in Theology* but not the first two elements. Many students have been riveted by a reading of Lonergan's *Method in Theology*, which held out the promise of an explanatory scheme to account for an incredible range of theological material, but some students were not persuaded by what appeared to be an overly abstract presentation of a system that seemed almost too neat to be true. But even for the majority of students who were impressed by the scale of Lonergan's accomplishment, it was still apparent to me that without some greater sense of the historical parameters around which theological method is circumscribed, a familiarity with some, or even all, of Lonergan's great book could not serve as a satisfactory substitute. What was needed somehow was a more rounded appreciation of just what reflection on practising theology means. Hence, I speculated about whether it would be possible to describe, in a relatively brief format, just those very parameters of theological method in a way that might lead – perhaps not inexorably but at least smoothly – into the kinds of questions and solutions that Lonergan offers like no one else.

Thus, in this book, the main objective is to survey and analyse the history of Christian reflection regarding *how* we speak of God and the life of the world in relation to God. By no means can a single volume cover even the most important figures, church traditions or theological movements in this respect. But it is my hope that this book might serve as a bridge to the more extensive engagements with theological method that might be undertaken subsequent to a reading of this expository account. Since this book deals with the first element of describing the ways that theologians have ordered theology, I do not deal with the more formidable introduction to philosophy that is no doubt a necessary aid in understanding theological method. Nor do I engage in extensive discussion of Lonergan's own positions on theological method, as appealing as that was to attempt.

Nevertheless, there is some analysis of figures and texts employed with the help of Lonergan's insights, which are kept at some distance from the immediate task at hand. Particularly when it is apparent to me that theological method has run into some dead ends or limitations of some kind, I tend to mention an aspect of Lonergan's work that is germane to a diagnosis of that limitation. But, given the relative brevity of this book and its veritable fountain of possibilities lurking at every turn, I severely limit the ways I introduce Lonergan in order to do justice to both the material at hand and thereby retain the fast clip in which material is introduced. In addition to which, I might add, there is a considerable secondary literature available on Lonergan's theological method. I have no wish to duplicate that material here. Nevertheless, I am convinced that some of the secondary material in Lonergan studies is in need of complementary insights and judgements from a deeper engagement with the Christian tradition as such, but this work can only begin to indicate ways forwards in that vast and comprehensive task. This book does not substitute for a presentation of the relationships between philosophy and theology – Diogenes Allen's *Philosophy for Understanding Theology*, 2nd edition (Nashville, Tenn.: Westminster John Knox Press, 2007), is an ideal text that meets that particular objective. What this book does do is provide a wide-angle lens on the horizon of Christian theology, with the peaks and valleys of theological method revealed in cursory snapshots over the bulk of its 2000-year history.

Introduction: Is there a theological epistemology?

There are many books about theology which refer to how theological claims are made; that is, to theological method. These books demonstrate *how* thinkers think about God and related themes. However, far fewer books deal with methodology as a topic unto itself, and there are some good reasons for this relative neglect. One positive reason for this neglect is that theologians are justifiably more interested in the contents of theology: God, salvation, biblical interpretation, natural theology, the historical Jesus and so forth. The negative reason for the neglect of theological method lies in the belief that theological method is uninteresting or too philosophical, or both. As one cynic once put it, clarifying one's theological methodology instead of doing theology is like sharpening a knife without cutting into anything. An implicit objective of this book, therefore, is to challenge the belief that thinking about method is dull or irrelevant. The sharpness of one's knife determines how well one is able to cut. If one's theological method is consciously chosen, then the scope and precision of the theological claims being made are bound to be clearer.

It is evident from a survey of contemporary theology that discussions of method are becoming increasingly urgent. This might appear to be an exaggeration. But, the evidence suggests two contradictory trends over the past few decades: there has been, on the one hand, an ongoing high level academic engagement with the topic of theological method, especially since the mid-twentieth century. Yet, it is becoming increasingly clear that the ongoing conversation has not resolved to anyone's clear satisfaction the question of whether one method is better than another.

The explicit objective of this book is to survey and analyse the theological methods evident in a historically diverse range of figures of the Christian tradition. It would be impossible to provide a comprehensive account of theological method within the space of these covers. That would take a multi-volume encyclopaedia to fulfill. This book seeks to achieve a more modest goal, which is to enliven and probe the key writings and figures of the Christian tradition for evidence of theological method.

The goal here is to give the reader 'extensive glimpses' into the craft of Christian theology over much of its 2000-year history. Such an outline is now made much more feasible because of several giant leaps in understanding about methodology that have been introduced by certain theological and philosophical giants over the past 75 years, and whose names will grace these pages at several points. I am referring, for instance, to the legacies of Bernard Lonergan, Rudolf Bultmann and Karl Barth.

It is now a common belief that the discipline of theology has been sidelined in Western culture for two major reasons. First, there are the practical effects stemming from the rise in agnosticism and atheism, testimony to a fairly widespread scepticism concerning the plausibility of God. This 'metaphysical' scepticism is linked to empiricism, the epistemological view that knowledge is that which is known only through the five senses. Scepticism over God's existence is also associated with the relative decline in the centrality of theological studies in Western universities. Second, there continues to grow a diversity of theological methods, owing to different interpretations of theological sources, despite more recent attempts to render theological coherence through fresh reconsiderations (see Chapter Eight). This is nothing new, because theology has always been practised in diverse ways. What is still relatively new, however, is the extent to which the viability of certain theological sources is contested.

Prior to the sixteenth century, the debate which preoccupied theologians concerned the relationship between two sources: scripture and tradition. The Protestant Reformation introduced a new distance between Christian thought and philosophical reason.

The reaction to Enlightenment reason and industrial, planned economic forms of society in turn brought an explicit attention to human experience as a source for theology. This turn is reflected in the writings of Friedrich Schleiermacher (1768–1834), whose contribution we will examine in some detail in Chapter Six. Since the rise of liberal Protestantism in the late nineteenth century, the writings of Bernard Lonergan, Paul Tillich, Rudolf Bultmann and – to some extent – philosopher Hans-Georg Gadamer, Christian theology has become more preoccupied with method. As a result, it is more self-aware as a discipline. Along the way, a great deal of thought has gone into the relationship between theology and the natural sciences. On one side, figures such as Karl Barth, Dietrich Bonhoeffer, Karl Rahner, existentialist theologians like John Macquarrie and liberation theologians, have pushed for a theological agenda which makes salvation history, biblical texts and personal experience the loci of concern. On the other hand, Lonergan and contemporary theologians such as Wolfhart Pannenberg, Alister E. McGrath and J. Wentzel van Huyssteen have made a theological engagement with science and philosophy central to their approaches. More recently still, there has been a turning away from methodological concerns as the struggle between contested epistemologies dies down.

Immanuel Kant (1724–1804) is regarded as the most important Enlightenment philosopher whose interpretation of epistemology has fundamentally affected how theologians and church officials do theology. For Kant, there are two basic kinds of knowledge. The first kind is scientific knowledge, which Kant conceived as knowledge derived through the senses. The second is metaphysical knowledge, which for him meant specifically three things: God, human freedom and human immortality. For Kant, we do not possess certainty that our senses or our minds provide objectively – apart from the categories through which our minds operate. Kant's epistemology was widely welcomed, especially in Protestant areas of continental Europe, where it was interpreted as a philosophical justification for theological knowledge, protected from the critiques of science and rationalism, or so it was thought. Similar efforts occurred later in the Catholic world in the nineteenth and twentieth centuries and, to some extent, more recently in the world of Eastern Orthodox theology.

One thorny issue which confronts the student of theology is to what extent theological method needs to be articulated in 'purely' rational terms. The most profound difficulty with regards to a systematic theology and method is the tendency to over-abstraction. The concern over the relationship between the demands of rationality and the distinctive spiritual basis for theological reflection is a constant methodological worry. Mark McIntosh has articulated this problem rather accurately:

> theology without spirituality becomes ever more methodologically refined but unable to know or speak of the very mysteries at the heart of Christianity, and spirituality without theology becomes rootless, easily hijacked by individualistic consumerism . . . Part of the difficulty is that the ramifications of such a divorce are obscure until one sees the proper integrity of contemplative encounter and dogmatic theology; for apart from their mutual interaction the true functioning of each becomes easily misconceived.[1]

Spiritual or religious experience is often cited by theologians to differentiate theological reflection from other forms of reflection or knowledge. The acts of praying, worship or contemplation are the kinds of acts that put into question a strictly epistemological approach to theological methodology. Then again, it does depend on how epistemology is understood in the first place, and it is this philosophical question that is much disputed. It should not be surprising that this dispute has profound theological implications.

Motivated by the concern for truth and coherence, most theologians would allow philosophy's influence while denying ultimate authority to philosophy over properly theological problems and theological responses. This book will trace the efforts of various theologians to convey meaning based on a range of specific theological sources mindful of this philosophical influence. Some of these figures draw on philosophy explicitly, while others do not. There are five identifiable methodological issues that will enter into the discussion with varying degrees of significance for the texts and figures involved. Apart from philosophy, there is also the issue of criteria for making theological claims, the relative weight attached to sources (the Bible, experience, tradition and reason), the nature of the theological task overall and the procedure that one follows. Of course, these methodological issues are interrelated; but, as we will see, some of these issues are highlighted differently, depending on the figure or text under analysis.

For now, there are four preliminary notions that concern every theologian in regards to method: the term method itself, hermeneutics, revelation and tradition. Method and hermeneutics are general terms, while revelation and tradition are regarded as specific theological terms. I will begin with a summary of the problem of method itself, its distinct philosophical elements and theological landscape.

Method

Theology was famously identified as the 'queen of the sciences' in the medieval period. This phrase summarizes an ideal from one historical epoch, and it is justly associated with the approach of Thomas Aquinas, who sought to render faith coherent with reason. By contrast, in ancient Greek thought, theology did not exist in the same way. Aristotle practised a very different form of 'theology', at least if we are to believe a ninth-century Arabic translation of a set of works by Plotinus entitled *The Theology of Aristotle*. However, it would be more accurate to say that the ancient Greeks practised speculative metaphysics, not theology, at least as Christians understand the term.

The distinction is based on how we assess the quest to articulate the nature of being, the divine 'principle' 'lying behind' the reality of the visible universe. Ancient philosophy endorses this task, even though philosophers disagreed on the terms by which it should be pursued. In Plato's *Timaeus*, for instance, the creator agent, known as the Artisan, is inferred from the regularity, order and goodness of the universe. There is no special method outlined to arrive at this inference. The *Timaeus* is unique among Plato's works for its overtly mythological character, yet it is consistent with other ancient texts that speak of a Godlike being in non-analytical terms. Aristotle himself speaks of a Godlike being in terms of first cause or unmoved mover. Plato contrasts an immutable, unknowable and inaccessible God with the worldly change that is methodologically analysed through an understanding of how we know reality.

With the Greek philosophical approach to God, we notice distinct differences with Christian theology. Theology is only partly dependent upon the abstract analysis of the philosophical quest for wisdom or the precise basis for inferring to an abstract being.

Christian theology is much more dependent upon an interpretation of a set of contingent events in history, beginning with the testimony of the preaching of Jesus of Nazareth and his death and resurrection. Central to Christian theology, as a whole, is the history of Israel, a history which continues to be of ongoing significance for understanding Jesus, and the relationship between the Old and New Testaments and the ongoing experience of God within contemporary Judaism, not to mention the doctrinal heritage of the Christian tradition. In fact, the twentieth-century discoveries into the historical Jesus have revolved around a highly methodological question: *how* do Christian theologians understand Jesus and his role in winning salvation from among sometimes divergent narratives and sources? This question bears on the understanding of sources and the relationship between an understanding of the truth and the relative importance of these sources to each other. There is a more fundamental question that pertains to the meaning of salvation. What does salvation mean, and will biblical sources be able to fully answer that question when interpreted rightly?

Having a method is presumed to constitute a superior form of inquiry since the Enlightenment and, especially, since Descartes' great work the *Discourse on Method*, published in 1637, was popularly received in European universities. In this work and others like it, the discovery of method was an embrace of a 'prejudice against prejudice', a move against the bias Descartes perceived on the part of the teachings of the Christian church and the prejudice that this tradition thus fostered. According to Descartes's sense of method, historical Christian theology is antithetical towards methodology; but Descartes's understanding of method proceeds according to doubting everything except the fact of one's own thinking. Is this correct?

Beginning in rudimentary ways, Greek philosophers embraced certain methodological priorities – for instance, in Aristotle's repeated insistence on the observation of things. *Epistêmê*, as the Greeks called knowledge, is not equivalent to the established methods employed by modern scientists. Modern science typically holds up the ideal of precise observation, hypothesis and verification, usually in that order. Yet without the modern stress on hypothetical claims, ancient thinkers, including Christian theologians, turned to reason to correlate and corroborate certain experiences and theological claims. Correlation is expressed at numerous points in the New

Testament between an interpretation of Jesus and a description of God or an Old Testament prophecy that is already known. By the fourth century, the choice to include in the Christian biblical canon four gospels rather than one gospel itself represents an implicit methodology of correlation. Different interpretations of several disciples' experience of Jesus (and the churches with which some of them were individually associated) with the person, message and work of Jesus Christ are forced to co-exist.

There is a difference, of course, between an implicit method and an explicit method. Thanks to Descartes, Kant and many more philosophers and theologians, Christian theology has devoted increasing attention to being explicitly methodological. Being explicitly methodological can mean that we come to see earlier theological claims differently from those who made the claims originally. This is especially true of Christian theology, which is an interpretation of Jewish claims about God. For instance, Janet Soskice notes that 'The christological question for the early Christians, as they began to pray to Jesus and see in him their salvation, was not about how Jesus was different from the God of Israel but how could he be *the same*.'[2] This observation shows effectively just how method enters into every question and problem of contemporary theology. First, Soskice invokes the early Christians: understanding how theology was carried out in the past – theology's history – has direct implications for engaging in theological reflection today. We shall touch on this when speaking of the role of tradition as a theological source. Method in Christian theology is not necessarily a 'prejudice against prejudice', but perhaps a prejudice against pure novelty. Second, Soskice alludes to the self-perception of Christians in relation to their ancestors in faith: Jews and Judaism. Much depends on whether Christians presuppose their theology as continuous with Judaism or opposed to it. In the past, some Christians believed that their claims were obviously in contrast with those of Judaism, not continuous with the faith of Israel. As we will see in Chapter One, understanding Paul's theology in the New Testament is not just an understanding of Paul's continuity with Judaism, it is a continuity that is methodologically established by Paul himself. As biblical scholars have shown, understanding Paul's theology in this way is a function of our application of better methodologies to the task of understanding the New Testament texts and Paul's religious and social world.

Bernard Lonergan develops his own understanding of method in theology in a very precise way. It is worth keeping in mind his formulation for using the word 'method'. For Lonergan, method is 'a normative pattern of recurrent and related operations yielding cumulative and progressive results'.[3] In theology, as with any other discipline, it is important to understand what goes into the act of understanding. Otherwise we are vulnerable to constructing theological arguments that stand in danger of being arbitrary, or at least disconnected, from other theological claims. Yet the demands of method are hard. Consistency, as one criterion by which a method is successfully applied in a discipline, is difficult to achieve.

A theologian is obliged to affirm that it is the subject matter which he or she is probing that guides the methods employed to understand that subject matter. This is as true in chemistry as it is in theology. In theology, the subject matter seems easy to define – namely, God – and God is mediated to the theologian through texts, language and traditions as a chemical problem is mediated to the chemist through the intelligibility of chemical equations, the template of the periodic table and the instrumentation of the laboratory. Theology historically identifies four sources of mediation between the theologian and God: holy scripture, tradition, experience and reason. The idea that the subject matter determines the method is an ancient idea. Aristotle articulated this realist doctrine when he stated: 'the subject itself led them to the right road and guided their inquiry . . . Thinkers were carried along by truth itself.'[4] The difficulty, then, arises in assessing the competing claims from these four sources, in addition to the claims that impinge on theology from other disciplines and the cultural context of the theologian.

One thinker who has identified the importance of truth as a quest that survives and informs the critical analysis of various philosophies is Hans-Georg Gadamer. In his landmark book *Truth and Method*, Gadamer proposed a second meta-category in the search for truth. Apart from the methods of the sciences, there is, in the humanities, the educational process known by the German word *Bildung* or 'formation'. Through his emphasis upon 'Bildung', Gadamer indicates that 'method' is an inadequate way to speak about certain procedures of knowing, including those of theology. He also wants to ensure that in the humanities, the focus be maintained on true subjectivity, with a person's capacity and willingness to understand their own prejudices and limitations. It is false, asserts Gadamer, for practitioners in the humanities to imitate scientific objectivity. In theology, a deployment of scientific method would imply that God is a being to be discovered – a negative claim, as Karl Barth insists. With Gadamer, theologians should not pursue a pure method so much as they should 'watch their language around God', as the saying goes.

Readers not already familiar with the ways of theology may expect to find, in this book, that theological reflection is 'scientific' or 'methodological' *analogously* speaking. This argument for some basic analogy between theological method and other methods is a way of describing Bernard Lonergan's view. More importantly, evidence for this view can be found in various ways throughout Christian theological history. That is, there are certain lines of reasoning, inferences and techniques that historical representatives of Christian theology have typically employed. Moreover, there have been discernible developments in how Christian theologians have practised theology. Allegorical ways of interpretation have become sparser over time, although it is possible to find defences of allegorization among contemporary theologians.[5] By and large, Christian theologians do not believe that the terms and relations of scientific method can produce the terms and relations of Christian thought. But, scientific method is itself not univocal; it is a way of describing sets of reasonable procedures. Philosophers have frequently expressed human reason as a universal phenomenon, although this assertion is controversial for postmodernists. To the extent that theologians have incorporated reason into theological arguments, theology has been obliged to think methodologically.

This is particularly noticeable among biblical scholars. Textual criticism, source criticism, form criticism and the newer methods of socio-rhetorical and reader-response methods vie for allegiance among biblical theologians. These methods can be grouped according to two types: synchronic and diachronic, those approaches that deal with the narrative structure of the text, and with the historical contexts of the text, respectively. As a result of this methodological pluralism, there is a profound disagreement between those who, for example, take the primacy of the intended meaning of the author of a text to be theologically relevant versus literary critics and others who take the primacy of the text in itself as theologically relevant. A great deal hangs on this hermeneutical choice. The former choice means encountering the text and allowing the author's intentions (of one author or many, edited or not) to shape the reader's self-understanding and his or her understanding of God. The second choice suggests no self-involvement or self-implication beyond a confidence in one's rational capacities and analytical skills as they are directed towards the text. The methodological dispute is most acutely felt in the contemporary academy between biblical scholars who are dedicated to the standard range of exegetical methods and theologians who seek to revive the practice of a theological interpretation of the biblical texts.[6] On the surface, this dispute over how to interpret the biblical text concerns whether the text can or should be measured by criteria based in self-involvement. Many biblical scholars feel that involving one's own theological ideas in biblical interpretation violates the principle of avoiding prejudice in the interpretation of the text. Theological interpreters feel that any method that leaves the self out of the picture is methodologically obdurate. For the latter group, an approach to biblical texts that denies a role for self-involvement is itself prejudicial. As we will see from Lonergan's understanding of method, there is not necessarily a choice to be made here, so long as we think in terms of a division of labour, as a set of differentiated questions dedicated to different sorts of ends, each of them plausible and theologically relevant. Certainly, if Lonergan is right, those scholars who are suspicious of theological interpretations of biblical texts from the perspective of methodological purity will have to re-think the preconceived naturalism that defines only their methods with academic rigour. The converse problem is real enough for theologians who downplay the findings of historical critical methods in biblical studies. Ted Peters has proposed that 'theology is inescapably apologetic'.[7] But to what kind of claim and at what point in a theological argument is an apologetic defence of Christianity proposed? Can a more sophisticated theological method really incorporate historical and social scientific approaches without radically undermining the epistemological framework that is presupposed in making *theological* claims?

The methodological position identified by Lonergan constitutes both a comprehensive response to this dilemma and a real challenge for theologians who are seeking methodological clarity. It is what animated Bernard Lonergan to write *Method in Theology*. There, Lonergan deals with the whole shape of theology, rather than particular, individual fields such as biblical studies or systematic theology. In tackling the discipline as a whole, Lonergan focuses his attention not on any one particular source or field, but rather on the distinct tasks of theologians. Instead of appraising a method for understanding scripture, experience, tradition or reason, Lonergan accounts for how these sources are employed in distinct kinds of tasks, such as the task of interpretation or the task of formulating doctrine. What is really compelling for Lonergan is the authenticity or truth of understanding, whether one is trying to understand a biblical source or one's own experience. More vitally, the methodological issue for Lonergan is whether theologians can integrate understandings with particular judgments and ways of life that themselves become the new context for doing theology. The context for doing theology that is always changing in form is the context of the individual theologian him- or herself.

One of the unmistakable elements of Lonergan's *Method in Theology* is the extent to which method is authorized not by particular rules or correct procedures, but rather by a criterion of authenticity. Theology, on Lonergan's reading of it, is a discipline that is self-correcting just as much as it concerns the knowledge of any one particular source or claim. Theology, for Lonergan, involves oneself, which is not the same (though it is easy to see similarities) as the existentialist thrust of Rudolf Bultmann's view of theology. For Lonergan and Bultmann, theology is always two-sided in a way that chemistry and even political science, for example, are not. This can be easily misunderstood to mean that theology is reducible to a personal spirituality that may or may not be informed by Christian sources. Not for Lonergan. For him, as with Christian theologians generally, a methodical theology simply means that a theologian who thinks and lives authentically is objectively better able to grasp the sources, meaning and truth claims of Christian theology.

Method always involves asking the question of whether there is a way of knowing that is unique to theology. That is, does a theological epistemology exist? To deal with this question with any authority, one must address the one factor that impinges upon the question of method at every turn: the question of revelation. Christian theology makes claims about God and God's activity in the world. This activity is described through the shorthand concept of revelation. If the church knows what God has revealed, however imperfectly and 'through a glass darkly', that knowledge is subject to an analysis according to how it was arrived at. Thus, in some analogous sense, there is such a thing as a theological epistemology. Theologians draw inferences, including claims made on the basis of obvious deductions, inductions and retrodictive claims on the basis of hindsight. Thus, theology does involve human cognition, but it also points beyond the world of inference and language in ways that other disciplines could not and would not imagine.

Revelation

Perhaps the most important methodological concept in the discipline of theology is revelation. In fact, it is known as a 'doctrine of revelation' in many Christian churches. Differences in relation to how to understand God's revelation are some of the most contested in contemporary theology. From the Greek *apokalypsis*, revelation literally refers to God's initiative to 'remove a veil so that something can be seen'. (An important caveat here: the concept of revelation is to be sharply distinguished from the biblical book with the same name.) For Christian theology, the question is how and for whom God removes this veil. For that matter, what is this 'veil'? Is it the ignorance and deceit that overcomes us as a consequence of human failure, our sin? That is one decidedly influential answer. If God is involved in revealing himself, to what extent may theologians claim a human component to theological knowledge? Is it human language that constitutes the specifically human part of divine communication? As we will see in the forthcoming chapters, the theological methodology of a number of historically significant theologians shows that there are several ways to formulate how one models God's acts of revealing Himself.

For instance, revelation is understood as mystical insight (Dionysius, Chapter Four), as experienced and correctly interpreted scripture (Augustine, Chapter Three) and as doctrinal reflections of scripture (Karl Barth, Chapter Seven). In these and other models of revelation, the customary use of the term 'revelation' is distinguished from natural theology. Some theologians advance an idea of general revelation and this is common in the high regard for nature by believing scientists. A concept of general revelation is thought to suggest that God communicates Himself in nature alongside what is traditionally seen as God's 'special' revelation. The category of general revelation blurs the distinction between natural theology and a theology of revelation, traditionally regarded as two kinds of theological literature.

Clear thinking about theological method can be thwarted if a concept of revelation has not been clarified. The disagreements over the meaning of revelation in Hans Frei, George Lindbeck and other 'post-liberal' theologians illustrate this challenge dramatically. With post-liberalism, to affirm God's revelatory activity is to conjoin the contents and method of theology in a way that upholds tradition and scripture at the expense of certain sorts of reason. Christian theologians refer to revelation in specific terms: 'the revelation given in and by Christ Jesus',[8] or as 'the threefold form of the Word of God'.[9] As Kevin Vanhoozer suggests with reference to the idea of God's 'speech acts', the meaning of revelation is undoubtedly tied to the meaning of scripture.[10] This leads to the question of how we read and interpret the Bible, the area of hermeneutics. For theologians, God's communication with us is bound up with our interpretation of the Bible as 'Holy Scripture.'

Hermeneutics

From the Greek word *hermeneia*, the term 'hermeneutics' refers to 'the theory of the operations of understanding in their relation to the interpretation of texts'.[11] Students looking for a purely ideal theological system or a theological logic which demonstrates full methodological precision will inevitably be disappointed by the recurrence of the key role played by the human interpreter in the expression of theological claims. Human interpreters undertake a wide range of cognitive 'operations of understanding' when interpreting texts; but this fact does not suggest epistemological relativism. The philosopher Michael Polanyi has said that 'we know more than we can tell',[12] by which he means that we possess, at any given moment, a cacophony of images, concepts and perceptions that guide our knowing and which determine our judgments according to different priorities at different times. This is the 'human factor' that invariably constitutes the basic pattern by which variances in theological expression can be judged. Hermeneutical theory is the field that identifies the 'tacit dimension' of human knowledge in determining how textual sources are interpreted.

From the earliest centuries of Christian theology, there are different hermeneutical choices concerning ways to interpret biblical texts. Most clearly, from the second century forwards, there are differences between the Antiochene 'literalists' and the Alexandrian allegorists. These distinct ways to read the texts demonstrate how theological method works from an early date; and it is true that the diversity of these approaches has caused difficulty from the earliest moments of the Christian church. In fact, Jesus is the first to treat scripture in a non-literalist way. When Jesus sums up 'all the law and the prophets' in Matt. 5 (the Sermon on the Mount), he is making a dramatic summary interpretation of the Torah's 613 various commands or obligations set out in the Hebrew Bible. The occasional Christian tendency to an excessively literal interpretation is thus problematic in light of Jesus' own approach to the biblical text. Indeed, hermeneutical considerations determined which books were included in the biblical canon in the first place. Therefore, theological commitments both shaped the structure of the New Testament canon and were, in turn, deeply shaped by it. This is a classic case of the 'hermeneutic circle' in operation.

Theological hermeneutics stresses the transcendent purpose of reading. An analogy from literary studies indicates the meaning of this context. In a characteristic declaration of praise of Shakespeare, literary critic Harold Bloom alights on the importance of the bard's words for 'you', the reader:

> You are more than an ideology, whatever your convictions, and Shakespeare speaks to as much of you as you can bring to him. That is to say: Shakespeare reads you more fully than you can read him.[13]

In these sentences, if we substitute 'the Bible' for 'Shakespeare', one may see a way to understand how the authoritative role played by the canonical biblical text was conceived. We are 'read' or understood by God more fully than we can understand God, although this possibility does not preclude our quest for understanding. For Bloom, the question at stake is the human condition and the classic source for self-understanding is none other than William Shakespeare. Analogously, the question in theology is God and the classic source is the canon of biblical books. Obviously, this idea of reading and 'being read' is very suited to theology, especially Protestant theology, for which there is a well-known emphasis on scripture as the prime instrument of God's revelation. This idea of mutual readings – God of us and us of God – is an important qualification to make with regards to the elaboration of a theological method in comparison with scientific method. 'Being read' is one way to describe what the religious concept of revelation means: a flow of communication and meaning from a source other than ourselves that appears inexhaustible across great historical time spans.

One concrete instance that helps specify this context of mutual 'reading' is the problem of Christian identity *vis-à-vis* the people of Israel. Since the Holocaust, Christian theologians have reflected on how to understand the people of Israel and the Old Testament in light of God's promises to the Jewish people and in light of the church's self-understanding as the people of God. Since World War II, new hermeneutical perspectives have been proposed which suggest alternatives to 'supercessionism', which is the term that conveys the notion that the covenant between God and the Jewish people has been revoked since Jesus Christ. Christian hermeneutical theology has now changed, not in expressing the churches' doctrines necessarily, but in its way of thinking of the church as a 'carrier' of the scriptures of Israel. In light of the Shakespeare analogy above, it is perhaps more methodologically significant to think of the Church as received by Israel's scriptures, not vice versa. To think of Israel's scriptures as a subject 'receiving' the Church and its scriptures might sound counterintuitive, but this way of thinking of God's covenant(s) is coherent with much of contemporary theological scholarship.

For instance, adherents of the 'New Perspective' in Pauline studies are calling for a better exegesis according to the norms of socio-rhetorical, historical and other analyses. These advances are important for biblical studies and theology. But, an even closer analysis bears out the conclusion, as we shall see in the next chapter, that, for Paul at least, the resurrection of Jesus places the Christian church communities within the ambit of divine providence. God is 'reading' the gentiles through Israel and Jesus. A *theological* hermeneutics has to read the New Testament mindful of this reading of us by God. Given God's prior reading of us through the people of Israel, it is hermeneutically possible to say that the Christian church is received into the scriptures of Israel.

Therefore, the question of hermeneutics in theology is that of letting oneself be shaped by God's word as one interprets the biblical text. This is what it means to construct a theological commitment. Hermeneutics thus concerns worldview, whether it be the theologian's worldview (such as Paul's worldview, examined in Chapter One and deemed authoritative for Christian churches) or a worldview communicated by the church itself. Hermeneutics is not simply a matter of striking some always vulnerable *via media* between the principles of systematic theology on the one hand and the historically shaped contingencies of the text that are revealed by exegesis on the other hand. It is not an issue of trying to strike a balance but of understanding the demands placed by the text on the reader in multiple ways; and the reverse is also true – understanding the demands placed on the text by the reader.

The criteria by which early Christians shaped the canon and the alleged diversity of the early churches have come to dominate many discussions of hermeneutics. What strikes some historians and social scientists who highlight different strands of belief within early Christian thought is that theological hermeneutics runs the risk of being an imperialistic exercise of trumpeting one interpretation of Christian faith over a number of other possibilities. Beginning with the 1947 discovery of the Nag Hammadi texts in Egypt and continuing with the discovery and contested translation of the gnostic Gospel of Judas, Christian origins has become one of the most discussed topics pertaining to the methodology of early Christian theology. The emphasis upon various contingencies in the development of Christian thought is now a widespread viewpoint. Views of history shape interpretation; therefore, if one sees struggle between essentially equal interpretations of Christian faith, then one is more liable to see equivocation in the biblical texts that pertain to some historic Christian doctrine. If, on the other hand, one sees a strong thread of what was later called 'orthodox' thought, then one is less likely to interpret biblical texts in ways that wildly contradict historic church doctrines. Heresy and orthodoxy are thus categories fraught with historiographical and hermeneutical significance. A recent book on this subject argues persuasively that our view of early Christian history has been distorted by those who emphasize the diversity of first-century Christianity over its orthodox coherence.[14]

Christian hermeneutics has to deal with the prevalent belief that different historical epochs are simply different and relative to one another, with no one culture or period being of greater value than the other. This relates to what English speakers call the 'Whig interpretation' of history. In this view, progress is like a vital force always propelling us towards more liberal, humane and compassionate standards of theology, law, philosophy and social custom. Other beliefs also play an important role in shaping hermeneutical expectations. Alleged discoveries and even fictional claims, parlayed through popular novels and movies (e.g. *The Da Vinci Code*), about Christian history, biblical interpretation and Jesus himself constitute a powerful counter-narrative to the narrative of Christian salvation. Far from being isolated from such controversy, theological method is affected by the various implications of historical Jesus research. Especially notable are claims that Jesus was a wandering Cynic philosopher. This view is associated with the biblical scholar John Dominic Crossan, who portrays a Jesus remarkably in step with the egalitarian politics akin to those of late twentieth-century liberal Western academics.[15]

What is the best way to respond to these questions of interpretation which pervade the very purpose, structure and meanings of the source texts of Christian faith? I doubt whether an adequate theological response lies simply in reiterating data that shows Jesus to be something other than a wandering Hellenistic philosopher. Neither would it be adequate, theologically or methodologically, to respond by affirming a point from the Creed. A key to resolving this interpretation of history begins with probing Crossan's hermeneutic and comparing it with the hermeneutic of biblical interpreters who come to different conclusions. Unless there are evident hermeneutical, historical criteria by which Christian theologians make theological claims on the basis of biblical texts and other sources, it is difficult to see how Christian theologians can move beyond simplistic reactions to successive, culturally rooted, controversial claims.

Before becoming embroiled in debates over views of history, hermeneutics meant something like the expression and translation of language. Certainly, the issues associated with language are central in biblical interpretation and that is much truer now than in the pre-modern period. Biblical exegetes rely on exacting linguistic analysis through complex inferences of comparisons and contrasts in order to determine original meanings in texts. One example concerning the identity of God is the lofty Hebrew prose of Exod. 3.14, usually translated in most biblical texts as 'God says to Moses "I am who I am"'. Many exegetes now suggest a rather different meaning of the text by paying close attention to the complex verb form of the Hebrew. The result of this analysis is the different English rendering 'I will be whom I will be'. Exegesis and linguistic analysis are unquestionably vital in the understanding of God that arises from this newer translation. The sheer effectiveness of such methods of linguistic analysis in turn affects how more general theological principles of interpretation and doctrine are proposed.

Werner Jeanrond comments in his book *Theological Hermeneutics* that in 're-reading a text . . . we never read a text "objectively" or "neutrally"'.[16] But this statement can easily mislead. From the thought of Bernard Lonergan, we can say that there is a significant difference between the two concepts of objectivity and neutrality. Lonergan offers the view that while we each read a text within a perspective, it is also the task of some theologians to articulate as precisely as is possible just what that perspective is. Whether Christian believers or unbelievers, we are never neutral, but if one has been sufficiently attentive, intelligent, reasonable and responsible, then according to Lonergan, one has achieved a significant measure of objectivity. Inasmuch as we can identify the contours and background of our individual perspectives and the ways in which these perspectives inform our reading of texts, we read objectively. This does not mean we are neutral in the sense that Jeanrond uses the term. But then the search for neutrality is a puzzling historical phenomenon. Historically, Christian theologians claim that theirs is not a quest for neutrality at all, but rather a quest for truth and goodness, goals with deep commitments that thankfully get in the way of strict epistemic neutrality.

Understanding biblical interpretation and principles of biblical interpretation relates to the understanding of literature and meaning generally. As we will see in almost every case of biblically oriented theologians, interpretive quests also involve an inherently existential quest. Modern theologians such as Rudolf Bultmann (see Chapter Seven) see the biblical narratives in existentialist terms, while his erstwhile theological opponent Karl Barth sees existential theology as leading to the denial of the divine revelatory initiative in scripture. What remains hidden from view in the famous debates held by partisans of liberal and neo-orthodox theology in the twentieth century is that both Bultmann and Barth agree on the centrality of conversion in theological method. This does not negate the serious drawbacks that have been associated with both of these theologians. In fact, as one biblical scholar put it, Bultmannianism died with Bultmann himself in 1976.[17] The role of conversion in theology means that theologians need to attend to their own prior positions, perceptions, images, theological concepts and related intellectual commitments that guide a reading of the Bible. And, as I will suggest in various ways, this is a healthy state of affairs.

Clearly, the role of conversion signals a difference between theology and scientific method. Or does it? Other philosophers see methodical inquiry in other disciplines, including the natural sciences, as a process of being *converted* to the truth. Thomas Kuhn, a historian of science who wrote the famous text *The Structure of Scientific Revolutions*, maintains that there is a dialectical movement between periods of normal science and revolutionary science. In periods of normal science, ruling intellectual paradigms shape the scientist's orientation to the truth, but this orientation is distorted when anomalies are discovered which disrupt the coherence of the entire predominant worldview, all at once. Theologian Hans Küng argues that a similar process takes place in theology; but it is German philosopher Hans-Georg Gadamer, in *Truth and Method*, who argues more substantively for the role of 'tradition' in the ongoing, authentic interpretation of classical texts.[18] Tradition concerns the entire set of social, epistemic and metaphysical components that go into the formulation of theological claims.

Tradition

The biblical canon of 27 New Testament books was not set by Christian church authorities until after Athanasius (d. 373). This single historical fact suggests that the role of tradition in theological method is decisive. All Christian churches and theologians operate on some assumption about the authority of tradition in theological practice. While Catholic and Orthodox theologians are more often explicit about the authority of church tradition in the process of developing doctrine, other theologians proceed on the basis of particular concepts or methodological priorities (e.g. 'sola scriptura'). The latter theologies themselves possess an entire tradition of formulation, revision, integration and expression.

Frequently, 'tradition' in Christian theology refers to the post-biblical heritage of the Christian church. This sense of the word turns up in various ways; for instance, in the phrase 'deposit of faith', which is used by the Roman Catholic Church in referring to the teaching role of bishops. Tradition is associated with the institutional agency of the communication of faith. This agency cannot be ascribed to scripture, to individual theologians or even to individual church leaders singly. Tradition is something broader and more corporate than these individual agents. One way to think about tradition in terms that are understood by contemporary culture is through reference to 'beliefs', or public knowledge. The beliefs of a tradition are central to the way that the scriptures, religious experience and reason are received and cited by theologians. Beliefs are not forms of private knowledge at all; they are a matter of one's heritage, and beliefs are present in a variety of disciplines. Beliefs are as central to the practice of science as they are to the reflection on one's faith. Of course, in Christian history, certain traditional concepts have become very important for distinguishing the nature of the tradition and the heritage of what is Christian belief. Apostolicity, for example, has often been cited as a criterion for true belief. It matters, according to churches which regard themselves as apostolic, that one belongs to a church that can claim tangible links with the first Christian apostles who received and handed on the faith in Jesus Christ.

Yet apostolicity, like other aspects of tradition, can be interpreted differently. It means somewhat different things for the authority vested in bishops, for instance. It means different things for Catholics and Orthodox Christians. Like scripture itself, theological traditions and the whole Christian tradition can be interpreted through human experience, reason or through some theme derived from scripture. For philosophers, tradition implies the general sense of a continuity of meaning. This is what Enlightenment thinkers sought to expose and disrupt by advocating that one should think for oneself. For Gadamer, tradition is associated with nothing less than the historicity of understanding. For him, we should not be waylaid into believing that the fruit of understanding is merely the application of a technique. Against a strictly negative understanding of prejudice, Gadamer stresses the 'meaning of "belonging" – i.e., the element of tradition in our historical-hermeneutical activity . . . fulfilled in the commonality of fundamental enabling prejudices'.[19] Tradition specifically allows hermeneutics to function properly, where the 'discovery of the true meaning of a text or a work of art is never finished; it is in fact an infinite process'.[20] This claim bolsters the case for theological reflection as a methodical, critical reflection. Theology is a discipline that seeks to articulate the true meaning of God, as revealed to us. This true meaning is expressed according to different cultural and historically contingent priorities. Revelation can be conceived of as being a 'first word' theologically, but theology seeks to elaborate on that word according to different questions and historical priorities. Theology also is obliged to reflect on how revelation is to be understood conceptually, not to smooth over its perceived contents, but in order to give shape to its meaning for human beings who use language. We are, after all, as Aristotle said, linguistically reasonable creatures: *zoon logon echon*.

Theological traditions contain elements that are both authentic and inauthentic, and Lonergan offers the term 'major unauthenticity' to denote an entire tradition's failure and its judgment by both 'history' and divine providence. 'Minor unauthenticity' is the failure of individuals to live up to the goodness of the tradition(s) that nourished them.[21] Complex relationships between the church and society historically show multi-layered interplays of various expressions of both major and minor unauthenticity. In theological method, what might appear as a division between conservatives who value tradition and liberals who do not, is, in fact, a more nuanced reality. 'Liberal theologians' typically draw on traditions of thought, but they notice the unauthenticity of particular traditions with respect to history. Conservatives, on the other hand, notice the unauthenticity of individuals with respect to the truth of theological traditions. History is marshalled in both cases to buttress these different interpretations of tradition.

For many Christian churches, the apostolic character of the church is deemed to be a criterion of ecclesial value and historical centrality for the Christian tradition as a whole. The Christian narrative stresses the sending of God's son and the sending of the apostles by the Son. So, Andrew Louth says: 'tradition in the sense of the tradition of the Church is the continuity of the divine sending, the divine mission, which the Church has received from her Lord and which she pursues in the world.'[22]

However, a stress on tradition to the exclusion of a critical hermeneutics of church practice and doctrine can lead to an 'anti-methodology'. This is what some theological respondents suggest is wrong with Karl Barth (Chapter Seven) or 'radical Orthodox' theology (see Chapter Eight). Yet, as we will see, sometimes an apparently anti-methodological stance such as that of Radical Orthodoxy's John Milbank and Catherine Pickstock helps clarify theological method more swiftly than a procedurally cautious theology. Inasmuch as theological method involves evaluating the tradition within which the theologian operates, the church theologian can feel vulnerable, as we shall see in Chapter Six when we deal with the idea of the development of doctrine. Perhaps the best theology is practised by those who embrace the tension of practising their faith in a full engagement with the tradition writ large while also engaging in the intellectual task of analysing and evaluating the tradition in discerning the distinct authentic and unauthentic elements in it. From the survey of theological method that follows in subsequent chapters, we will begin to see what constitutes best theological practice. With Lonergan and others as our guides, we will be better able to make judgments about theology that is methodically adequate versus theology that is not. Our first theologian, whose methodological instincts in theology are more resolute than many assume, is Paul.

CHAPTER ONE

Paul the theologian

In the field of biblical studies, one viewpoint, sometimes still heard, is that 'in scripture there is not a line of theology'.[1] While this may be a plausible interpretation of some of the biblical books, it is difficult to square this assessment with the life and writings of Paul in the New Testament. Paul was a theologian, albeit not a 'professional', 'scholastic' or an 'academic'. He is not a very sophisticated exponent of Christian philosophy – a hybrid literature that would emerge in later centuries. Yet, in our day, a major contemporary philosophical academic movement studies Paul as a philosopher. However, when it is time to identify Paul, most scholars do not hesitate. Noted biblical scholar Joseph Fitzmyer terms Paul 'the first Christian theologian', and F. F. Bruce claims that Paul is the Christian church's 'greatest theologian'.[2] Yet, as the church's 'first theologian', Paul was often portrayed in contrast, or even in opposition to, the pure 'religious posture of Jesus'.[3]

Certainly, Paul is an interpreter of Jesus, *the* interpreter of Jesus *par excellence*. First and foremost, Paul is the author of what were later established as canonical letters. While he is an interpreter of Jesus, he is also a reader of the biblical books of the Old Testament. He is a convert whose faith is therefore hermeneutical. That is, Paul interprets his faith through scripture and he interprets the scriptures through faith. His faith is informed by an interpreted experience of Christ's death and resurrection, which is his way of 'reading' the Jewish scriptures. There is a circular interdependence of scripture and experience through which Paul's own theological method becomes clear. Or, at least, this is the outline of a Pauline method. I shall argue in this chapter that Paul's method is basically a method that is hermeneutical with regards to Israel's scriptures and to Christ, while it is apostolic (or communicative) with regards to the church. These two adjectives – hermeneutical and apostolic – capture the thrust of Paul's theological method by and large. Such adjectives are sufficiently general to take into consideration the contingent occasions for which he develops theological arguments, yet they are specific enough to rule out the idea that Paul is only an occasional writer with no concern for coherence.

A comprehensive approach to scripture developed slowly within the Christian church from the middle of the second century onwards. New Testament texts are cited by early churchmen, such as Ignatius of Antioch, alongside texts from what would later become known as the Old Testament, and were henceforth regarded as wholly authoritative. Paul's own theology forms the bulk of the New Testament, even if it is technically true that some of the letters attributed to him have been judged by modern scholars to have been written by others. But, as first-person accounts go, his experience of Christ and his interpretation of the Hebrew Bible are unique, partly because of the fusion of distinctive Jewish elements with his Christian faith.

What is undeniably unique with regard to Paul is that methodically speaking, the pivotal point upon which his theology turns is his conversion experience on the road to Damascus, as recounted in the Book of Acts. (I retain the term 'conversion' because of its associations with Lonergan's understanding of conversion as authentic faith, reason and ethics, despite the fact that the guild of New Testament scholars now generally disapprove of it to describe Paul's apostolic call.) Thereafter, Paul is a preacher and 'apostle' of Christ, 'evangelist to the gentiles' as tradition identifies him. Yet, in his letters, his prose often comes across as enigmatic or contradictory, and he seems at times taciturn. Paul claims in 1 Corinthians, on the one hand, that 'I have the Spirit of God' (7.40), yet he comments in self-reproach later on that 'I am the least of the apostles, unfit to be called an apostle' (15.9).

As a singularly important figure in the Christian tradition, we are justified in asking to what extent Paul actually adopts anything like a theological method. Partly as a consequence of his reference to his conversion, some scholars regard Paul as neither systematic nor consistent.[4] Others would say that the question about method makes little sense to ask. Indeed, William Wrede alleged that Paul pushed Jesus 'the greater one, whom he meant to serve, into the background'.[5] Thus, one could argue that against a methodical perspective, Paul is a freelance genius. As Freud put it, Paul 'has a gift for religion, in the truest sense of the phrase'.[6]

But if Paul is to be called a theologian, as I believe is justified, what method or methods did he follow? One common way of approaching this question is to examine Paul's letters from a literary or textual point of view, comparing, for instance, tropes and metaphors as they are developed in different letters. One prominent instance of this approach is through the analysis of similarities and differences in the way that Abraham is treated in the *midrashim* of Romans and Galatians. Therefore, even if one claims that Paul is not a 'theologian' in the proper sense of that word, one could at least affirm that Paul follows a pattern in his writing.

If we adopt a more descriptive approach, we would conclude that Paul is drawing on a variety of sources for constructing his theology. He fuses his own experience, the Jesus tradition of the Christian churches scattered around the Mediterranean, Jewish scripture and philosophical Stoicism. Paul employs various hermeneutical strategies in order to lay out the narrative coherence of his good news for the diverse audiences and recipients of his ministry. This diversity is evident in his letters. Paul identifies himself as 'called to be an apostle' (Rom. 1), a form of ministry with a didactic orientation, as distinct from the more passive orientation of (mere) discipleship. There is a psychological dimension to Paul's self-identity as a teacher and apostle, as one who bears the burden of responsibility. This role clarifies his *way* of communicating theological insights.

J. C. Beker, a leading scholar of Pauline theology, has thought a great deal about Paul's methodology and describes Paul's letters as documentary evidence of a balance struck between 'contingency' and 'coherence'. Contingency characterizes the communicative mode by which Paul conveys the meaning of the gospel on various occasions to different audiences. The coherence of the gospel is a reference to a centre of Paul's thought that underpins the variety of occasions on which he speaks. Beker is not alone in arguing for a centre to Paul's theology while fully aware of the variety of theological interpretations of Paul that are attributed to the array of images and concepts Paul uses to convey his faith in Christ. Beker is also aware of the dangers of erring on the side of coherence. He is aware, for instance, of the early Protestant 'consensus' on the 'justification by faith' doctrine that was taken by Luther and others to be the essence of Paul's thought. However, as recent scholarship has stressed, this alleged 'essence' of Paul's theology only begins with Luther's reading of the Books of Galatians and Romans. So, for instance, the eschatological mysticism of Albert Schweitzer (1875–1965) is a reaction to this historic Lutheran interpretation of Paul. Yet Schweitzer ironically established a new theme that he claimed to be the core of Paul's theology. Such is the trajectory of scholarship in Pauline theology as it waxes and wanes over contested core theological storylines. With the current popularity for 'nonfoundationalist' and postmodern ways of interpreting biblical texts, the search for a core of Pauline thought has become somewhat discredited.

In light of the debates that swirl in this theoretical tug-of-war, I argue for a pattern in Paul's theology comparable to Beker's framework of contingency and coherence. In this chapter I will take up four key issues which demonstrate an implicit theological method in Paul. Each issue can be understood through the analysis and interpretation of key texts. These issues exemplify Paul's theological method, though, of course, by no account do they exhaust what that method means. The four issues are as follows.

a) Justification by faith is a doctrine famously attributed to Paul, especially by Lutheran theologians during the Protestant Reformation and thereafter, as already noted. As a means of combating what Protestants viewed as the Catholic Church's efforts to convey a works-based concept of God's grace, Luther and his various successors drew on what they perceived as the gospel of grace in Paul's letters in order to communicate a *theology* of God's grace known and won through simple faith. The question that has arisen in the twentieth century is whether such a (Lutheran) doctrine is a misreading of Paul himself.

Without agreeing exactly with the historic Lutheran theology of grace on the basis of Pauline texts, I argue that Paul does develop something like a doctrine of justification. He does so methodo-logically. He interprets scripture, especially by correlating his own understanding of Jesus with those understandings nascent in the traditions of the ancient Christian church, which are evident in the gospels. What this means, from a twenty-first-century perspective, is that Paul's way of articulating justification is intentionally aligned with the basic sense of forgiveness that we read about in the parables of Jesus in the gospels. Both the gospel writers and Paul articulate an understanding of salvation based in part on the sense of God's mercy found in the Old Testament. To that extent, justification is not a doctrine that is Paul's alone. It is a doctrine, or at least a well-founded idea, that plausibly extends the meaning of Jewish scripture through the prism of Christ. Thus, Paul's theological method is one which arrives at a doctrine (or a proto-doctrine at least) by interpreting scripture in light of his powerful conversion experience. If there is coherence to Paul's thought about justification, then that coherence results from methodically thinking about the salvation that is now possible for Gentiles, in unity with Jews. This salvation is made possible by Christ through faith and marked by baptism. Now, justification does not rely upon Israel's law.[7]

b) Paul's expression of a holiness ethic stems from an understanding of righteousness, which is the life of faith. For Paul, an ethic of personal and corporate holiness has both communitarian and sexual applications, as we can see from 1 Thess. 4.5 for instance. While Paul refrains from addressing moral issues systematically in the way of Greek philosophers, he nevertheless fosters the spirit of a comprehensive moral view which follows as a consequence of Christian faith. So, for instance, Paul does not advise Philemon to free his slave Onesimus in the Book of Philemon, yet the church was already 'fully conscious of the inconsistency between this institution [of slavery] and the inner freedom and equality which was the Christian ideal'[8] a freedom that Paul advocates such that slavery is rendered morally untenable. I will untangle a bit further the methodological steps taken in Paul's account of Christian holiness, which demonstrates both the coherence and contingency of his theology.

c) On the question of the Fall and original sin, Paul has been both authoritative and controversial. Is Paul's interpretation of the Genesis account of the fall of Adam an ad hoc doctrine, or is it consistent with Jewish tradition and early Christian belief? When Paul encounters and reflects upon the significance of sin and the first human family in his writing, does he bring to his reflection anything resembling a methodical account of human fallenness? To be more specific, is the Adam/Christ typology of humanity in Rom. 5 an argument that is organized properly? To his credit, I think Paul does bring some consistency to bear on the question, a constructive theological position that serves as an important jumping-off point for subsequent Christian systematic theology.

d) One other theological issue on which Paul demonstrates a methodological disposition is his affirmation of something like the doctrine of the Trinity. Of course, unlike the later, more abstract statements of the church fathers for whom terminological precision became a matter of meticulous debate, Paul is much more interested in settling the kind of experience that justifies talking of God's threefold disclosure. Paul's experiential grounding of Trinitarian ideas does not necessarily entail a doctrinal approach. But, his experiential reference points are sufficient grounds for what, in hindsight, I would term a proto-doctrine of the Trinity in Paul. A number of passages in his letters tend to suggest a relationship between experience and doctrinal judgement. Some of this doctrinal judgement is Paul's. Subsequently, theologians and the church would follow his lead in the dialectical debates that followed in subsequent centuries.

Together, these four examples in Pauline theology lend support for the early church maxim 'lex orandi lex credendi'. The mediated, doxological experience of God is a key criterion that permeates early Christian theology, notably Pauline thought. Paul expresses, perhaps more than many patristic figures, the trajectory of theology from experience, worship included, to doctrine. The *lex orandi* expression comes to be formulated in a text of Prosper of Aquitane, a fifth-century monk who assisted Pope Leo the Great as secretary and interpreter of Augustine. It literally means that 'the law of worship is the rule of faith'. Taking Paul's conversion experience and his constant exhortations to pray, we see that, for him, the striving to render theological judgments (proto-doctrines, if you will) based on his experience is a prime example of the *lex orandi* rule in operation.

In order to assess Paul's theological method through an analysis of these four questions, it is first of all important to underline several crucial factors that characterize his methodical outlook. The contemporary literature dealing with the *influences* on Paul's thought and writing is vast. The sheer amount of this scholarly discourse complements the more voluminous material that continues to analyse Paul's actual theology. Still, both sets of literature dwarf the literature dedicated to a study of his method.

Talk of method in Paul can run the risk of making him out to be the logical philosopher that he was not. One thing that nearly all scholars agree upon, however, is that Paul's faith is rooted in his belonging to the house of Israel, a sense of belonging made tenable in self-consciously Christological terms. The friendship with God, to which he attests time and again, stems from both his Jewish and his Christian identities. This dual identity is the key context to all of his theology. Even if Paul self-consciously alters the terms of his Jewish identity because of what God has done through Jesus Christ, the template of Paul's theological outlook is still recognizably Jewish.

Also important is Paul's Hellenistic background, which plays a considerable role in shaping his somewhat limited education. Being from Tarsus in Cilicia, Paul was a Roman citizen according to the Book of Acts – information that is probably trustworthy, despite some lingering doubts over the historicity of certain claims in Acts. He was formed early on in his life by a literary culture. In fact, Strabo claimed that 'the people at Tarsus have devoted themselves so eagerly, not only to philosophy, but also to the whole round of education in general, that they have surpassed Athens, Alexandria, or any other place that can be named where there have been schools and lectures of philosophers'.[9] As we are told in Acts 22.3, important segments of Paul's education came from his learning at the feet of an important Jerusalem rabbi and seer, Gamaliel. This suggests that Paul's early exposure to the written Torah, poetry and basic Greco-Roman philosophy was complemented by later formation in the 'oral Torah' at Jerusalem.

However, an understanding of Paul's background context, while necessary, is insufficient for determining his theological method. In the field of Pauline studies itself, there is a dialectic that runs between those who emphasize Paul's background and those who want to focus on the logical patterns of thought and speech that make up the narrative thread of his letters. There is a dialectic between thinking of Paul's context as determining his theology versus thinking of Paul's theology as more or less independent of his context. What is evident in this dialectic is a distinction in theological tasks, or 'functional specialties', as Lonergan calls them. On the one hand are scholars who are convinced that Paul's thought is reducible in some way to being an expression of Jewish piety that is historically, rhetorically and psychologically peculiar, even esoteric. Others marry Paul's Jewish perspective through his understanding of Christ and this is what the so-called New Perspective on Paul brings. In turn, this perspective provides a helpful, and perhaps necessary, corrective to the older, traditional view of Paul's view of justification. For the New Perspective, it is vital and plausible to retrieve the Jewish context which moulded Paul as a person of faith, action and belief. For the New Perspective, no constructive theology ought to contradict Paul's Jewish experience of Jesus Christ.

So, there are now more theologians and scholars who want to prioritize the fresh, conceptual and even doctrinal significance of Paul's thought which emerges from his Jewish outlook. Typically, constructive theologians take it as their task to understand Paul in this sense. According to this analysis, the priority is to understand what it is that Paul wants his hearers or readers to understand. The issue which arises in this second, 'more theological' perspective concerns intention: what did Paul and those who were involved in the writing of his letters *intend* to mean in their choice of particular words, phrases and arguments? Attention to the question of Paul's intentions brings out the full range of Jewish meanings that he interprets and makes new through Christ.

If it is true that Paul's letters convey something of a coherent theological perspective, then it is vital to say how this coherence is won. Coherence cannot be claimed if there is little or no evidence for it, and it is the Jewish framework to which the New Perspective has pointed as the most obvious way to understand Paul's overall message. For instance, there is a tremendous amount written concerning the notions of 'grace' and 'law' that originate with Paul. For many theologians, not least Martin Luther himself, the concept of grace, interpreted through the phrase 'justification by faith', became the central organizing principle of his entire theological system, as it did for many others thereafter. We are right to ask whether Paul thinks methodically about his sources when *he* speaks about 'grace' or 'law.' It is certainly true that Paul engages in theological reflection not in an abstract way, but in a 'rabbinic' way, since Paul lays claim to a pharisaical training. This is important to make clear in order to ensure that we do not interpret Paul in a purely philosophical way, as interesting as that might be. Such an image of Paul is offered, for instance, by the Slovenian philosopher Slavoj Žižek and by the French philosopher Alain Badiou.[10]

Keeping in balance the questions of Jewish context and those of theological intention, we can say that, heuristically speaking, Paul's rabbinic style is inseparable from his theology. But, by way of drawing conclusions concerning his methodology, how does the New Perspective's better understanding of Paul give us a more methodologically coherent Christian theology?

With this sort of question in mind, Francis Watson says, 'Paul's "view of the law" is nothing other than his *reading* of Exodus, Leviticus, Numbers and Deuteronomy. Paul speaks of the law not as a propounder of dogmatic assertions but as an interpreter of texts.'[11] Watson does not mean to suggest here that Paul is *only* an interpreter of the Jewish law. As the distinctive (and numerous) employment of phrases such as 'through faith in Jesus Christ' (Rom. 3.22) suggest, Paul's hermeneutic is decisively Christological. But what Watson wants to say is that Paul's repeated engagement with texts puts hermeneutics at the forefront of how we can attempt to assess Paul's theological method. And, it is clear that this matter of hermeneutics has actually been made more possible through the New Perspective, a methodical interpretation mostly unavailable to earlier generations of theologians. It is with this hermeneutical question in mind that I will approach the four issues that I have selected as exemplary of Paul's theological method.

Justification by faith

Historically, according to Christian tradition, the *loci classicus* of Paul's emphasis on the Christian's justification by faith are twofold: the first few chapters of Romans, in particular Rom. 1.17, 3.21–4.25, and Galatians, in particular Chapter Three. The traditional Christian debate over Paul's definition of justification, God's declaration of the Christian's guiltless standing before Him, centres on these passages. But, any assertion of a methodology in Paul's thinking on this subject usually implies several closely related theological claims. For instance, if we go with Ernst Käsemann's argument that Paul's doctrine of justification through faith is something unique to Paul – as a thesis to be defended by a *subsequent* recourse to scripture – then methodologically, we might be inclined to believe that Paul's doctrine is something that he arrives at independently of (Jewish) scriptural tradition. Käsemann takes up the constructive task but it is shorn of the most obvious religious motivation within which it is meaningful. A claim such as Käsemann's is an abstract claim about God's righteousness, to which scriptural passages are then selectively cited post hoc to prove that doctrinal proposition. Is that what Paul does? I think we need to say 'no'.

If, on the other hand, we agree with contemporary theologians that Paul's theology is a hermeneutical construction of his interpretation of both the Old Testament and his own experience as a Jewish believer, who has decided to become a follower of the resurrected Lord Jesus, then a different picture begins to emerge of his theological method. As discussed at length by Francis Watson in *Paul and the Hermeneutics of Faith*, it is in precisely a hermeneutical way that Paul's faith and his reflection upon faith emerges as a theology. Paul's theology is not something that strikes him fully formed from the beginning of his apostolic career. Paul's theology of justification, if we can use that phrase, is not conceptually pure. And for this reason then, the key methodological concept which we need to introduce in regards to what Paul is doing in his letters is 'intertextuality' (or 'intratextuality', if we consider the whole canon as a single text).

As the New Testament scholar Richard Hays has amply demonstrated with special reference to Romans, the term 'intertextuality' refers to the way in which Paul draws upon the topics, metaphors, images as well as direct quotes from the Old Testament in his own writing. Thus, there is an interplay of two texts, with one dependent upon the other; but Paul's intention is that the meaning of Old Testament texts be rendered dependent upon the meanings and emphases that he brings to light about Christ, hence 'intertextuality'.[12]

So, how is Paul's notion of justification arrived at? The variety of interpretations prevents us from making a comprehensive assessment. Reacting against the predominantly Lutheran estimation of Romans as a pure gospel, the idea of a more doctrinally poignant *kerygma* than the four actual gospels themselves, Albert Schweitzer dissented. He asserted: 'the doctrine of righteousness by faith is . . . a subsidiary crater, which has formed within the rim of the main crater – the mystical doctrine of redemption through the being-in-Christ.'[13] The problem with Schweitzer's alternative 'mystical' view of Paul's theology, as with numerous other interpretations that followed Schweitzer's, is that it tends to promote an overly conceptual approach to understanding Paul's theology of justification. In seeking simplified explanations of ranking ideas in Paul, many have not paid sufficient attention to Paul's methodology in assessing his semantics. In short, many have not paid sufficient attention to Paul as an interpreter of the Hebrew Bible or Old Testament.

With regards to one's justification by faith, in Rom. 1.17 (cf. Gal. 3.11), Paul addresses the power of the gospel by writing: 'For the righteousness of God is revealed in it, by faith for faith. As it is written: "The one who is righteous by faith will live."' Paul's choice of words is awkward. Nonetheless, as Watson convincingly elaborates, for Paul there is both a semantic and lexical connection between the idea of justification he puts forwards and the original meaning of (the Old Testament passage) Hab. 2.4 being cited. What this means, in essence, is that Paul is neither repeating verbatim a passage from Jewish tradition, nor is he concocting a theological construct by going around the tradition. In short, Paul is mounting a constructive effort to uphold and interpret the justice of God spoken of in Habakkuk in order to corroborate his experience of God's call to bring in the Gentile nations in the final days.

He is, to use Lonergan's way of describing the distinct tasks of theologians, engaging in the historical interpretation of Habakkuk and simultaneously announcing his own foundational framework of understanding God. Paul is convinced that God acknowledges and accepts the righteousness of faith. God's invitation to a faith, which attains righteousness among both Jews and Gentiles, is valid from the perspective of the prophet Habakkuk and from the perspective of the gospel that Paul has experienced so powerfully.[14] What does this imply? To summarize Paul's position, there is no one doctrinal or conceptual statement that succinctly communicates the meaning of the righteousness that comes with being close to God. For J. R. D. Kirk, who assesses both the historic Lutheran and the vaguer mystical alternative of Schweitzer, 'labeling either justification or participation in Christ as the gospel is a category mistake'.[15] New Testament scholars, who are increasingly sensitive to the theological worldview of Jewish-Gentile equality before God in Romans, are cognizant of the complex hermeneutics involved in Paul's reasoning. As a result, Kirk and others see Paul's identification of the resurrection as the most significant event through which faithfulness makes sense. What we can say with regards to justification is that Paul is corroborating the text and the resurrection event through an inference of likeness between the text and the new reality that the resurrection posits. As we shall see in terms of other issues as well, Paul's theology is largely one of setting his own foundations upon the interpretation of an *event*, the event of Christ resurrected, in the light of an interpretation of the Jewish *scriptures* in his own tradition, for the benefit of the church of Jews and Gentiles. This is Paul's hermeneutic circle, the virtuous circle of interpreted meaning from *text* and the foundational meaning of the resurrection *event*.

A holiness ethic

Paul is frequently dismissed, not without justification, regarding his moral teaching, by those who cite his pastoral concerns and the demanding criteria of his ever-changing culture as the reason for his alleged scattershot approach to moral issues. Indeed, one popular and well-known way of interpreting Paul, especially in regards to his views on the public role of women and of homosexuality, is to dismiss his views as necessitated by 'his context', hence of little relevance to the contemporary reader. But what is this context? Paul's context, in fact, involves a panoply of concerns around which he interprets the most important categories of early Christian belief. His concerns are couched in terms of the vital categories: Jew and Gentile, law and grace and his invocation of God's judgment of history in the light of Christ's crucifixion and resurrection. I think it is too quick to dismiss Paul's moral thought as simply a function of his context, if by context we are referring to one strand of the Christian moral tradition which developed and changed in subsequent history. When it comes to articulating holiness, Paul's context is, in fact, a multi-layered fabric of theology laced with occasional, strategic appropriations of philosophers' moral views. As such, it has remained, in some sense, a permanent fixture in Christian theology ever since, but is always complemented by ever-increasing accretions of other views. Whatever the occasional nature of Paul's moral counsel, it is surely connected to the most vital theoretical categories of ancient Christian faith.

Two of the most controversial aspects of Pauline studies are the questions of his Jewish identity and the applicability of his moral counsel. What is especially controversial is the way in which these two issues come together in his letters. The contents of various controversies are well known, but the question for a methodologist is how and why does Paul engage in moral counsel at all? How does he presuppose that theology bears on moral questions or vice versa? The question turns on his relation to Judaism and the Law, because of the fact that Paul, despite his emphasis on faith and justification, continues to presume a basic Jewish principle that good behaviour will be rewarded while bad behaviour will be punished. When all is said and done regarding Paul's theology of grace, Paul still retains this template for thinking about God and God's relations with us even though it is no longer filtered exclusively through the Torah. Paul's idea of the justification by faith is a clear yet complex background factor in his offerings of moral instruction. He admits in the book of Romans that it is not the hearers of the law but 'the doers of the law who will be justified' (Rom. 2.13), something which presents a clear problem for any narrow view of Paul as someone concerned with faith to the exclusion of works. But, the relationship between law and grace matters because Paul is the first Christian theologian to account for God and the implications of faith in God in connection with the moral life.

A number of passages are candidates for analysis in regards to this tension, but I will focus on the points Paul makes in the first letter he writes to the Thessalonians. Before moving into that analysis however, let us briefly consider Paul's reference points for a moral code which he makes elsewhere. In Rom. 2.15, Paul remarks that the Gentiles, who do not possess the law but 'do instinctively what the law requires' are those who 'show that what the law requires is written on their hearts, to which their own conscience also bears witness'. Nevertheless, the Jewish law is still a worthwhile measure of moral behaviour, a visible indication of the standard of virtue that must be upheld. Since it is coherent with certain philosophical ideals of moral virtue, the Jewish law buttresses Paul's famed description of the tensions between the spirit and the flesh.

For Paul, the human conscience (a conceptual pillar of the [later] natural law tradition in moral philosophy) is insufficient as a complete measure of the good. The exercise of conscience is inevitably insufficient as means for choosing morally. Evidence for why Paul thinks this way comes from his critique of 'pagan morality', evident, for instance, in Rom. 1.20, and in Gal. 5.24, where Paul is convinced that in contrast to pagans, 'those who belong to Christ

Jesus have crucified the flesh with its passions and desires'. In 1 Cor. 6.10, Paul sees a contrast between the moral profile of the Christian community and those outside it: 'Do not be deceived! Fornicators, idolaters, adulterers, male prostitutes, sodomites, thieves, the greedy, drunkards, revilers, robbers – none of these will inherit the kingdom of God.'

Paul's frequent allusions to love are pivotal to his theocentric ethics as well (Rom. 13.8-10, 1 Cor. 13, Gal. 5.14), thus giving the solid impression that for Paul, a moral conscience is unable to establish a moral code without the additional ingredient of a basis in God's love for us and our love for God in return. Because of the love framework, Paul engages in various kinds of exhortatory or 'parenetic' rhetoric in order to convince his hearers of his particular moral perspective – for instance, on sexuality and marriage. Thus, Paul's moral theology, while rooted in being a response to God's love and grace, is more than that. On the other hand, without Paul's theology, we would not read at all about his moral outlook, which is framed in terms of the urgent future.

1 Thessalonians demonstrates Paul's balance of a theocentric and an eschatological ethical outlook, because of the way in which he offers practical advice for Christians living in Greco-Roman, Mediterranean culture. Paul's exhortation to the Thessalonians reaches its crux in 1 Thess. 4.3-8, when he advises the Thessalonian Christians to seek holiness in contrast to those Gentiles who 'with lustful passion' 'do not know God' (v.5). Here again, we see Paul making a distinction between Christians' holy behaviour and the pagan Gentiles whose behaviour is rooted solely in the passions. Yet, as we read of Paul's efforts to advocate holiness in this letter, there is some inconsistency with his advice offered in Romans and Philippians (4.8), where his call to virtue – for its own rewards – harks back to the Greek tradition. In his letters overall, however, Paul seems to advocate the theological virtues (faith, hope and love) and uses them to interpret or re-interpret the general, already valid philosophical virtues (justice, courage, temperance, prudence).

Paul is operating with two parallel dynamics regarding his moral advocacy. On the one hand, he can draw on pagan culture's native philosophical tradition, which promotes moral behaviour among non-Christians, while nevertheless allowing certain kinds of misbehaviour to flourish. On the other hand, within the Christian community, notably among the Corinthians, there are misbehaviours that contradict holiness and the call to perfection, these misbehaviours being effects of the pagan culture that contradict the Christian's body which is united to Christ in his death. Appeals to general natural law types of moral argument are present in Paul, but these appeals do not rule out Paul's overarching theological narrative in which the theological virtues are the key for Christians in order to understand moral obligation in light of Christ's death and resurrection. Sometimes Paul sets out general moral injunctions, such as 'whatever is true . . . just . . . honourable . . . pure' in Phil. 4.8, or that which might be 'good, acceptable and perfect' in Rom. 12. These general moral categories conform to the expected descriptions of those who live according to God's grace, even though their immediate origins are socially and culturally prompted within the confines of Greco-Roman society.

In 1 Thess. 4, Paul intensifies the contrast by articulating the goal of *hagiasmos* (holiness) with *porneia* (often fornication but really implying a general category of sexual immorality) and *akatharsia* (impurity). Paul's ethic of chastity is clear from his injunction of sexual self-control. What is interesting about this particular exhortation is that Paul draws explicitly upon holiness, a notion of separation. Interestingly, this word is not used in secular Greek discourse. The category of holiness is one which serves to filter the divinely authored event of grace and is in fact what God wills for believers (4.3). Cognate references are found in 1 Cor. 1.30 and 6.11 as God's sanctification of us. Thus, holiness is not transferable to the categories of the Greek virtues nor is the call to holiness restricted in Paul's mind to a soteriological sense, whatever compatibility may exist, practically speaking. Paul intends the ethical sense here, despite repeating in 5.23 that 'being made holy', or sanctification, is God's work.[16]

The category of holiness serves Paul's eschatological ethic. His advice concerns the way Christians should behave in the time between the coming of Christ and the end of time. Thus, we should not take E. P. Sanders' remark that 'Paul developed neither a developed halakah to govern behaviour nor a system for the atonement of post-conversion transgressions' to mean that Paul did not think through the moral demands of being a follower of Christ.[17] If Sanders were correct, it is hard to see why Paul would deliberately choose the word holiness in the context of his correspondence with the Thessalonians. Rather, Paul simply recognizes that the gift of holiness that God wants Christians to express in their lives is a gift which has to be grasped as a vision of the resurrected life. True, it is not reducible to a code or to a particular hermeneutic of interpreting Jewish scriptures. Neither is it a situational ethic of a subjective moral attitude, devoid of particular contents. We know enough about Paul's proscription of homosexual behaviour to be able to say that holiness does mean something definite.

As his repeated concerns over sexual matters in Thessalonians and in Corinthians (where there is more of a connection with the Christian meaning of human embodiment, especially in 1 Cor. 6) and with the repeated concern for how Christian brothers and sisters treat one another (1 Thess. 4.6), Paul has very specific types of transgressions in mind. Paul's holiness ethic, at least insofar as 1 Thessalonians is concerned, is an ethic that is two-sided. It is one of interpreting the sense of law and righteousness that comes from the Jewish legacy of a separate holy people, and it is eschatologically oriented to the communal life of Christians whose bodily existence should anticipate a resurrected existence, hence union with Christ. Paul's theological method of interpreting the tradition and setting foundations for a struggling and future church consistently shows itself. He is consistent by being able to draw on both a natural law ethic in one context (cf. Rom. 1) and a theological category of holiness that is rooted in grace to articulate a moral theology which is plural in its sources (the gospel and the virtues) yet focused in its meaning.

Original sin

Given the legacy of doctrinal frames of thinking about Paul, Christian theologians have historically grown accustomed to believing that Paul expresses a doctrine of original sin. Some say that Paul interprets the 'fall' of Adam in a way that specifies an actual formulation of basic human depravity from which we are saved by Christ. Paul has thus been seen as the first doctrinal figure in Christian theology because of what he says about sin and 'original' sin. But, modern exegesis has disabused us somewhat of the idea that there is a Pauline 'doctrine' of original sin. Modern exegesis settles instead for a more truncated understanding of what Paul was trying to communicate. In the process, it has become clear that between Paul and later theologians, such as Augustine and Gregory of Nyssa, there are significant differences of meaning. These differences are not only differences of theology but also differences of theological method. In Paul, for instance, we do not find the precise Augustinian concept of biologically inherited original sin. This is not to suggest that Paul's and Augustine's expressions of the causes of sin are at odds with each other, but there are notable differences in scope between them. These differences can be understood in part as methodical differences.

The locus of Paul's theology of sin is the enigmatic statement of Rom. 5.12: 'Sin came into the world through one man . . . because [or 'in whom'] all men sinned.' The power of sin is described in Chapters One and Two as a challenge for individual Christians, against nature and conscience (2.14), causally connected to death (Rom. 5.20, 8.20), known in light of the Torah (5.13) and demonstrative of the struggle between spirit and flesh (8.8-9). Particularly troubling for interpreters is Paul's admission, on the one hand, that 'I do not do the good that I want, but the very thing I hate is what I do' (Rom. 7.15). Yet, for Paul, Christ has died to sin with the probable meaning that, in some sense, Christians are impervious to sin and its consequences. He even refers to the life of sin, 'aroused by the law' (Rom. 5) in the past tense. Thus, Paul is seemingly caught up in a series of contradictions concerning sin, explaining its origins and claiming its defeat, while admitting it as a problem for the present moment. He affirms its power over himself while denying its power over Christians. In the later Augustinian formulation of sin, Christian life means the possibility not to sin, over against the expectations and power of an age in which it is impossible not to sin. For some critics, such paradoxes imply a less than methodological outlook. Yet methodology and consistency are not to be confused. Paul can be methodical without being necessarily consistent. Moreover, there are plenty of clues to indicate that, however disparate Paul's message, he is mindful to structure his claims.

First, it is obvious that Paul is constructing his view of sin on the foundations laid by Judaism. Primarily owing to the interpretation of Bultmann, Paul has been viewed by moderns as equating the law with the reality of sin. Bultmann was interested in portraying the law negatively in order to stress the centrality of grace as its dialectical opposite in Paul. But, not only is this not based on a good reading of Rom. 7 in particular, it also implies a false portrait of the *structure* of Paul's argument concerning sin. In Rom. 7.7-11, Paul interprets Gen. 3 and Exod. 20.17 in a midrashic way, claiming that the Jewish law is not responsible for sin per se, but that it does illustrate sin and its consequences.

Second, Paul is able to regard sin as having been depleted of its power in light of Christ. For Paul, based on his Christophany, his experience of Christ on the road to Damascus, an apocalyptical or revelatory age has begun. This new age is an accomplishment of Christ. In the person of Christ is encapsulated a realized eschatology, a hope that springs forth in the gospel, 'my' gospel as he terms it at several points. Here is Paul's stance, his foundational perspective that governs his interpretation of sin and the history of sin since the beginning of time. For Paul to mark out the reality of this new age, he uses language that evokes this panoramic vision. The repeated use of 'in Christ' (*en Christo*) and its equivalents in the Pauline corpus was sufficient to lead Schweitzer, as well as the biblical scholars Adolf Deissmann and Wilhelm Bousset, to advocate the Platonic 'Christ mysticism' as an alternative to justification by faith as the single lens through which to understand Paul's soteriology. While this proposal is not the alternative that they imagined it to be, it is a motif by which we see how Paul leads his readers to see Christ as the representative of this new age. Christ is the herald of this arriving new age and the means by which it comes about. As the representative for this new age, Christ represents a new humanity, as distinct from Adam, the representative of the old humanity.

This is the framework that Paul sets up to understand sin, and the somewhat contradictory lines of thought in Rom. 5–7 on the scope of sin and the means by which sin is confronted are, for Paul, evidence of a confused state of affairs that characterize the present age, caught between the past and the future. Paul's own presently experienced existential struggles over sin are absurd for him in contrast to the *metanoia* that he has experienced in Christ. The existential tension between sin and God's acceptance of him is also a tension between the present 'now' and the 'not yet' of eschatological hope. Methodologically, this means that his arguments will appear haphazard, if only because they reflect the chaos brought on by sin and the weakness that it causes Christians, even though their status 'in Christ' is already won. This tension is captured well by Luther in the expression (*simul justus et peccator*), which serves as a hermeneutic for scriptural interpretation and doctrinal development within Protestantism from the sixteenth century onwards. Indeed, this way of doing theology from the explicit cognizance of internal struggle can be traced all the way back to Paul. That statement needs clarifying, however. Paul is doing theology as a preacher and a correspondent. He is not elaborating his thought in a deductive manner or in the manner of a philosopher providing a logical exposition of thought. The juxtaposition of Adam and Christ, the two representatives of humanity, is Paul's way of expressing the reality of sin and, therefore, his means of expressing the danger that lurks to prevent his union with the glorified Christ.

Third, as with other themes present in his letters, Paul expresses the reality of sin and salvation through particular metaphors and analogies. Compare the treatment of sin and Adam/Christ in Romans with Paul's contrasting of Adam and Christ in 1 Cor. 15.21-22. In 1 Corinthians, he writes 'For since through a man came death, also through a man came resurrection of the dead. For as in Adam all die, so also in Christ, shall all be made alive.' The first statement contains a chronological sequencing of Adam and Christ, figures connected to the beginning and the end, respectively. Implied in this sequence is a narrative telling of two figures and their sins/benefits. In the second part of this passage, however, Paul draws an analogy between Adam and Christ, distinct figures or 'types'. The analogy is meant to highlight the semantic differences without necessarily restating the dependence of the second on the first. This form of analogy repeats what is present in Rom. 5.12 with respect to Adam and Christ, and in Rom. 5.18-19 with respect to the misdeed or righteous act.

Thus, on the subject of sin, Paul incorporates arguments that take a quasi-narrative structure as well as a more analogical structure.[18] His arguments here also follow a rhetorical structure of syllogistic reasoning that would have been familiar to his first-century readers/hearers. These are two different methodological strategies which communicate a message in complementary ways. The invocation of a narrative and the employment of an analogy are examples of two aspects of Paul's theological method. On the one hand, we see Paul reflexively joining his claims to the rabbinic tradition in order to establish continuity with the past. On the other hand, Paul is constructing analogies by way of setting out a kind of proto-doctrine or concept for assent, which might serve to guide his hearers. This is Paul's hermeneutic: interpret God's promises and revelation as set out in the Hebrew scriptures, but guide that interpretation in the light of the spiritual foundation revealed in an experience of Christ.

The holy trinity

Paul's experience of God is a vivid experience of Christ and the Spirit. And, according to Trinitarian doctrine, these are two 'missions' through which God makes salvation to be both possible and even intelligible. Indeed, the participative 'in Christ' metaphor that Paul develops in his letters is supplemented by many references to the Body of Christ and the sending of the Spirit, these images being sufficient grounds to suppose a proto-doctrine of the church and the Trinity in Paul. While calling any idea that Paul adopts as 'doctrinal' is an exaggeration, the main point is that Paul, by referencing his own experience of God in distinct ways, does clarify some rudimentary elements of a Trinitarian God. I want to focus on this suggestion for its relevance to theological methodology.

Especially crucial is the idea that Paul is constructing his images of God on the basis of his own experience, not strictly upon a prior belief. From his references to Christ and the Spirit, we see that for Paul, it is not mere belief that justifies his interpretation of God or some cognate subject. Of course, it is impossible to delete from Paul's new experiences of God the Torah monotheism that frames those experiences. The hermeneutical circle is thus operative in a Trinitarian way for Paul, so long as we take 'Trinitarian' to refer to a pre-doctrinal sense of God's threefold presence.

According to New Testament scholar James Dunn, for Paul, there is 'no distinction that can be detected in the believer's experience' between the exalted Christ and the Spirit of God.[19] And yet we see in both Paul's letters and the 'deutero-Pauline' letters, including Ephesians, a variety of ways that he invokes Christ and the Holy Spirit. Methodological considerations can help us clarify, I think, what Paul is up to, since at first glance, we need to probe Dunn's implication that Paul is being rather arbitrary in assigning names and powers to the action of God in his life and the life of the Christian churches.

Rather than being arbitrary, Paul is simply being ambiguous. Paul is expressing in terms that are not yet conceptually precise what his understanding of God looks like. A clear example of this ambiguity can be gleaned from considering his frequent allusions to the 'Spirit of God' and the 'Spirit of Jesus' (cf. Rom. 8.9; 1 Cor. 2.11, 12,14; Gal. 4.6; Phil. 1.19). As Gerald O'Collins points out, the 'of ' or genitive form of the noun can mean three distinct things: (1) the Spirit that brings us to God or Christ; (2) the Spirit that comes from or is drawn from God or Christ; or (3) the Spirit that simply is God or Christ.[20] Whichever it does mean (and it is impossible to know for sure), we can nevertheless affirm that Paul at least understands a relationship among three distinct aspects of God. We can also see that for Paul, it is the more subjectively nuanced Spirit who enables our union with Christ. The connection between the Spirit and Christian experience is especially poignant for Paul. In Gal. 4.6, God has sent the Spirit of His Son into our hearts. In Rom. 5.5 and 1 Cor. 12.7-8, the Holy Spirit 'has been given'. The passive voice in these examples is also key, as it indicates an experiential hermeneutic for affirming God's being. Rom. 5.5 affirms that God's love 'has been poured into our hearts through the Holy Spirit', and Gal. 4.5-6 picks up on this by adding: 'that we might receive adoption as children . . . God has sent the Spirit of his Son into our hearts crying, "Abba! Father."' In 1 Thess. 1.4-6, the Holy Spirit has inspired the Thessalonians to receive the Word joyfully and withstand persecution; and in vv. 9-10 of the same chapter of Thessalonians, Paul emphasizes, as he does elsewhere, the action of God in raising Jesus from the dead. There are other instances, but these examples suffice to show that Paul does not issue timeless propositional statements in regards to the Trinity. Instead, he claims that through the direct power of the Holy Spirit functioning cognitively and affectively, God acts graciously to transform us from within. This experience of empowerment, the beginning of our salvation, is our access to the Trinitarian character of God.

Paul can adapt this experience of God to correlate with already existing traditions of triadic formulae. We see some evidence of these formulae in Ephesians, but also, more prominently, in Rom. 1 and 2 Cor. 13.13 – two passages that appear at the beginning and end of those two letters. In fact, the formula at the end of 2 Corinthians appears to be an experiential gloss: 'The grace of the Lord Jesus Christ, the love of God, and the communion of the Holy Spirit' attributes particular characteristics to each of the persons of the Trinity. The Father, Son and Holy Spirit each function to produce certain effects. So, Paul's method, in regards the threefold God, is experientially inclined with doctrinal effect, but not necessarily doctrinal intent. The ambiguity over the respective roles of the Holy Spirit and Christ simply constitutes evidence of this inclination. Paul's ambiguity does not indicate an insufficiently doctrinal instinct. Paul is not trying to explain the Trinity, the nature of each person of the Trinity or the relations between them. But guiding Paul's experiential perspective is the idea that the revelation of God is an event to which he wants to respond with some degree of understanding. Clearly, the crucifixion and resurrection stand out in Paul's soteriology precisely because they are events that have transformed his perspective towards God in a Trinitarian direction, yet corroborating what Paul already understands from scripture.

The experiential perspective adopted towards the triadic God does not contradict the hermeneutical perspective towards God which Paul takes from the Torah. At the centre of Paul's appropriation of the tradition of Israel lies his adoption of the name 'Father' for God. And so, for Paul, as with other names, images and metaphors on other issues, what is perhaps marginal in ancient Judaism becomes central for him. Images and motifs galore from the Hebrew Bible assist Paul in speaking about the significance of Christ's resurrection. For instance, one important parallel concerns Paul's reference to Christ's resurrection from the dead as 'the first fruits of those who have died' (1 Cor. 15.20), which is based on the elevated temple offering of the first fruits of the harvest in Lev. 23.9-21.

More significant is Paul's employment of the term 'Lord' or *kyrios* for Jesus. The Lord is applied to Christ twenty-four times in 1 Thessalonians alone, the earliest book of the New Testament. In the Hebrew Bible, including its Greek translation, the Septuagint, 'kyrios' refers to YHWH, the tetragrammaton or special name for God that is applied by Israel to the one God. For Paul, the title 'Lord' is applied to Christ as well, an affront to Jewish monotheism, yet an interpretation of the resurrection, after which divinity is ascribed to Jesus. Paul feels able to apply 'Lord' to Christ by calling on texts from the Hebrew Bible to support his interpretation, such as the citation of Joel 2.32 in Rom. 10.13: 'Everyone who calls on the name of the Lord shall be saved.' And at the end of the kenotic hymn in Phil. 2.10-11, Paul adds 'at the name of Jesus' to Isaiah 45.23-24, where the prophet writes in the name of the Lord, 'To me every knee shall bow'.[21]

The belief that Christ is Lord extends to cognate concepts as well, notably the concept of 'the day of the Lord'. Going on the numerous references in the Hebrew Bible that mention God's intervention 'on the day of the Lord' to combat the wickedness of Israel (Jer. 17.16-18; Am. 5:18-20; Ezek. 7.1-27; Zeph. 1.14-18; Joel 2.1-2), the forces of Babylon and Egypt (Isa. 13.6-9; Ezek. 30.3), to judge sinners (Isa. 2.11-12; Jer. 30.5-9) and to restore Israel (Zech. 14.1-21), Paul applies this eschatological imagery to Jesus' return at the *parousia* (1 Thess. 5.2). He conflates the two elsewhere, such as in 1 Cor. 1.8: 'the day of our Lord Jesus Christ' and 2 Cor. 1.14: 'the day of the Lord Jesus.' Paul mostly seems to presuppose sonship on the part of Jesus. This shows up in the fifteen references to Jesus as specifically 'God's son' in the seven authentic letters attributed to Paul, amid other allusions. He also seems to presuppose some sort of pre-existence for Christ. Again, what is notable by its absence is an extended argument for Jesus' pre-existence of the sort that we see in the patristic literature. There is not even any elaborate language of 'Logos' that we find in John or even in Luke. What there is, instead, is a focus on the soteriological purpose of God sending His son to free us from sin, God *pro nobis*.

Hermeneutically speaking, the novelty of Paul's Christian messianic faith is more noticeable when it comes to Christology, novel in relation to early Judaism. Yet even on this question, there are still resonances with the Hebrew Bible, concerning, for instance, the extraordinary parallels that Paul draws between Isaac and Abraham, Christ and God and Israel and the Gentiles. The exegetical details of these parallels are complex, yet it is sufficient at this point simply to note that Paul's Christological and ecclesiological readings of the interpolations he brings forwards about God's Old Testament promises and covenants is wide ranging, especially in Romans and Galatians. His ability to set off Abraham from Moses is, in itself, an extraordinary hermeneutical feat, especially when it comes to grappling with the Judaizing party he confronts in Galatia.[22]

The main methodological point of this discussion is that Paul's portrait of God does not concern an abstract Trinity. Paul's Trinity is the Trinity of God's agency which is known through its functioning in the economy of salvation. Unlike Luke and John, Paul does not make an argument for the pre-existence of Christ, although it is certainly plausible to infer that Paul is presupposing Christ's pre-existence. Moreover, Paul does not affirm that Jesus himself sends the Holy Spirit; yet, true to his more ambiguous style, Paul does say that the risen Christ, the last Adam, has become the life-giving Spirit (see 1 Cor. 15.45). Paul's qualifier of the Spirit as 'life-giving' is typically Pauline in the sense that Paul identifies the Spirit by its role or salvific function. Methodologically, Paul's theology bears evidence for being consistently two-sided. There seems to be a persistent movement between the background acts of theological interpretation of scripture (the Septuagint) that are guided by his foreground positions and perspectives rooted in his own experience of Christ and the Spirit. It is sufficient to serve as the basis for later doctrinal developments, even if such developments within Paul's own writings are not doctrinal pronouncements per se. What Paul provides are vivid images, metaphors and categories on which later thought is highly dependent.

Conclusion

One of the longstanding claims of Christian theologians regarding Christian doctrine is that it is best conceived on the basis of a particular form of experience as opposed to the idea that doctrine is a form of knowledge rooted in abstract reasoning. The Latin saying *lex orandi est lex credendi* ('the rule of prayer becomes the rule of belief') is frequently introduced as an antidote to the persistent mistake of conceiving beliefs in an exclusively cognitive, rational way. Paul, whom we have been considering, is an exemplar of *lex orandi est lex Credendi*. His writing bears the stamp of this claimed relationship between prayer (or even mystical experience) and belief. Paul's theology does not exemplify a straightforward Hellenistic Judaeo-Christianity of the kind that might have developed in a hypothetical interaction between Philo and Hellenistic Christians in Alexandria. What we have seen in this chapter through the examples of justification by faith, a holiness ethic, original sin and the Trinity, is that Paul's experience of God is a hermeneutically filtered experience. It is not *sui generis* in the way that some critics have tried to isolate Paul from his religious tradition or other Christian contemporaries. Paul is not a unique religious figure, disconnected from his Jewish and his Christian traditions that some have described.

With particular cogency in relation to Galatians but throughout his letters (at least to some extent), Paul adopts a twofold strategy in developing his theological arguments. The one strategy is to argue from points of scripture and the second is to argue from the priority of his own experience. Richard Hays asks 'is the scriptural text to be illuminated in the light of Spirit-experience, or is Spirit-experience to be measured by normative constraints laid down by the text?' This is the methodological question *par excellence* and Hays answers resoundingly: 'Paul's unflinching answer . . . is to opt for the hermeneutical priority of Spirit-experience.'[23] Let us take this to mean, however, that by experience, Paul is not endorsing *all* of his experience as foundational. His ruminations on his own sinfulness make it clear that he is being selective. The experience which guides his hermeneutical instincts is that which aligns with the revelatory experience of his conversion to Christ, an alignment that is the work of the power of the Spirit. What we have in Paul is therefore a method of one who is working in terms of the practice of scriptural interpretation and foundational categorization.

These two practices are what Bernard Lonergan would come to call the 'functional specialties' of theology. Specifically, interpretation and foundations are Lonergan's second and fifth functional specialties, and we shall say more about them as specific theological tasks in Lonergan's schema of theological method from time to time in this book. For now, it will suffice to note that they are located on either side of the background/foreground distinction already discussed. Scriptural interpretation, while not chronologically prior to foundations, is a practice that Paul takes up in order to extend the cognitive meaning of his conversion. In Paul's case, since he is already vastly familiar with Hebrew scripture, his conversion is all the more potent since God's creating and saving purposes in the world are already well perceived from his Jewish upbringing and rabbinic context. What his conversion allows, however, is a self-conscious correlation between the meaning of his conversion and the new meaning that he is able to attribute to scripture. Paul's frequent use of metaphors and analogies is precisely his means of securing such a correlation between interpretation and foundations, between God's past saving action and his present activity through Christ and the Spirit.

In this sense, Paul's theological methodology, while canonical, is nonetheless not unique, because these very same devices are deployed by Irenaeus, Origen and other patristic theologians of the second to fifth centuries as their own theological methodologies. In the case of the patristics, however, as we shall see in Chapter Two, the reliance upon allegory expands the methodological scope of acts of interpretation. Over subsequent centuries, the deepening reliance upon philosophy likewise expands the methodological scope of their respective efforts to establish theological foundations. In the process, theological method begins to take on more complexity in Christian history as orthodox and heretical positions become distinguished. Doctrines begin to be probed systematically as worldviews begin to shift in the light of attraction towards and repulsion from Platonic and Stoic philosophies. Paul's theological methodology shows us that whatever the logical complexity of subsequent developments, a robust theology can be crafted through the deployment of a mere two theological tasks: interpretation and foundational (categorical) theology. We will now turn to the patristic period for examples of figures that expanded Christian theology's methodological horizons, which were largely laid by Paul.

CHAPTER TWO

The patristic era

This chapter pivots from an analysis of the familiar figure of Paul and his theological method to the much more unfamiliar figures and themes of the patristic period. The patristic era, which is often dated from approximately the end of the first century until (arguably) the eighth century CE, was foundational for the development of theology and theological method. Here I shall only be able to touch on a few salient issues relating to theological methodology in early Christianity. To supplement this preliminary discussion, we shall dedicate the entirety of the following chapter to Augustine's *De doctrina christianae*, the most important text dealing preponderantly with matters of theological method, which was a mainstay of the theological curriculum for most of the thousand years after Augustine's death.

The first and most obvious difference between Paul and the patristic theologians of the second century is the authority which is granted to particular sources. For Paul, as I argued in Chapter One, there is a twin appeal to the Old Testament and to the event of Christ's crucifixion and resurrection, about which he claims a personal experience. The authority behind theological claims for the patristics is more diffuse than it is for Paul. Yet, there are particular methodological foci that become default patterns for patristic theology and the Christian church thereafter. Beginning with Irenaeus and proceeding with Origen and Athansius, this chapter will examine the degree to which a patristic pattern of theological judgement takes shape.

Irenaeus

Irenaeus (c.130–c.200), the first theologian to be considered here, was made bishop of Lyons (France) in 178. His theological significance goes far beyond any cursory enumeration of his fundamental insights. Nevertheless, although we cannot capture the totality of his contribution to the development of theology here, it will be helpful to hinge our analysis on four pillars of his thought. Irenaeus: (1) is one of the first to develop a sense of tradition as authoritative in the practice of theology; (2) he adapts interpretively the famous notion of recapitulation or *anakephalaiosis* in Christology from its New Testament usage; (3) he adopts the motif of orthodoxy, the 'rule of faith' as a marker of belief in God the trinity of three persons, in order to oppose the heretical Gnostic movement; and (4) he generates novel ideas in the areas of the doctrines of creation and eschatology. In these and other topics, Irenaeus distinguishes himself as one of the greatest and most innovative of early church fathers.

Methodologically speaking, one of the most significant aspects of Irenaeus' thought is his preliminary attempt to systematize Christian doctrine. Like other early patristic theologians, he was deeply aware of the resources available to him from the Greek philosophical tradition. Rhetorically, for instance, despite his early claim in his well-known book *Against the Heresies* (*Adversus Haereses*) that he is unfamiliar with rhetorical form, he structures the book in a way that resembles the main Ciceronian divisions of rhetorical principle. Irenaeus' treatment of various topics is said to reflect general arrangements laid out by Aristotle.[1] He is obviously heavily influenced by Plato, although he may not have been aware of this influence, given the pervasiveness of Platonic thought in ancient society. Yet one of the more significant aspects of Irenaeus' legacy is the very different impressions he has made on modern scholars. On the one hand, as German theologian Adolf von Harnack emphasized, Irenaeus' theology seems internally split on how salvation is wrought between creation and the final consummation. On this view, there is a contradiction between a soteriology that stresses moral growth or gradual healing on the one hand, and the soteriology of restoration to our original status before Adam's original sin on the other.[2] If we were to agree with Harnack, we would implicitly affirm that Irenaeus was unmethodical by falling into such serious contradiction.

On the other hand, there is evidence to support the claim that Irenaeus is the first truly systematic theologian of the church. On this interpretation, the term 'systematic' can denote both 'methodical' and 'comprehensive' or 'coherent'. Such evidence is derived from two surviving texts, especially the *Demonstration of the Apostolic Preaching* and *Against the Heresies* (hereafter *AH*). In both of these texts, Irenaeus weaves together the two hands of God as the actions of creation and salvation history, respectively. He also sees scripture as a unique communication by God which is summed up in the whole person of Christ and explained through the concept of recapitulation that he expands from its original, scriptural mention.

The role of Christ is accentuated in Irenaeus so much that it is possible to speak of a contrast with the earlier Platonic exegesis of Justin Martyr. Irenaeus sees, for instance, Christ speaking with Abraham, Noah and with Moses from the burning bush (*AH* 4.10.1). With Paul, intratextuality is alive in his theological imagination. The Platonic category of participation, which animates so much later patristic and medieval biblical interpretation, is also implicit in Irenaeus through his spiritual appropriation of philosophy. This category is a methodologically significant move for Irenaeus, since it contrasts with the earlier hermeneutic of Justin Martyr, who concentrates heavily on the role of the Logos concept. Irenaeus' presentation of Christian faith identifies the Logos with Christ, the Son of God, in a much clearer fashion. His thinking resembles, therefore, the soteriological and Christological registers of recent neo-orthodox and radical Orthodox thought. This does not make Irenaeus modern, of course. But, it does support the idea that, like his patristic, medieval and more modern theological descendents, his thinking is worthy of being called systematic. Thus, Eric Osborn, in a comprehensive study of Irenaeus, disagrees with the idea that Irenaeus is confused. Osborn claims that the four concepts of (divine) intellect, economy, recapitulation and participation 'govern all that he says'.[3] These concepts do not bespeak method *per se*, but Irenaeus is methodological to the extent that he is systematic.

His dedication to the idea of doctrine is where his methodological instincts prove even more enduring. Irenaeus was dedicated to the propounding and the understanding of Christian doctrine as an explanatory tool for distinguishing between true and false judgements about God, Christ, scripture and the life of faith. In this regard too,

Irenaeus shows considerable development from Paul and other early apostolic fathers. He moves from the mere reception of the central categories of faith to the more theologically sophisticated stage of formulating judgements that explain the stance of ecclesial Christian faith as a viable position that can be explained and theologically rationalized. He is not as differentiated in his doctrinal formulations in comparison with later patristic figures, of course; but his efforts in formulating doctrine are methodologically significant, a leap up the ladder of complexity from the basic dialectical categories of faith (scripture and experience) that we find in Paul. Now, this leap in complexity does not substitute for Paul's kerygmatic clarity. As Lonergan explains in *Method in Theology*, the difference between offering foundational categories and formulating doctrine is the difference between laying out a personal stance and formulating it with the help of categorial knowledge. Doctrines add a theoretical dimension to the categories that animate one's faith in general, something which Irenaeus sees. Paul's clarity is not explanatory, or if it is, it is suggestive of explanation, as proposed in Chapter One.

Irenaeus' need to explain Christian faith and belief arises from his labours to counter the teachings of various Gnostic schools of thought, especially the thought of the influential figures of Valentinus and Marcion. In that sense, Irenaeus faces a contingent situation of conflict, as did Paul on a number of occasions. *Gnōsis*, as it is identified by Irenaeus, is a kind of knowledge about God, creation and nature that enjoyed remarkable popularity in the ancient world as a loose system of thought that sees God as responsible for the existence of suffering and evil present in the material world.

Irenaeus believes that he is able to trace a genealogy of Gnosticism that begins with Simon Magus through Marcion and Valentinus. He believes that his defence of orthodoxy, of 'Catholic' faith, in defiance of Valentinus especially, serves as a workable model for how to confront other heresies. Historically speaking, despite significant overlaps in belief, there are distinct differences between Marcion, Valentinus and other forms of Gnosticism. Nonetheless, one heresy is singled out by Irenaeus for special mention; namely, the idea of two gods – the creator God of the Old Testament and the redeemer God revealed by Jesus. This Gnostic belief, ascribed most plausibly to Marcion, was held for very different reasons by various figures. It prompted Irenaeus to affirm the unity of God and refute the idea that God is divisible. This stance allows Irenaeus to affirm the witness of the entire set of scripture as testimony to one God. This hermeneutic of scripture implies strongly not only a doctrine of the canon, which was still almost two centuries from being formalized, but it also allows Irenaeus to articulate a strong theology of revelation. That is, knowledge of God is a knowledge gained from scripture, but the speculative knowledge that is claimed by various heretics on the basis of other sources is suspect because it is speculative and is based on divergent experiential and textual sources.

What this position immediately suggests is that there is a profound tension between claims that are based on a proper reading of scripture and claims derived from other ecclesially unsanctioned sources. The Trinity is a case in point. For Irenaeus, interpreting Jn. 14.9, 'He who has seen me has seen the Father' (and Jn. 8.19), the Son is what is visible of the Father, while the Father is what remains invisible of the Son. The rough shape of a Trinitarian doctrine is present here because Irenaeus depends on the scriptural account as grounds for proceeding. On the other hand, the Valentinians develop a distinction that owes its language and conceptuality to Platonic sources. Theirs is the distinction between the Father and Mind (nous) and the Word or Logos, which Irenaeus cannot accept for its confusion between the Father and Mind (*AH* 2.17.3). Some scholars, seeing Irenaeus' distinction between God visible and invisible, ascribe to him Gnostic sympathies which get snuck into his arguments. If we take this point to mean that Irenaeus relied on a philosophical meaning to be attached to visibility and invisibility, then that criticism is mooted. Both Gnostics and the orthodox rely on reason. Nevertheless, Irenaeus resisted undue philosophical influence on the whole. In this respect, he differs methodically from Justin Martyr. Irenaeus' debt to scriptural sources and an overwhelming Christological hermeneutic are still the most vital factors in his development of a doctrine of God. These two factors also distinguish him clearly from the Gnostics despite some shared reliance upon philosophical vocabulary.

Indeed, Irenaeus' relationship to philosophy is not cut and dry. In the *Heresies*, Irenaeus does not draw on the resources of scripture all the time. In Parts 1 and 2 of the 5-part work, he spends a great deal of energy refuting Gnostic ideas in logical terms, without any substantial reference to scripture or even tradition. This is a remarkable fact in itself for a theologian who is so well known as a theologian of tradition and orthodoxy. In Book 2.25-28, Irenaeus is said to have borrowed from the methodological canons of the empirical school in medicine and a certain form of scepticism.[4] Irenaeus spends most of his time dealing simply with what he regards as inconsistencies in Valentinian exegesis, especially the interpretation by one Ptolemy of the Johannine prologue regarding the Logos.

Irenaeus refutes the Gnostic approach to scripture by making his focal point the way in which human beings are transformed or educated. Whereas the Marcionites and Valentinians seek to ignore both the Old Testament and the gospels of John, Mathew and Mark, because of their insufficient repudiation of the Law, Irenaeus defends God as the creator. But, he does more than that. He tries to draw the argument away from the nature of God, perhaps because of the many difficult passages of war and violence in the Old Testament with which he would have had inherent hermeneutical difficulties. Instead, he focuses upon the appropriate validity of each covenant for its own time, a linking of the Old and New Testaments to the same 'educational' purpose, the teaching of human beings. This is the famous concept of maturity, brought out by the modern theologian John Hick, among others.

For Hick, Irenaeus' theology is significant for elaborating an evolutionary account of revelation.[5] Such an account justifies a theodicy, a reason to explain the origins of evil. Irenaeus himself is focused on the needs of human salvation itself, a gradual ability 'to accept God's revelation'. In *Adversus Haereses* 4.38.3, he claims:

> Now it was necessary that Man should in the first instance be created; and having been created, should receive growth; and having received growth, should be strengthened; and having been strengthened, should abound; and having abounded, should recover [from the disease of sin]; and having recovered, should be glorified; and being glorified, should see his Lord. For God is He who is yet to be seen, and the beholding of God is productive of immortality, but immortality renders one nigh unto God.

Irenaeus is not so simplistic as to oppose Gnosticism with the Bible straight off. Rather, he introduces an anthropology to mediate the discussion. Akin to the way that Reinhold Niebuhr would conduct theology in the twentieth century, Irenaeus' attention to the significance of sin carries both doctrinal and methodological weight. Doctrinally, the presence of sin counters an exclusively evolutionary worldview, which, incidentally, is something that contradicts Hick's reading of Irenaeus (*AH* 4.39). For Irenaeus, as for Paul, sin serves to block human transcendence, a *de*volution that counteracts evolution. Therefore, the consequent need for salvation from sin mitigates against the pursuit of a naturally constructed knowledge of God.[6] Sin cannot simply be bypassed in the quest for immortality.

Irenaeus' arguments against Gnostic speculation and for the knowledge gained through reading the Bible are not arguments in favour of scripture *per se*. What is not so obvious, but what is crucial to appreciate, is the anthropological aspect of Irenaeus' methodology: human beings are limited in what they can understand and appreciate. Against the Gnostics and foreshadowing Calvin to some extent, Irenaeus responds to critical (speculative) queries about the nature of the relationship between God the Father and the Son by stating simply that 'God knows', thus implying that 'Human beings do not' (*AH* 2.28.6).[7] Our unknowing is linked to the disease of sin – sin being the limiting condition under which we labour.

The relationship between scripture and tradition, a methodo-logical sticking point in Christian theology for most of the church's history, is a live issue in Irenaeus' theological method too. Eric Osborn detects a bias in much Irenaeus scholarship, which he says has too readily characterized Irenaeus as thinking of tradition as saving scripture from its inadequacies. And yet a cursory examination of both *Heresies* and *Demonstration* reveals a far greater number of references to scripture than tradition.[8] Osborn delineates eight principles of scriptural interpretation that stand as distinct ways in which Irenaeus analyses scripture. None of these ways depends on a particular aspect of the church's embryonic tradition as such. Of course, this is not to suggest that such principles of interpretation are introduced as systematically as later hermeneutical thought demands. Unlike Justin Martyr before him, Irenaeus is convinced that the substance of the Christian message of salvation is captured by the 'rule of faith', or *regula fidei*. This 'rule of faith' is grounds for attributing those writings later termed as the New Testament to be scriptural, alongside those of the Old Testament. Paul is to be granted equal authority to the other apostolic writings too. The rule itself is a summary term denoting the main points of early Christian preaching and teaching that Jesus Christ died, was buried and rose from the dead for the forgiveness of sins. As such, the 'rule' served as the conceptual content of the church's tradition which is 'handed down' from the apostles, according to the famous phrase (*AH* 3.3.3). For Irenaeus, the sense of tradition he possesses through handing down is no metaphor, because he had, in his youth, heard Polycarp of Smyrna, a man he regarded as an 'eyewitness to the Word of Life', whose reports concurred with scripture.[9]

Irenaeus advocates, in a sense, a historical metaphysic of scripture. He offers a doctrinal and foundational lens through which scripture is appreciated as a complete knowledge, a revelation. This is taken to mean several things. The fourfold gospels, for instance, reflect the four zones of the world, the four directions by which the wind, like the Spirit, blows (*AH* 3.11.8). This recourse to a metaphorical or aesthetic criterion for scriptural truth is, of course, motivated by Irenaeus' stance against Gnostic attempts to divide scripture. While interweaving citations to each of the four gospels, Irenaeus allows for a plurality of expressions which hold together through a Christological prism. For Irenaeus, Christ is the unifying reality of scripture and of the response of faith. The preaching of the apostles corroborates the stories and prophecies of the ancient patriarchs that foretold Christ's advent in the history of salvation. For Irenaeus, the prophets are a pointer (but not in any final pivotal way) to understanding the kind of salvation which followers of Christ speak about: 'So Abraham was a prophet and saw things of the future, which were to come to pass, the Son of God in human form – that he was to speak with men and eat food with them . . . All such visions signify the Son of God speaking with mankind and being amongst them.'[10] Christ is present, for Irenaeus, in the words and acts of the patriarchs Moses and Abraham, and is therefore active in the covenant of the Word with the people of Israel (*AH* 4.9.1). Conversely, the Law points to the gospel. Christ is 'inseminated' in scripture (*AH* 4.10 and 4.23-26).

It is in this context, then, that the other aspect of Irenaean theology, which is so well known – his theory of recapitulation – begins to make sense, and in a methodical way too. Rooted in a reading of Eph. 1:10 and in the Roman rhetoric of the period, recapitulation for Irenaeus is a term that captures the summing up of scripture and history in the headship of Christ in contrast to that of Adam: 'There is . . . one Christ Jesus who is coming throughout the whole economy, recapitulating all things in himself. But in this "all" is man, the handiwork of God; and thus he recapitulated man in himself, the invisible becoming visible.' (*AH* 3.16.6). The broad theological scope of the language should not distract us, in the end, from noticing what Irenaeus does methodically. According to John Behr, it is the Roman rhetorician Quintilian who identifies recapitulation, stemming from the Greeks, as 'the repetition and regrouping of facts . . . [serving] to refresh the memory of the judge and to place the whole case before his eyes.'[11] Christ does this for salvation history before God, according to Irenaeus. The point, however, is that Irenaeus, like Paul, is free to deploy a rhetorical device at theology's disposal.

More importantly, recapitulation gives us a clear sense of how Irenaeus thinks concretely whereas the Gnostics speculate. John Behr summarizes this nicely: 'The apostolic proclamation, the Gospel, is made up of the texture of Scripture, no longer proclaimed in the obscurity of types and prophecies, but refracted through the Cross and proclaimed clearly and concisely in a résumé.'[12] What Christ brings is clarity, in contrast to the enigma that went before and in contrast to the aimless musings of Gnostic speculation. Christ is an event and, as such, reveals the Word. So, for Irenaeus, the methods of allegory that would come to dominate later patristic exegesis are not only downplayed in his writing, they are necessarily in the background so as to make the history of salvation's climax in Christ clear. It is not surprising to read that Irenaeus, discussing his own anti-Gnosticism, downplays the importance of knowledge itself: 'Preserve therefore the proper order of thy knowledge, and do not, as being arrogant of things really good, seek to rise above God himself, for He cannot be surpassed; nor do thou seek after any one above the Creator, for thou wilt not discover such.'[13] As a consequence, Irenaeus upholds the remembrance of the event of Christ's death in terms of Eucharistic action, a harbinger of the great *lex orandi lex credendi* rule of early theology: 'Our teaching is consistent with what we do in the Eucharist, and the celebration of the Eucharist establishes what we teach.' (*AH* 4.18.4-5). The *lex orandi* method stipulates that doctrine emanates chiefly through worship and prayer. Irenaeus makes this rule explicit, partly through arguing against the Gnostics' preference for speculation. In summary, therefore, we can say that Irenaeus marks a turn towards explanatory reflection in theological method. His deeper thinking implies a turn that not only necessitates the distinction between orthodoxy and heresy, but also necessitates a humble anthropology that twins conversion with judgement for the sake of the church in the light of Christ.

Origen

Of all the early church fathers, Origen is perhaps the most enigmatic and yet one of the most vital for understanding the trajectory of theological method as it evolved in the Christian church during the second and third centuries. Born *circa* 186 and dying from wounds related to his torture under the Decian persecution in 255, Origen was hounded by his theological and political opponents for most of his career. After his death, his theology became the subject of great vexation, and eventually he was condemned by the Fifth Ecumenical Council in 553.

The most distinguishable feature of his theological method is the mode of biblical interpretation known as allegory, which he promoted and utilized unremittingly. In service to his systematizing impulses, Origen adopts a form of biblical interpretation already present in Paul, for instance in Gal. 4, where Paul explicitly states that his interpretation of Abraham's two wives, Hagar and Sarah, is itself an allegorical interpretation.

Yet, some historical theologians have been disquieted by Origen's use of allegory, given its apparent arbitrariness. In this section, we shall endeavour to explore some of the grounds for such charges as well as the evidence for Origen's theological practice that seem more reasoned and coherent. Origen is also justly remembered as the compiler of the *Hexapla*, a lost work of the authorized Hebrew and five Greek translations of the Hebrew Bible in parallel. Only a dedicated philological and exegetical mind could manage the detailed textual analysis which such a task involved, and, evidently, he did manage an entire team of students in compiling this edition of the Bible.

Origen is mainly associated with the idea that the Bible is to be read most of all for its spiritual sense. The spiritual sense is the most significant of the three famous senses of scripture that Origen distinguishes: the literal or historical sense, the psychic (perhaps equivalent to the moral sense) and the spiritual sense. For Origen, the spiritual meaning of scripture is the mysterious reality to which the biblical texts point, most poignantly, as allegorical signs. Strictly speaking, Origen develops a way of reading the Bible that is present in Irenaeus' more limited use of typologies. But, his way of elaborating on the power and scope of allegory is far more comprehensive, to the extent that a hundred years after he died, Basil the Great and Gregory of Nazianzus compiled a number of Origen's texts in the *Philokalia*, through which much of Origen's corpus of work came to be distinctively known and preserved thereafter.

What is remarkable about Origen's sense of allegorical biblical interpretation, however, is not the greater number of applications of allegory to various biblical texts. Rather, what is noticeable is the sheer faith that he places in allegory as a systematic way to interpret the Bible. Paradoxically, Origen utilized non-biblical sources, especially the Platonic philosophy of Philo to unravel the meaning of the Bible's underlying spiritual meaning, despite his insistence in his most famous work *Contra Celsum* (*CC*, *Against Celsus*), that the Christian gospel does not require any external criterion as proof of its veracity (1.2). We will see more examples of this methodical argument in future chapters as theologians who value the integrity of specific theological sources feel obliged to identify an epistemological or metaphysical warrant to justify the priority given to these sources. It seems to be a paradoxical hermeneutical situation that is unavoidable.

Allegory is rooted in the ancient sense of *hyponia*, the 'subliminal intent' or hidden sense of meaning concealed by the surface meaning of the text. It is associated already with the use of metaphors in biblical and other texts. In connection with the biblical writers' penchant for metaphors, Origen buttresses his claims by stating that allegorization is mandated *by the scriptures themselves*. The recourse to the allegorical construction of theological meaning is rooted in the Alexandrian tradition in which Origen was schooled, probably by Clement. Allegory also extends what Irenaeus held concerning the 'Rule of Faith', the way of summarizing the entire Bible as the diversity of histories, events and individual figures that are related to one another in an overarching story which Origen re-tells in light of Platonic philosophical categories. The *Peri Archon*, Origen's book *On First Principles*, which was intended as a handbook for the orthodox interpretation of scripture, is the best-known work, and it has led modern scholars to reclaim Origen's theology from the heretical margins to which his work was assigned by the sixth-century condemnations.

What makes Origen's commitment to allegory so compelling is that it expresses a kind of isomorphism of human anthropology and textual hermeneutics. On the one hand, human nature is that spoken of by Paul in 1 Thessalonians: 'Spirit, soul and body.' On the other hand, biblical texts themselves require interpreting at a spiritual level, a moral level of disciplining instincts and a physical level of what is going on in the external history of the world. The nature of scripture and human nature are thus parallel. And just as not everyone is capable of reaching the higher level of human wisdom, so it is that not everyone is capable of understanding the higher meanings of the biblical texts. In fact, even in Origen's work, one can detect a division between his efforts to elucidate the moral meaning of texts in his homilies (meant for wider audiences) from the biblical commentaries which employ the allegorical method in order to elaborate on the spiritual sense of texts.[14] Scriptural interpretation is dependent on the task and audience that one is obliged to address.

Origen's reliance on allegory has won modern praise. For instance, Henri de Lubac, who was a central figure in the twentieth-century Catholic theological renewal movement, *La Nouvelle Theologie*, alongside Henri Crouzel, an Origen scholar, laud Origen's allegorical approach to the Bible. For de Lubac, allegory suggests a twofold foundation to biblical interpretation and theology in general. The objective historical events of salvation history require a subjective, imaginative Christian reader who allegorizes the mysterious elements of the biblical text in order to render the biblical account of salvation history coherent. But, as de Lubac argues, the 'mysterious character of the Bible is not affirmed to the detriment of its historical character. The Spirit does not wish to harm the letter.'[15] In this context, de Lubac notes that, for Origen, the biblical stories of the flood and ark, as well as the Tower of Babel, are true (CC 4.21, 4.41).

Therefore, for De Lubac, Origen's acceptance of the historical sense disproves the opinion that Origen is an extreme allegorizer, a crude hellenizer of the gospel. De Lubac also notes that Origen's biblical interpretation was widely acknowledged as authoritative in the fourth century and beyond, even while his dogmatic theology fell into disrepute.[16] The implication here is that modern theology is within its rights to admire Origen's hermeneutical strategy while leaving aside his doctrinal novelties. But, R. P. Hanson has criticized de Lubac because Origen's frequent habit of forbidding a literal meaning for various biblical passages does not, in his view, allow a recognizably Christian exegesis to unfold. Maurice Wiles famously claimed that Origen wants to have it both ways: he appears to treasure both the particular historical details of the biblical text and its hermeneutical unity simultaneously. Joseph Trigg observes that Origen admits that the Bible contains errors in order to placate pagan critics of Christianity while affirming the Bible's divine inspiration nevertheless.[17] Trigg sees Origen's Platonism as a fairly straightforward matter, with salvation being the communion with God that is won through a process of separating ourselves from 'purely sensual concerns',[18] yet in a way subtly different from the Gnostics against whom Origen wrote. In fact, it is because of his opposition to the Gnostic doctrine of fate that Origen trumpeted human freedom. Where Origen's emphasis on freedom becomes problematic, however, is with regards to divine justice, the attempt to understand God's response to human goodness and evil. His exegesis of passages, such as God's apparent miscarriage of justice towards Esau and Jacob in Genesis, is one example. If God judges rightly our positive response to the offer of salvation, then why are Jacob and Esau treated so differently despite their equally upright behaviour? For Origen, the doctrine of the pre-existence of souls is introduced in order to save a difficult biblical narrative. Pre-existing human souls exercise agency – including in ways that are sinful – prior to birth. Arguably, Origen's rejection of Gnostic fatalism therefore leads him into another kind of determinism, and a speculative form of determinism too; but the personal, soteriological character of his exegesis, as opposed to a purely metaphysical cosmology, is retained nonetheless.[19]

What does Origen's doctrinal novelty suggest therefore about his own understanding of the relationship between doctrine and scripture? In him, I believe that we see the first tangible signs of an emerging distinction in Christian theology between those theological doctrines that pertain to the rule of faith on the one hand and those that are more speculative ideas on the other hand. The speculative ideas function centrally for the Gnostics, though not so for Origen. This distinction between doctrine and speculation becomes critical if we are to appreciate the growing body of theological literature in subsequent centuries that is increasingly speculative. The distinction is also key to appreciating why so much of subsequent theology becomes dependent on the deployment of philosophy. The idea of human freedom is one example that perfectly demonstrates the sort of methodological schema Origen creates. For him, the existence of human freedom is something that is known in light of the revelation of God's judgement. From his book *First Principles*, Origen posits the idea that the origin of human freedom is a necessary corollary of God's summons to us 'to live a good and blessed life and in every way to avoid sin'.[20] While scripture reveals the existence of human nature and its ultimate source, it does not deal with the nature of human freedom. This is what Origen feels he needs to explain in terms of metaphysical principles such as movement. Origen's notion of the pre-existent agent souls might be said to contradict his doctrine of human freedom, we might say now. However, on Origen's own grounds, we could also say that the pre-existence of human souls is a speculative idea that would not interfere in principle with the revealed fact of human freedom; it would be simply a paradox.

More central to our concern for theological method, however, is Origen's stated belief that investigations into human freedom are indicative of a broader distinction among doctrines or truth claims. This distinction is between those doctrines preached by the apostles as 'necessary ones . . . delivered . . . in the plainest sense to all believers, even to such as appeared to be somewhat dull in the investigation of divine knowledge' and 'other doctrines . . . about which the apostles simply said that things were so, keeping silence as to the how or why; their intention undoubtedly being to supply the more diligent of those who came after them . . . those who train themselves to become worthy and capable of receiving wisdom.'[21] As Lonergan explains in his own distinction between doctrine and systematic theology, there are church and theological doctrines and then there are the grounds for affirming such doctrines. As we can see from Origen, the latter grounds are not necessary for understanding doctrine. But, doctrines do not simply supply their own grounds. Theological doctrines can be investigated on the basis of questions such as those that Origen indicates begin with 'how' or 'why'. It is only with Augustine and the medieval theologians that we see the word 'question' appearing in the titles and headings of various works. This is one way to understand how Origen's methodological distinction between necessary doctrines and other doctrines becomes a presupposition for later theology.

Is Origen's theology, in the end, simply too unwieldy? Porphyry, a contemporary opponent of Origen's, claimed that he 'played the Greek' and that he took 'things said plainly by Moses' as 'riddles, treating them as divine oracles, full of mysteries'.[22] In fact, opposition to Origen was based primarily on his use of allegory. Theodore of Mopsuestia and Diodore of Tarsus worked to develop a fixed relation between history and the spiritual sense, bypassing allegory more or less altogether because of its tendency to render the biblical text mythical and inaccurate.

Contemporary scholarly debates still retain traces of earlier debates that arise from reading Origen's extant writings. Was he a systematic thinker in the mode of a Platonic philosopher? Or, was he really a Christian believer seeking to interpret the Bible in an ad hoc fashion? It may be impossible to summarize Origen in terms of either of these options because it may simply constitute a false dichotomy to contrast these impulses in Origen. What we can pinpoint with more accuracy are the terms of Origen's theory of interpretation.

Objections to Origen's allegorical method lie in the perception that his deviations from the emerging Christian orthodoxy form part of a wider vista of incoherence. Certainly, Origen's belief in the pre-existence of the human soul and the redemption of Satan are two ideas that distract attention from his allegorical method, leading some to credit both Origen's doctrine and his way of reading scripture as similarly arbitrary. Others allege that anyway, Origen's allegorical method works against his own interest in scripture, since allegory is hostile to real poetry. Once allegory takes over, scriptural categories can be distorted. The prime case in point according to this line of thinking concerns Paul's contrast between 'Spirit' and 'Letter', which Origen interprets *as* the contrast between the spiritual and literal interpretation of scripture. Origen does have the tendency to impose his own theory for how allegory works onto scripture.

On the other hand, Origen's theological ideas are alluring for their spiritual and pastoral brilliance. The category of beauty, for instance, is an innovation associated with Origen's writing, and it arises largely because of his epistemology which stresses the act of seeing. While not a directly methodical matter, Origen puts great stock in Jesus' saying that 'he who has seen me has seen the Father', a model of what it means to 'see' God (*Homily on Luke* 3.1, 14). Central to his epistemology, however, is the allusive Platonic category of participation. To know is to participate in something. Knowing is, moreover, a function of God's love, and so to know God is ultimately an act that is initiated by God at the outset of a chain of participatory acts. This explains why Origen ends his most well-known work, *Contra Celsum*, with an emphasis on worship in contrast to those public duties recommended by Celsus. Evocative of Irenaeus, worship is, for Origen, becoming 'absorbed in the word of God and the divine law'. (CC 8.75) And true to his ascetic vocation, Origen posits that while 'knowledge of God is beyond . . . human nature . . . [yet] by God's kindness and love to man . . . knowledge of God . . . extends to those . . . after He was made known to them.' (7.44) Worship and Christian participation in the life of God are important explanatory factors in Origen's theology because of the way they underlie Origen's overarching hermeneutical concern: the faith of the simple believer. Other allegories established by Origen have become Christian theological staples; for instance, the interpretation of Israel's sojourn in the wilderness as an allegory for the Christian soul's journey towards perfection. Also, the wider salvific parallels between Israel and Christ, which Origen exploits in his writing, have become normative in Christian practice and doctrine.

As far as allegory goes, Russell Reno comments astutely that for Origen:

> interpretation is preparatory. The primary function of exegesis is to get us moving in the right direction. It cannot bring us to the destination the way a syllogism can bring us to a conclusion. For the end or goal of exegesis is to dispose the reader in such a way that he or she can 'see' Christ.[23]

Along with Irenaeus, Origen wants to establish scripture's single origins in an invisible God, seen as the pivot point between scriptural exegesis on the one hand and the doctrinal traditions of the church on the other hand. Unlike Irenaeus, however, Origen wants to project a systematic character to the coherence of scripture and doctrine. In doing so, we may worry that Origen's allegorical exegesis is too dependent on irrational word associations. Nevertheless, we can be consoled by the fact that he recognizes that his systematizations do not constitute, as he says, a part of church doctrine; they are speculative. Moreover, Origen's exegesis is not only an exercise in attention to words, grammar and historical context. For him, the presuppositions and purpose of exegesis make for an altogether more important kind of interpretation, affected but not predetermined by doctrine. The communication of the biblical Word, whether originally inspired in the gospel writers, for instance, or even, by comparison, in exegesis itself, *is* a 'spiritual structure which consists in proclamation and written characters', as Origen says.[24] For Origen, in conclusion, the significance of scripture is its role in communicating the divine economy in and through the vast array of historical particulars found in the Bible.

His theology is therefore best conceived methodologically as providing both foundations and a systematic attempt to push beyond doctrine. He grounds biblical interpretation and doctrinal formulation in mutual correlation. In interpretation, the spiritual sense is not the provision of doctrine at the expense of the literal sense. De Lubac was not the last to notice that Origen is not preoccupied with matters of dogmatic theology.[25] Origen is much more interested in the Christian life as a whole, including the moral life, a perspective that is in continuity with Paul. Allegorical exegesis yields a coherent sense of the whole of reality, a system in fact. As de Lubac says, Origen's work is that of a 'mystical exegete', an ascetic experience. According to Origen, the whole plan of God's salvation is revealed in glimpses contained in the words and images of the Bible. The wholeness is evident in a key passage from *On First Principles*:

> Everyone . . . who is desirous of constructing out of the foregoing a connected body of doctrine must use points like these as elementary and foundation principles . . . Thus by clear and cogent arguments he will discover the truth about each particular point and so will produce, as we have said, a single body of doctrine, with the aid of such illustrations and declarations as he shall find in the holy scriptures and of such conclusions as he shall ascertain to follow logically from them when rightly understood.[26]

So, principles are needed for the proper cohering of various doctrines, which are illustrated by scripture. While further examples and points of connection are necessary so that the truth of these doctrines can be discovered anew, the overwhelming impression is that Origen is interested in providing for a systematic character of Christian faith. Overall, in key respects, this foundational and systematic orientation to scripture constitutes a foreshadowing of the early modern preference for system, something that supplies the impetus, in Origen's time, for a foundational reading of the canonical biblical text.

Athanasius

Bishop of Alexandria in Egypt between 328 until his death in 373, one of several great episcopal centres of the ancient Christian world, Athanasius is one of the most formidable patristic figures of Christian history. Most of his writings are occasional in form, usually letters, not unlike the form of theological expression in Paul. His theological method is elusive to try to conceptualize precisely. This is particularly because Athanasius' name remains so bound up with the controversy over Arius and Arianism. As with Irenaeus and Origen, Athanasius had his disputes to resolve, which he attempted to do, in part, through writing. Nevertheless, there are some broad patterns and recognizably Athanasian elements of theological method that have become important reference points for historical Christian self-understanding.

Because of the Arian crisis which gripped the Christian world and fourth-century Roman society, the reception of Athanasius' theology has, for most of Christian history, been associated with Christological doctrine. Athanasius attended the Council of Nicaea as a protégé of Alexander, the bishop whom he succeeded. He publicly defended the faith of the Nicene formula against the Arians in apologetical works, especially in his two-part work *Contra Gentes* and *De Incarnatione Verbi*. (Athanasius' reception has also been tinged by historically inaccurate treatments of writings that were later found to have been inauthentic.) In his work *On the Incarnation* is contained one of the most significant aspects of Athanasius' thought, his discussion of deification, the transformation of human beings brought about as a consequence of the Incarnation of the Word of God. The anti-Arian works were directed against the Arian party in Alexandria as well as beyond that city. This tumultuous controversy led to no less than five exiles from his episcopal seat, where his support solidified eventually among the desert monks.

In his struggle with Arianism and local Egyptian dissenting movements, Athanasius tried to protect the tradition of the universal church against what he saw as the personal theories of his opponents. It is true that Athanasius is typically portrayed as fomenting a rallying cry in defence of *homoousios*, the Greek word for consubstantial, indicating Jesus' equal divinity to the father. Remarkably, however, more recent analysis has alighted on the fact that Athanasius did not simply repeat the word in its defence. Rather, he relied upon subsidiary arguments in regards to the relation of Christ and the Father. The term 'consubstantial' is not used by Athanasius before 350, according to W. H. C. Frend, one of the foremost historians of Christianity.[27] According to Andrew Louth, the term does not seem 'to be a natural part of Athanasius' theological vocabulary until 362. Either way, Athanasius does not resort to a doctrinal term until at least 30 years after Nicene orthodoxy was definitively formulated in 325.'[28] This is actually a good clue as to what Athanasius' theological method is not. He is not simply a formulator, originally or in imitation of others, of Nicene doctrine, despite his obvious interest in doctrinal formulation. What chiefly interests Athanasius is the careful refutation of heretical theology as one part of expounding a wider theological vision. His chief methodical intent seems to be engaging in dialectical argument with an eye towards some foundational resolution. That is, Athanasius' doctrinal discussions are in service to the task of refuting heresy. But beyond refutations and in the process, he arrives at some foundational stances that allow for new doctrinal novelties that have important implications for the future.

One instance in which Athanasius articulates foundational aims is his argument for the inseparability of the divinity and the humanity of Christ. The concept that unites the divinity and the humanity is the Incarnate Word. It is used in response to the Arian criticism that he and the Nicene party are 'worshipping a creature' by retaining the full divinity of Christ while maintaining the full humanity of Jesus. This apparent paradox led the Arians to suspect the impossibility of worshipping Jesus. This paradox is one that the Arians could not abide. For them, the Nicene party could be blocked more readily if it could be shown that their worship was deficient. If we recall that *lex orandi lex credendi* is a way of explaining the doxological source of doctrine, then this Arian charge is serious. The Arians are suggesting that the Nicene doctrine is not only incorrect in its judgement, but that it is also incorrect in the *way* that it is rendered as a judgement.

Athanasisus responds to this charge with a development of theological doctrine that is expansive. Though not focusing on the experience of worship that underlies the development of doctrine, Athanasius does not remain at the level of doctrine *per se*. His rhetoric, for instance in his *Letter to Adelphius* in 370, focuses on the Incarnation and the fate of the body. Athanasius wants to place Christological doctrine within a wider horizon of relating Word and flesh:

> We do not worship a creature. Never! Such an error belongs to the pagans and the Arians. But we do worship the Lord of creation, the Word of God who has become incarnate. While that flesh, on its own, is a part of creation, it nevertheless became the body of God. And neither do we separate the body from the Word and worship it on its own, nor do we cast the Word far from the flesh.[29]

There is, as Khaled Anatolois has remarked regarding this letter, a conviction in Athanasius' theology of a single salvific unity to Christ's person.[30] As such, Christ is a single object of worship and his embodiment represents no impediment to worshipping Christ. Underlying Athanasius' logic is a reflection on the significance of Christ's body, or God's human body, as Athanasius calls it. In this passage, as elsewhere in the letter, he refers to creation, the fact that God has created a world which ought not to be neglected in discussions of Christological doctrine. For Athanasius, it is not a reflection on the more abstract terms 'person' or 'nature' that settles the Nicene doctrine, at least not by themselves. Rather, the question becomes the coherence with which the Nicene doctrine fits with the already relatively settled doctrine of creation. God is able to become a body because creaturely embodiment, despite sin, is good. The notion on which Athanasius is relying is known as the 'communication of idioms'. This notion serves as a premise of

Nicene and later Chalcedonian orthodoxy, and it stipulates a mutual
relationship between humanity and divinity in Christ's person.
This foundational premise undercuts Arius' belief that Christ is
only a creature. It also thwarts semi-Arian arguments that were
premised on the sharing of divinity from God the Father *towards*
the Son. In fact, Athanasius also manages to provide support for
the *homoousion* doctrine without confronting the verbal issue head
on. After the Council of Nicaea in 325, there were two different
interpretations of what *homoousion* meant. According to some
interpreters, it meant the sharing of the same substance, such as
two tables sharing the characteristics of wood, while for others,
homoousion meant the oneness of an entity; namely, God. The
debates over Nicaea's use of this word and the related problems
over the Greek words *ousia* and *hypostasis* are the most complex in
the entire history of Christian theology.

Again, curiously, Athanasius is not committed to dealing with the
doctrinal issues in terms of Greek metaphysics or the philological
tricks of formulae. He is not dedicated to the hair-splitting techniques
associated with the distinction between the unoriginate and the
originate, or the unbegotten and the begotten. His chief recourse is
regarding the permanent meaning that he believes should be attached
to the biblical terms 'Father' and 'Son', notably in light of the Lord's
Prayer. To be sure, Athanasius picks up on this relationship and
adds to it a metaphysical explanation. In *Contra Arianos* (*Against
the Arians*), he describes the relationship as follows:

> For the Son is in the Father . . . because the whole being of the
> Son is proper to the Father's *ousia*, as radiance from light and
> a stream from a fountain; so that whosoever sees the Son, sees
> what is proper to the Father and knows that the Son's being, as
> from the Father, is the Father and is therefore in the Father. For
> the Father is in the Son, since the Son is what is from the Father
> and proper to him, as there is in the radiance the sun, and in the
> word the thought, and in the stream the fountain: for whoso
> thus contemplates the Son, contemplates what is proper to the
> Father's *ousia*, and knows that the Father is in the Son.[31]

What such metaphysical language preserves, from Athanasius'
viewpoint, is the ineffable nature of language about God. But,
he is trying to avoid falling into the trap that he perceives in

the Arians: a cold rationalism. His reference points in biblical literature, worship and the relational character of the Father and Son are intended to uphold this mystery. Influenced by Irenaeus, Athanasius is interested primarily in describing God in a way that fits soteriological criteria. By dealing with the Incarnation in terms of the personal relationships between the persons of the Trinity, Athanasius establishes the prayerful, relational foundations for the doctrinal formula he chooses to defend mainly in his later life. From this foundation comes the so-called soteriological principle, best summarized by Altaner as meaning 'we should not have been redeemed, if God himself had not entered into humanity, hence if Christ were not God'.[32]

Athanasius also references creation in his work, something which also deserves our attention, since the doctrine of creation anchors the Nicene proposition in order to corroborate it. For Athanasius, the will follows the understanding and thus 'the Word is first, then the creation'.[33] God is, then God does, which additionally supports the Nicene doctrine that the Word is eternal action, rather than a creature that comes into being, as the Arians would have it. Like Origen, Athanasius gives grounds for linking points of doctrine systematically, but without the full systematic thrust which characterizes Origen's theology. Given Athanasius' admiration of the monastic founder St Antony of Egypt, which he expressed in his biographical account, *Life of St. Antony*, as well as due to his deployment of principles and soteriological criteria, it is best to think of Athanasius as a foundational theologian. He is obviously aware of the fully dialectical and doctrinal dimensions to his theological agenda, but these are in service to the fruits of conversion, both religiously and intellectually speaking. This judgement does not preclude us from correctly understanding the historical work that has uncovered no small amount of bullying that he waged in self-defence. Nevertheless, his work as a theologian is to be judged on how he made his life's work a matter of reflection and the means by which he chose to reflect on God. To see his work as foundational does not detract from his doctrinal significance either. It is simply to suggest that Athanasius is more than a mere formulator. He is one whose theology endured, partly due to his ability to function methodically in a way that transcended the parameters of theological argument that he encountered.

Conclusion

From our cursory examination of three seminal patristic theologians, a clear picture of early Christian theological methodology has come into view. First, we must resist the temptation to view the fathers of the church as merely doctrinal theologians, or as simply 'more doctrinal' than Paul. It is true that they are doctrinal in ways that Paul is not; but this is only in the sense that they are offering explanations for their faith. God, scripture and faith are conceptualized in particular ways, and so are not to be conceptualized in other ways. Irenaeus is not quantitatively more doctrinal than Paul. Saying this would not adequately explain what it is that he is doing in his theology. Where Irenaeus differs from Paul is that he is seeking explanations where Paul did not. Irenaeus is seeking to understand such explanations as well as trying to see, through recapitulation for instance, how doctrinal concepts are internally coherent with one another. In terms of Lonergan's functional specialties, therefore, Irenaeus is not doing theology in one or other way in a quantitatively different way. He is functioning in a different theological key. He is doing something qualitatively different. Cognitively, Irenaeus is seeking and making judgements and then seeing what those judgements mean, whereas Paul was keen only to grasp those images and categories that burst forth from his mind in the aftermath of his decision to convert to Christ. Origen's systematic theology and Athanasius' foundational language and principles are distinct strategies that construct a tradition that is faithful to scripture and dialectically opposed to the Arians respectively.

The significance of the early patristic sense of theological method lies in the promise of the distinct theological tasks that they each express. What is perhaps surprising with respect to each of these three and their theological method is to appreciate how little philosophical concerns dictated theological conclusions. Of course, this will not be a surprise to those who know the period and its theologians well. For these early church fathers of theology, the issues that they each face of a doctrinal or speculative nature are both theological problems and spiritual matters of great personal interest. For them, the fruit of their imaginative labours is not a purely cognitive, intellectual pursuit. Rather, theology is naturally conducive to philosophical reasoning, but more obviously, it is a question of cohering sources (scripture, doctrinal formulae, the 'Rule of Faith') in the way that is most practical. As we will see in the next chapter, the practical focus of Augustine ends up producing a theological work that not only reveals a theological method that is at work, but whose author is explicitly self-aware of his theological method in the execution of it. That is something that is relatively new, and to Augustine's *De Doctrina Christiana* we now turn.

CHAPTER THREE

Augustine and the method of Christian conversion

In this chapter, we will focus our attention on Augustine, regarded as a 'doctor of the church' by Catholics and as a figure of authority by Protestants as well, although we will not look at his entire corpus. We will instead focus on Augustine as the progenitor of what is called the first work in Christian hermeneutics, *De Doctrina Christiana* (*DDC*).[1] This collection of four books is most often translated in English as *On Christian Doctrine*, but some think it would be better to translate it as *On the Form of Teaching Suitable for Christians*.[2] In fact, the term 'doctrine' incorporates a great many things, because in Book I it refers primarily to the contents of faith, in Book II to the contents of scripture, Book III to a theory of signs and rules of biblical interpretation, while in Book IV he focuses on Christian preaching. By terming this book the first in Christian hermeneutics, I am thinking about Augustine's explicit efforts to make the 'strange world of the Bible' appear relevant for the church of his time. It is worthwhile to recall that by the time Augustine wrote this work on Christian education, he and his church were already separated from the biblical events by almost 400 years.

In the words of Rowan Williams, Augustine is trying to conceive of a rhetoric that can communicate and cultivate a 'counter-culture'.[3] Methodologically, this is a highly significant observation, since many Christian churches in our own contemporary culture perceive that theology is at its best when it serves the task of establishing a counter-culture.

For Augustine, what is important is the construction of a counter-cultural way of referring to God, biblical texts and theological principles. His attention is to the meaning of words, to language. For Augustine, the ways that human beings signify realities that lie behind other realities are the key to understanding biblical texts. He wants to probe the complexity of linguistic representation. *DDC* is divided into two parts. Books I, II and II constitute the first part and they pertain to scripture as Christian teaching. Book I deals more with things (*res*) and books II and III with signs (*signum*). Things and signs methodically and cognitively shape Christian teaching. Book IV, on the other hand, is about professing or expressing doctrine in the best way possible. It is in Book IV that Augustine deals specifically with the rhetoric that makes for good theology. He begins by noting that Christian doctrine has to do with two things: things and signs.

The difficulties begin when, as Augustine says, 'Things are learnt through signs.' (*DDC* I.2.2) The nature of the difficulty partly concerns how we discern the things of God that are signified by the verbal signs (*signa data*) of scripture. More challenging, however, according to Augustine, is the task of understanding how some things are themselves used to signify other things. The classification scheme that Augustine introduces to differentiate different kinds of signs and things turns out to be somewhat complex. The significance of it all is the culture clash that Augustine envisages between different patterns of signification. These patterns are discernible according to whether there are human or divine institutions that form the process of signification.[4] Does this suggest a rejection of pagan culture? Confusingly perhaps, the answer is no. In Book II (19.29–42.63), an expansive yet qualified use of pagan culture and disciplines is recommended to the extent that these human institutions contribute to an understanding of signs, symbols and words, the very stuff of literature, which cannot be inimical to Christian faith.

Rather than throw himself into the biblical world by working on the assumptions of open allegorical textual meaning (as Origen did), Augustine wants to bring organization to such a commitment first. As Werner Jeanrond comments, 'The semiotic dimension of Augustine's interpretation theory frees the reader of biblical texts both from any crude literalism and from the dangers of arbitrary allegorization.'[5] The *DDC* is thus well known as a treatise that introduces a plan for how Christians interpret the Bible with the assistance of secular disciplines, specifically the *trivium* and the *quadrivium*. These are the seven classic disciplines of Augustine's day: grammar, rhetoric and logic, along with music, geometry, mathematics and cosmology. The secular disciplines are found, however, embedded in pagan learning. The saying that sums up the Christian way to use pagan disciplines is like Israel's taking away of the gold and silver from the pagan Egyptians, 'dug, as it were, from the mines of divine providence' (*DDC* II.40.60). The implication is one that Augustine has earlier laid out in Book II: 'A person who is a good and a true Christian should realize that truth belongs to his Lord, wherever it is found, gathering and acknowledging it even in pagan literature.' (*DDC* II.18.28). It is precisely this attitude towards scripture and the wider knowledge to be gained of God throughout the world that would have a lasting impact on medieval and modern conceptions of theological method. Augustine's openness towards the world explains why allegorical readings of scripture unfurl the Bible's spiritual sense. As O'Donnell remarks, Augustine likely saved the spiritual sense of scripture from what might have been its elimination from exegetical practice. After all, Origen, who was regarded with great suspicion, was the only other major champion of allegorical interpretation in this period.[6]

Most of *DDC* was composed in the mid-390s as Augustine was beginning his career as bishop of Hippo. After breaking off towards the end of Book III, it would not be until 30 years later, in 427, that he would be able to complete it, an interlude that is explained by his heavy responsibilities as bishop, and attributable also to his other writing projects, especially the *Confessions*. In fact, it is helpful to consider *DDC* and the *Confessions* as two works in a complementary, even thematic, relationship. The *DDC* provides a theoretical approach to the interpretation of scripture and the *Confessions* is a personal narrative account of how Augustine saw his life in light of scripture, properly interpreted. To say that the *DDC* is theoretical is perhaps misleading, however. It is written with the aim of supporting the ministry of preaching, probably in the training of clergy. In fact, Book IV (e.g. at IV.17.34) emphasizes the role of oratory, an abiding concern for Augustine since his early formation in the works of Cicero. By emphasizing secular education to such an extent, Augustine opens the door to a systematic programme of Christian, especially monastic, educational formation that would become the cultural backbone for the church for over a millennium, despite its concessions to the pagan categories of Cicero and other philosophers.

Augustine's hermeneutical approach to scripture contains several strands that are revolutionary. The first strand that we should notice is his tendency to see many scriptural passages converging on key themes. Karla Pollmann goes so far as to claim that this tendency amounts to Augustine knowing what scripture will say before he reads it. A more generous and, in fact, more accurate way to describe Augustine's method would be to say that if scripture is to be meaningful for Christians, it must embrace love or *caritas*. He declares as much in Book I by saying that the use of scripture is to point to Christ. In accord with Irenaeus on this point, Augustine announces what his scriptural hermeneutic is to be, and it is Christ, the Word made flesh. If a passage cannot be interpreted in a way that informs the way of love, then it is not a useful sign of God:

> the fulfillment and end of the law [cf. Rom. 13.10; 1 Tim. 1.5] and all the divine scriptures is to love the thing which must be enjoyed and the thing which together with us can enjoy that thing (since there is no need for a commandment to love oneself). To enlighten us and enable us, the whole temporal dispensation was set up by divine providence for our salvation. We must make use of this, not with a permanent love and enjoyment of it, but with a transient love and enjoyment of our journey, or of our conveyances , so to speak, or any other expedients whatsoever (there may be a more appropriate word), so that we love the means of transport only because of our destination. So anyone who thinks that he has understood the divine scriptures or any part of them, but cannot by his understanding build up this double love of God and neighbour, has not yet succeeded in understanding them. (*DDC* I.35.39-40)

So, as this text seems to show, a second issue, which is the distinction between the Latin verbs *uti* (use) and *frui* (enjoyment) is absolutely critical to an understanding of *DDC*. For Augustine, God, and only God, is to be enjoyed, while the rest of creation is to be 'used' in order to serve this primary enjoyment. Choosing well in the interpretation of scripture is dependent upon what we desire in general. Scriptural interpretation is impossible to separate from human behaviour and culture. Rowan Williams comments that for Augustine, 'God alone is the end of desire; and that entails that there is no finality, no "closure", no settled or intrinsic meaning in the world we inhabit.'[7] While the *uti/frui* distinction does not appear elsewhere in Augustine's work, its bluntness in *DDC* offers an extraordinary open window onto Augustine's way of seeing God and the world. It is consistent with his depiction of the human condition in his other writings. It is summarized with regards to the 'right ordering of love' (*DDC* I.27.28). The ordering of one's loves is both necessitated and tempered by the reality of sin. Thus, it fits with the *Confessions*, his autobiography of travails, conversion and fleeting triumphs about which he claims ultimately: 'my heart is restless until it rests in you, O Lord.' But, the use/enjoyment distinction also offers, by implication, a glimpse into his methodological schema. Among those things of the world, words in particular are to be used, not loved, for their role in signifying God, especially the words of scripture. This is the quite distinct basis for Augustine's ready endorsement of allegorical or figurative uses for the words of scripture.

Augustine's intent, especially in Book III of *DDC*, is not to praise allegory *per se*, but rather to articulate the *non*-figurative propositions of Christian doctrine. The signs of scripture refer to the things of Christian teaching. In fact, the *uti/frui* distinction is parallel with Augustine's distinction between *signa* and *res*, signs and things. While the verbal signs of scripture may describe things or events in the world, their true meaning is to re-present ultimate things, of God and salvation. This entails the logical possibility that there are things spoken of in the Bible that can mean what they do not appear to mean, because their meaning has, for instance, been altered by Christ. The crucifixion, as a historical event, is the prime example of this process of altering the meaning of other biblical narratives.

In fact, Augustine alludes systematically to Christ's love, such that the meaning of figures and events in the Old Testament become signifiers of Christ. In the context of the relationship between the Old Testament and the New Testament, this way of interpreting a theory of signs has become mired in deeply problematic issues of inter-faith interpretation, especially since the Holocaust. Nonetheless, as a way of framing a relationship between scripture and the truths which it represents, Augustine's theory of signs plumbs explanatory depths not articulated by his theologian predecessors.

As an explanatory framework, Augustine's understanding of scriptural interpretation is quite distinct from the biblical interpretation that is aligned with foundational or doctrinal theology, which we have already encountered in the early church. Unlike Paul, Irenaeus, Origen and Athanasius, Augustine seems much more fully aware that he is constructing a method for interpreting scripture that is based not on this or that external priority, but which is coherent with human desire itself. Yes, Augustine's view of scripture is thus steeped in his high appreciation of ancient rhetoric. This in itself does not suggest that Augustine's theological programme will be superior in every respect to other patristic interpreters. It is, however, a leap in the history of theology that Augustine inaugurates with his hermeneutical approach.

For Augustine, the theologian should be aware of both the external factors at work in the biblical text and its historical circumstances, as well as the internal factors of human desire, socially and culturally conditioned as it is. The things represented by scripture and the intention which we bring to it are not ultimately separate issues. Moreover, scripture is like a code that is written with these divergent desires fully in view, despite its frequent textual crudeness. Here is why Christ, the Word made human, is precisely the prism through which we must take scripture and for which scripture was meant to point. Thus, a figural reading of scripture is not only possible, but often necessary because of the human-shaped problem that scripture has been written to address. The complexity and difficulties of scripture are the mirror image of the complex difficulties that mark the human condition. All told, interpreting scripture places the problem of thing and sign, use and enjoyment in full view and it is none other than the human predicament itself, the struggle to rightly understand sin and salvation.

Augustine's more purposeful methodology means that he for-mulates some clear rules as to how a theologian proceeds, notably with reference to scripture, which we must recall, is still the first and only explicit source for theology in the early centuries, while experience, reason and tradition lurk in the background in increasing magnitude. Arguably, as I have already mentioned, Augustine's most important legacy is to establish the hermeneutic of love, made genuine through acts of goodness. This is the hint provided in Book I's discussion of the need to order one's loves. Likewise, whatever else is derived from the interpretation of scripture, the communication of the love of God should be the primary meaning provided by the act of interpretation, according to Augustine. As he says, 'in dealing with figurative expressions we will observe a rule of this kind: the passage being read should be studied with careful consideration until its interpretation can be connected with the realm of love' (*DDC* III.15.23). He goes on to say how this works in connection with different types of scriptural passages:

> If the expression is a prescriptive one, and either forbids wickedness or wrongdoing, or enjoins self-interest or kindness, it is not figurative. But if it appears to enjoin wickedness or wrongdoing or to forbid self-interest or kindness, it is figurative. Scripture says, 'Unless you eat of the flesh of the Son of man and drink his blood, you will not have life in you' [Jn 6.54]. This appears to enjoin wickedness or wrongdoing, and so it is figurative, a command to participate in the Lord's passion . . . Scripture says 'If your enemy is hungry, feed him; if he is thirsty, give him a drink' [Rom. 12.20]. Here no one can doubt that it enjoins kindness. (*DDC* III.16.24)

So, here we see that the stress on moral conversion allows Augustine to turn and make a critical distinction about what constitutes the two different kinds of scriptural language or genre of biblical literature: literal historical language and figurative language.

One additional aspect to Augustine's rules for interpreting scripture is the conviction that scripture can be validly interpreted in various ways, both literal and figurative, without entailing a necessary confusion or contradiction. In *DDC* III.27.38, he asks rhetorically, 'For what more liberal and more fruitful provision could God have made in regard to the Sacred Scriptures than that the same words might be understood in several senses, all of which are sanctioned by the concurring testimony of other passages equally divine?' There is, in this section especially, a view of scripture that implies a more direct and broader theology of revelation, one that makes explicit the role of God inspiring the writer and the reader through the agency of the Holy Spirit:

> The person examining the divine utterances must of course do his best to arrive at the intention of the writer through whom the Holy Spirit produced that part of scripture; he may reach that meaning or carve out from the words another meaning which does not run counter to the faith, using the evidence of any other passage of the divine utterances. Perhaps the author too saw that very meaning in the words which we are trying to understand. Certainly the spirit of God who worked through the author foresaw without any doubt that it would present itself, because it too is based on the truth. (*DDC* III.27.38)

Truth cannot contradict truth according to Augustine, and this applies equally to those lesser, yet still significant, truths alighted on by readers of scripture. Contrary to an Origenist approach to allegory, Augustine places the intention of the biblical author as the primary locus through which one arrives at the meaning of scripture. Yet, foreshadowing the Enlightenment stress on individual intentional agency in interpretation, Augustine allows for an implicit theology of personal illumination which he makes explicit in other writings. Personal conversion or orientation to the truth, as opposed to a concept of the passive learning of information, is related to Augustine's view of revelation. The idea that God is directly experienced is a gloss on the theology of revelation that would be picked up strongly in the Middle Ages by Bonaventure. God's intention is to be revealed not just through the scriptures, but through the writer and the subsequent readers of scriptures as converted persons. The emphasis falls then, on the believer, first as convert and as reader.

Augustine also emphasizes that easier passages should be employed to illuminate more obscure passages (*DDC* III.26). In fact, it is better to interpret difficult passages through clearer passages instead of interpreting scripture through reason (III.28.39). To the extent that the reader is already a Christian convert, and this is certainly the audience that Augustine anticipates in writing this treatise, then these various hermeneutical rules – the rule of love, God's revelation in and through the human heart and the rule of interpreting the difficult passages through clearer ones – together constitute a single hermeneutical vision, a theological method.

But this vision is not without its dubious or less than compelling aspects. Augustine's symbolic system centres partly on the need to overcome what he believed was the theological and moral loss incurred by the Jews, who, as Augustine saw it, cannot see the full meaning of the usefulness of biblical signs. Going on what is, by contemporary standards, a caricature of rabbinic and biblical Judaism as being overly concerned with the rubrics of practice, Augustine sets up a dialectic between a Jewish tendency to take the figurative passages of the Bible as literal and the ideal Christian hermeneutic of taking the figurative passages in the Bible as symbolic of the mysterious ways of a transcendent God.

For Augustine, a theological method is needed for two distinct reasons. First, Christians must engage with 'secular' disciplines, despite Augustine's reticence over the role of reason in interpreting scripture. Augustine welcomes reason, contrary to the instincts of Augustine's Donatist opponents in particular, who were known to ignore extra-biblical sources. Second, a theological method is suggested by the very nature of the Christian dispensation. This is more difficult to grasp, but essentially, a theological method is required, according to Augustine, because of the kind of language in which God has allowed scripture to be formed. These two requirements for method lead Augustine, in his struggle with the literalist Africans, to rail against the taking of figurative language literally. He also tackles the opposite problem of taking literal language too figuratively. All of this raises the urgent question, which was mentioned earlier, as to how one may distinguish between literal and figurative language in general. I quote an extended passage from Book III of *DDC* to demonstrate what Augustine proposes:

> As well as this rule, which warns us not to pursue a figurative (that is, metaphorical) expression as if it were literal, we must add a further one: not to accept a literal one as if it were figurative. We must first explain the way to discover whether an expression is literal or figurative. Generally speaking it is this: anything in divine discourse that cannot be related either to good morals or to the true faith should be taken as figurative. Good morals have to do with our love of God and our neighbour, the true faith with our understanding of God and our neighbour. The hope

that each person has within his own conscience is directly related to the progress that he feels within himself to be making towards the love and understanding of God and his neighbour . . . But since the human race is prone to judge sins not by the strength of the actual lust, but rather by the standard of its own practices, people generally regard as culpable only such actions as men of their own time and place tend to blame and condemn, and regard as commendable and praiseworthy only such actions as are acceptable within the conventions of their own society. And so it happens that if scripture enjoins something at variance with the practices of its readers, or censures something that is not at variance with them, they consider the relevant expression to be figurative (always assuming that their minds are governed by the authority of the Word). But scripture enjoins nothing but love, and censures nothing but lust and moulds men's minds accordingly. Similarly, if their minds are taken over by a particular prejudice, people consider as figurative anything that scripture asserts to the contrary. But it asserts nothing except the catholic faith, in time past, present and future. It narrates the past, foretells the future and demonstrates the present, but all these things serve to nourish and strengthen this love and to overcome and annihilate lust. By love I mean the impulse of one's mind to enjoy God on his own account and to enjoy oneself and one's neighbour on account of God; and by lust I mean the impulse of one's mind to enjoy oneself and one's neighbour and any corporeal thing not on account of God. (*DDC* III.10.14-16)

The criterion of faith and morals is a crucial restriction on what should be meant literally. Almost as crucial, it seems to me, is his sense of the human condition that frames our capacity to interpret authentically. Augustine speaks about the major and minor biases of individuals and entire cultures that affect the ability of the human conscience to understand God and God's love. Opposed to the process of understanding love, of course, is Augustine's famous category of lust, inordinate human desire. There is no mistaking the moral features of Augustine's purpose, and so we must think of Augustine's theological method of scriptural interpretation as simultaneously a struggle to overcome the vice of lust (or enjoyment for enjoyment's sake, at least) and receive the theological virtue of (God's) love in its place.

For Augustine, a good interpreter must be converted in three distinct ways that are interwoven in this passage and in the entire treatise of DDC. There are distinct intellectual, moral and religious conversions that make up the ongoing process of becoming closer to God. One must be intellectually converted, by which he includes the judicious employment of pagan disciplines for the purpose of illuminating scripture. The limits of intellectual conversion are nevertheless profound, since Augustine is not exclusively interested in the conceptual clarity of belief statements, as necessary as that is for doctrinal formulation. It is true that Augustine lays out the properly 'doctrinal' propositions and beliefs which are most important for the Christian educator in Book I. He refers to doctrine this way in DDC when he refers to the 'Rule of Faith'. Augustine thinks of the Rule as a shorthand criterion of internal epistemic consistency that arises almost naturally as a consequence of having been won over to the love of Christ. It can even serve as a general guide to confront the confusion that arises in disputes over punctuation in the biblical text which offer divergent interpretations. In that sense, Augustine provides at least a principled perspective *vis-à-vis* scripture.

It is true too that Augustine lauds and classifies various arts and sciences in Book II. He extols the spiritual virtue of understanding what he terms 'unknown signs', and he reiterates the rules of interpretation offered by Tyconius, the Donatist, later in Book III. Here, Augustine agrees with his rival on a set of criteria that provide the true meaning of texts which are at variance with the original meaning proposed by scripture's human authors. Such textual difficulties in scripture are what one should expect to see, despite the primacy of the author's intentions, since for Augustine, theological education is a process, and revelation did not stop with the biblical authors.

As a process, the interpretation of scripture is 'a parable of our condition', the means by which God allows us to enjoy scripture, the supreme sign of his Word after Christ.[8] One of the most important intellectual gifts to be prized in theology is rhetoric, which Augustine praises when it provides clarity, a clarity which is sometimes lacking in the scriptures themselves. He develops this theme, in nuanced terms, in Book IV. Augustine certainly wishes Christian faith to be given intellectual support. Knowledge, for Augustine, is construed as the authentic search for meaning and is an irreplaceable component to Christian faith. This desire is reflected in his famous claim in

Book X of his *De Trinitate*, where he says that 'nothing can be loved unless it is known'. So, intellectual conversion, Augustine's exhortation to continual intellectual precision, is a running theme of *DDC*.

And yet, as we know from Augustine's theological account of his own conversion and his struggle to articulate the difference between literal and figurative meaning concerning particular biblical books (e.g. Genesis), our desires for knowledge are invariably frustrated. According to Augustine, as we see from *DDC* III.27.38, our desire to transcend the signs contained in the Bible is both anticipated and produced by God, who gives the signs which we are meant to receive. To understand these signs, moreover, is to realize that words and their meanings are human constructs which point to greater realities. As Augustine points out in the preface to the *DDC*, a danger lies in believing that the Christian can be illumined directly by God without resort to understanding the contingencies of human authorship and the tools available for understanding biblical texts properly. For some, the things of God are available without the signs of scripture; but, in this respect, Augustine is speaking of very few persons. Usually, revelation is mediated. For Augustine, theological method means using one's intelligence for the sake of faith: Platonism and Cicero for Christ. It means constructing a counter-culture that distinguishes itself from the surrounding culture from a stance of conversion, of being moved by God. Along the way, as Book II dramatizes, the Christian is to beware of language that seduces, words that are a 'perverse sweetness' and things that are enjoyed as creative instead of being used to turn us towards God, the Creator.[9]

For Augustine, whatever the virtues and necessities of skills in language, history and the other pagan disciplines, a collection of skills does not constitute theology. On a related matter, as he mentions in Book IV in regards to eloquence, rhetorical skills are best appreciated through the imitation of Christian preaching, a unique Christian rhetorical form that enjoins believers to goodness and faith. Therefore, Augustine the theologian is famously interested in the moral conversion that must attend a careful reading of scripture. Without moral conversion, one's reading of scripture will fall short of the understanding of scripture and of Christ which God has intended. Short of a morally converted will, we are blind to the supreme good, the '*summum bonum*' which we ought to seek for its own sake in order to be truly happy. We experience ourselves as divided, according to Augustine. As a composite of reason, memory and will, we are complex beings, whose destiny is sorely injured through the Original Sin of Adam. Taking over this idea from Paul's rendering of the contrast between Adam and Christ, especially in Romans, Augustine possesses an urgent sense of why scripture and proper interpretation matter: we need to avoid sin. His understanding of Original Sin frames the problems that beset any and all readers of scripture. True happiness, for Augustine, is not restricted therefore to the attainment of virtue, but also in realizing that such an attainment, for sinful creatures as we are, is impossible in this life.

Conversion for Augustine means happiness as an effect of our communion with God. Happiness is not reducible to particular virtues or even virtue itself, as Augustine makes clear in his claims against the Stoics in *The City of God*. Similarly, Augustine sees scripture in *DDC* and moral behaviour too, as means to an end, the end being friendship with God. Augustine's notion of God's grace lies behind such a move, because like scripture, virtue is a gift from God. The assumption is the classic Augustinian one: the individual must decide on how to live. How scripture is interpreted is not less than existential. Both Augustine's autobiographical account of faith and his approach towards a proper interpretation of scripture turn on a moral quest. But, a moral life can only be supported by a theologically coherent vision of faith. As we have seen from the hermeneutic of love introduced by Augustine for the proper reading of all scripture, a religiously converted individual needs to recognize that he or she is loved by God and must love God in return. The urgency of religious conversion presses Augustine at every turn in setting out a theological method. His method is no dry correlation of theology with philosophy or a set of rules. Nor is it a free-floating endorsement of individual interpretive skill, as we saw from his account of bias and cultural prejudice as well as his nuanced appreciation of allegory.

In conclusion, we might draw several conclusions about the relevance and significance of Augustine's *De doctrina Christiana*. It is clearly meant to, first, aid those in some position of leadership in the church to learn from the Bible and teach Christian doctrine from a basis in scripture, properly interpreted. But there is another level to the DDC that deserves mention far beyond what Augustine was doing for his own time and place. Matthew Lamb writes, for instance, that:

> modern critical methods assist greatly in establishing the texts, what Augustine calls the 'signs' or 'symbols.' But without an attunement of wisdom, justice and charity the reader or listener will not know the sacred realities to which those signs and texts refer.[10]

Augustine directs our gaze beyond the textual particulars, through the prism of the author's intention and re-directs it at ourselves, our self-understanding and the understanding of God. One interesting parallel between Augustine's approach to scripture and ours is that in both his milieu of educated Roman citizens and in contemporary postmodern Western cultures which doubt the veracity of religion, there is a scepticism regarding the legitimacy and the authority of the Bible. Augustine's distinct way of handling such scepticism is to avoid altogether a literalism which might offer an easy logic of reaction to an anti-Christian culture. So also does Augustine avoid an open-ended allegorizing approach to scripture. For him, there are truths about God that are found through the signs of scripture and through the authentic, converted heart which endeavours to scour the Bible for those truths. What makes Augustine's method stand out is his unswerving attention to the love of God and neighbour as a baseline message that scripture bears. This hermeneutical priority is present in the Word of scripture through the event of Christ. Augustine's legacy lies in avoiding the exegetical extremes. More profoundly, it lies in routing the presentation of theological method beyond simple rules towards a subtler understanding of the kind of person who engages in acts of interpretation. Augustine's insistence on the foundation of theological virtues and on the need for the conversion of Christians in intellectual, moral and religious ways means that theological method is no longer written off as an exercise in the attainment of purely intellectual skill. Augustine's great triumph, methodologically speaking, is his account of theological sources and theological inquirer in an interwoven web of meaning. His understanding of procedure is to place it at the service of the converted interpreter and Christian teacher. As we shall see in the next chapter, the heightened place of reason in medieval theology came to vie with the hermeneutical pillars of method set by Augustine; but the presence of a differentiated approach to the biblical text remains in the Christian theological academy, as does does the concept of the theological task as urgently soteriological. Both of these are Augustinian legacies.

CHAPTER FOUR

Medieval theology – Not just sacred doctrine

Those who use philosophical doctrines in sacred scripture in such a way as to subject them to the service of faith, do not mix water with wine, but change water into wine.[1]

In summarizing theological methods of any era, it is impossible to make a selection of theologians who perfectly represent that period. This is certainly true of the medieval era, a period of several hundred years, in which a great number of theological styles and methodical choices are in evidence. Yet, for the purposes of gaining some clarity on how theology was practised in this long period, I have chosen to focus on the thought of just three figures: Pseudo-Dionysius, Anselm and Thomas Aquinas. Noticeably absent are some formidable theologians, such as Gregory of Palamas, Bonaventure and Duns Scotus. Still, the three chosen theologians expressed themselves theologically in ways that have more than stood the test of time. Along with Augustine, their respective theologies are the focal point for entire traditions of theological reflection, beginning in the periods, religious congregations and churches with which they are each associated; and like Augustine before them, each one renders a particular set of meanings from carefully constructed scriptural interpretation, reason, tradition and, to some degree, experience. Most often, medieval theology is noted, usually negatively, for its dependence on philosophy. Of course, much depends on the meaning of the word 'dependence'. And, indeed, the relationship between philosophy and theology is the issue that comes to a head during the medieval period. However, this tangled relationship should not obscure some of the other vital themes that permeate theological method in these respective theologians. Let us begin with the most mysterious character of this book, Pseudo-Dionysius.

Pseudo-Dionysius

Cited almost 1,700 times by Thomas Aquinas, Dionysius or Denys (an anglicized form of his name) the 'Areopagite' is regarded as one of the most mysterious theologians in Christian tradition. The *Corpus Areopagiticum* or *Corpus Dionysianum*, originally taken to be a set of writings attributable to Dionysius the convert (who is mentioned in Acts 17.34), are now attributed to another writer (or writers) in the late fifth or early sixth centuries. He may have existed in the Syrian region of the ancient Mediterranean. His main works are *The Mystical Theology*, *The Divine Names* and *The Celestial Hierarchy*. These are works which gradually became accepted and widely read in the subsequent two centuries, thanks to diligent work on the part of John of Scythopolis and Maximus the Confessor. Yet, despite their mysterious progeny and in some ways because of it, Dionysius (as we shall refer to the pseudonymous writer in this chapter) meets with consternation and discomfort. This is usually owing to his highly Platonized rendering of Christian belief. Luther, for instance, in his *Babylonian Captivity of the Church* cites Dionysius this way: 'in his *Theology*, which is rightly called *Mystical*, of which certain very ignorant theologians make so much, he is downright dangerous, for he is more of a Platonist than a Christian'.[2] Such characterizations are intriguing, for they bear on Dionysius' theological method. Let us see whether it is a fair assessment or not.

Paul Rorem, one of the leading authorities on Dionysius, writes that 'a perplexed reader is in good company, for the history of Christian doctrine and spirituality teems with commentators and general readers who have found the Areopagite's meaning obscure, and yet his mysterious appeal irresistible'.[3] One of the most recognizable and simultaneously remarkable factors in Dionysius' corpus is his insistence that God is essentially unknowable. God is utterly beyond, even beyond the category of what so many other theologians before him and since have deemed 'transcendent'. As with other Neo-Platonic philosophers, Dionysius expresses God's being by prefixing words with 'hyper': *huperousios*, *huper noun*: God is beyond being, beyond knowledge, invisible, incomprehensible, inscrutable, unsearchable and infinite.[4]

For him, theology is simply the 'science of God' or 'the Word of God'. It is the collections of words that begin with words but which lift us up to the mysteries of God, divine simplicity. This has obvious implications for how we evaluate his theological method. The idea that God is essentially unknowable is an idea that we can immediately associate with the Neo-Platonic heritage of thought. According to Platonic epistemology, the divine is inherently eternal and therefore *terra incognita* for terrestrial human beings. The mystery that accompanies God's being and God's attributes is precisely what one should expect to realize in relation to that which cannot be fully known. In Christian tradition, this view of God is the thematic thrust of the 'apophatic' or 'negative theology' tradition. This theology says what God is not rather than what God is, in order to stress the ineffable nature of God. Indeed, the opening section of Dionyius' short *Mystical Theology* invokes the spiritual path that his epistemology implies:

> my advice to you . . . is to leave behind you everything perceived and understood, everything perceptible and understandable, all that is not and all that is, and, with your understanding laid aside, to strive upward as much as you can toward union with him who is beyond all being and knowledge.[5]

Mystical union is the goal of both the spiritual life and theological knowledge. Fulfillment is in God who is beyond all categories of thought. This approach does not endorse ignorance, but rather an 'agnosia', the root for the English term 'agnosticism'; and, for

Dionysius, this approach designates the active task of unknowing. Dionysius goes on in this short treatise to describe Moses' encounter with God. Moses 'plunges into the truly mysterious darkness of unknowing'.[6] Moses does not actually see God's face but treads around the peak of Mt Sinai, apprehending only the darkness of being in God's presence, the 'rationale of all that lies below the Transcendent One'.[7] Does this categorically summarize for Dionysius the significance of mystical experience at the expense of theological speech? Not precisely.

Dionysius articulates a threefold hierarchy of understanding – a theological epistemology that includes sense perception, intellectual knowledge and mystical union. These three levels of understanding mirror the threefold hierarchy of the legal, the ecclesiastical and the celestial. The extant Dionysian corpus lacks a lost treatise, which is referred to in *Mystical Theology* as *Theological Representations* (or *Outlines*), in which Dionysius spells out an affirmative (or cataphatic) theology, restricting himself, nonetheless, to a mention of Trinitarian and Christological considerations as well as 'other revelations of scripture'.[8] The contents of *Representations* seem to be repeated in *The Divine Names*, where he allows concepts such as wisdom, life and the good to apply to God. In another lost work, *Symbolic Theology*, he apparently allows for analogies to apply to God drawn from what we may perceive. So, it is unwise to think of Dionysius as exclusively a 'negative' theologian, and it is especially unwise to take him as the representative of an Eastern (Orthodox) theology that is exclusively apophatic as a consequence. There are substantive signs of complexity in his thought. And indeed, Dionysius' awareness of a balance between what can and cannot be said of God is one reason why Thomas Aquinas and Bonaventure incorporate Dionysius into their systematic theologies at the height of the Middle Ages.

Dionysius provides us with clues about the inherent limits of theological knowledge. God's revelation is given to us from above and is conceptualized in terms of the two key doctrines, the Incarnation and the Trinity. These doctrines speak to the attributes of God that stand in some tension with other Dionysian language, such as God's utter (unknowable) goodness or His infinity. But it is to these latter attributes that Dionysius' analogies from the material world are intended to provide meaning. These analogies fill out a picture of knowledge that is prominent in Dionysius.

In medieval thought, analogies are offered as forms of knowledge which compare two dissimilar objects or ideas by suggesting some basic similarity or likeness. As such, analogies always contain within them the disanalogies that pertain to any dissimilar things. Employing analogies, Dionysius proceeds from the material world in constructing a return movement of love and knowledge upwards towards the divine. The implicit portrait of knowledge is shared with other Neo-Platonists, and it becomes a part of Thomas Aquinas's view of God and creation as the movement of procession and return, the *exitus/reditus* from God to humanity and back to God in a contemplation won through salvation. Dionysius thus lays out a theological method that views all constructed human knowledge as ultimately a gift from God. The best way of returning that gift is through a passive, contemplative attitude, accompanied by a spiritual 'anagogy', of being led upwards. This ascent does not involve an accumulation of knowledge, but, if anything, it involves a shedding of prior knowledge, especially sensory knowledge and 'rational reflection' too.[9]

There is not a consensus about the Dionysian heritage, however. Chiefly, the dissent concerning Dionysius' view of knowledge comes from Vladimir Lossky and several Eastern Orthodox theologians who believe he has not articulated apophatic and kataphatic modes of theology as sufficiently complementary. Rather, Lossky, in particular, thinks Dionysius is suggesting apophasis as a form of prime experience, a spiritual awareness that cannot be categorized in terms of knowledge at all, and which cannot be balanced alongside katapahatic knowledge of any sort.[10] Further to this, John Jones has tried to show that in appropriating the theology of Dionysius' *Divine Names* specifically, Thomas Aquinas has erred by taking his theology as an organized programme to know God's essence. Since, according to the Eastern way of understanding God's being and keeping in mind Dionysius' intent in the *Divine Names* to write a liturgical, hymnological text, John Jones argues that Aquinas cannot construe a science of God, at least not on the basis of Dionysius, since human beings cannot know the divine essence according to Dionysius.[11] Rightly, as a drama of the spirit, Dionysius' theology is termed a 'liturgical theology'. The dramatic element of liturgical symbols and sacraments is supposed to articulate the most important part of deification, the coming into communion with God, a process which cannot be summarized in an exclusively intellectual way in the apophatic tradition.

His theology of symbolism is sharp, as one might expect from a Neo-Platonist. It has resemblances with both Augustinian sign theory and that of early church fathers. Symbolic theology is associated with the act of being initiated. It is contrasted with a philosophical theology 'which involves demonstration', a distinction noted with approval by Aquinas.[12] In *The Celestial Hierarchy*, Dionysius notes that symbols play two roles. The first is that symbols are placed in our midst because 'we lack the ability to be directly raised up to conceptual contemplations'. The second is 'that the sacred and hidden truth about the celestial intelligences [should] be concealed through the inexpressible and the sacred and be inaccessible to the *hoi polloi* . . . knowledge is not for everyone'.[13] Of course, because of such language, Dionysius has been accused of fostering an elitist spirituality along the lines of Platonic academies of old. True, there may be some congruence with such 'elitism'. There is speculation that the *Dionysian* corpus in fact originates among a number of followers of Origen. As with the spiritual ecstasy envisioned by Origen, Dionysius also conveys a theological metaphysic that stresses the role of the illuminated few – a latent form of Donatism, if some critics are to be believed. He is well known among students of theology for having developed the concept of hierarchy in relation to the Godhead and to earthly society, which is rooted in the philosophy of Proclus. Dionysius' hierarchy is a 'sacred order, a state of understanding and an activity approximating as closely as possible to the divine'.[14] Given the reference to bishops as church hierarchs, Dionysius is sometimes seen as merely another early medieval apologist for church power under the aegis of pagan terminology.

But, I think that given his insistence upon the complete otherness of God, a God who is completely self-giving, bestowing to all of creation a trace of the divine, it is better to credit Dionysius as being a theologian of cosmic reconciliation. One of the consequences of this style of theology is a somewhat lower view of scripture than that of earlier church fathers. Scripture's role in revealing God is limited because of the strongly limited capacity of human language to acquire such knowledge.

In summary, we may say that, for Dionysius, the limits of human categories and language itself implies a wholesale realignment of theological method. If we take Dionysius seriously, then the act of naming God as Good, Love, Life, Light and Beauty and all the other names discussed in *The Divine Names* means that we are transformed beyond ourselves. Theology is primarily existential in this sense because of the intellectual, moral and religious conversion that comes from simply naming God. What is not necessarily possible, however, on a Dionysian account, is a thorough interpretative, doctrinal, systematic or communicative theology. In fact, Dionysius' theology bears little relation to historical or dialectical categories. Even less tangible scriptural terms for God, such as 'Word', 'Mind' and 'Being', are no more successful in ascribing attributes to God than 'earthly' descriptions.[15] It is therefore difficult to relate the conversion to which he points as a conversion away from something. That Dionysius is able to express the mystical goal of conversion, there is no doubt. His accent is on the need for human surrender to divine love and praise as the proper attitude for doing theology. However, in contrast with other patristic theologians and medieval theologians after him, Dionysius is unwilling to analyse the ways that this approach to God coheres with the events of revelation in tangible ways measured by causes and effects. His theology downplays historical contingencies, to the point of downplaying the primacy of the names of the Trinity in favour of the other Platonic names. It is no wonder that his theology was admired and cited by the Monophysites as a consequence.

Dionysius' basic category for union with God is that of simple participation, of imaging God to the point of potential deification. Therein lies one of the basic elements of tension that has divided Western and Eastern soteriologies from even before Dionysius' time, and which continues to distinguish different approaches to theological method as well. To the extent that the Dionysian style is admired and appropriated by postmodern and Radical Orthodox theologians, we see evidence across the ages for pushing aside theological method in favour of a purely experiential approach, even to the point of conceiving of method as an idolatrous or anti-theological concern. The irony of some contemporary postmodern interpretations of Dionysius is that they selectively overlook the robust metaphysics on which Dionysius' language for God is erected. The anti-methodical impulse in theology is thus inherently conflicted over how and why to use certain kinds of language and concepts. Yet, by appreciating the Dionysian heritage in conjunction with both his forebears and descendants, the emphasis on the apophatic perspective, on doxology in fact, can round out an overall picture of theological method. Dionysius holds out for the basic theological task as being self-transcendence. Ironically, his fiercest critics, including Luther, are also reticent when it comes to adopting an explicit theological method.

Anselm

Italian by birth, Anselm (1033–1109) became a leading monk and one of the most well known of all the Archbishops of Canterbury. He is also regarded as one of the most important theologians of the early medieval period. His importance is underlined by the fact that Thomas Aquinas and other medieval theologians cite him frequently in their writings. In order to live a monastic life with more emphasis on study rather than other daily tasks, Anselm joined the monastery at Bec, in Normandy, rather than the reformist monastery of Cluny. At Bec, he was mentored by Lanfranc, a leading monk. Like other early medieval theologians, Anselm relied upon Augustine to a great extent, although there are hints of a more independent thinker in his writing, reading and through his interpretations of Cicero, Boethius and even the Greek fathers. Anselm writes theology very much in the spirit of Augustine, even though he does not simply repeat Augustine's arguments as would other medieval Augustinians. Certainly, what is present in Anselm's thought is a much more confident understanding of the role of language in theological affirmations than is the case with Dionysius. It is Anselm's theory of language that has captured much modern attention, not all of which is dismissive. However, where his ontological argument (for the existence of God) is concerned, Anselm's understanding of language is viewed by many modern theologians as categorically naive.

Anselm appears on the scene when theology is on the cusp of a revolution, a movement away from a reverential approach to sources to an approach in which disputation and interdisciplinary collaboration are formally incorporated into the teaching and writing of theology. His theology bears witness to this revolution in method. What this means with respect to particular works of his, however, is more difficult to determine. Anselm's theological method is somewhat difficult to summarize, chiefly because he altered his method between his early meditative works, the *Monologion* and *Proslogion* and his later philosophically oriented dialogues.

The most historically momentous aspect of Anselm's theological method is the principle '*fides quaerens intellectum*' – 'faith seeking understanding'. This great defining motto of theology appears in Chapter One of the *Proslogion*, which initially bore the motto in its title. It is from Augustine that Anselm obtains this principle. It is derived in turn from an Old Latin translation of Isa. 7.9: '*nisi credideritis, non intelligetis*' – 'If you do not believe, you will not understand.'[16] In thinking about the rewards of faith, the most obvious feature of Anselm's approach is his employment of dialectic. Anselm's dialectical presentation is evident through his use of the dialogue format. It is borrowed to some extent from Boethius, who is cited throughout the early medieval period as an authoritative logician. Dialectic for Anselm means, as it did for Augustine, trying to resolve questions left unanswered from scripture. This is partly what is going on in the *De Doctrina Christiana*, which was examined in the previous chapter. Yet logic cannot proceed towards a proof of any proposition on its own. Logic only supplies the form of the proposition, not the truth of it. There is also the need to be consistent with authority. For Anselm, the church's faith is conceived as a rule by which the fruits of philosophical reasoning can be measured, rather than the reverse whereby philosophy measures faith.

The balance between faith and reason in Anselm is inordinately nuanced. Not surprisingly, Anselm has been interpreted in two strikingly different ways by modern interpreters. The philosopher Étienne Gilson has characterized Anselm as an arch-rationalist who tried to prove the doctrines of the Incarnation and the Trinity from reason alone. The Reformed theologian Karl Barth, meanwhile, has tried to show that, for Anselm, reason always moves within a circle of faith and not outside it.[17] Gilson is a medievalist whose familiarity with intellectual life from the eleventh to the fourteenth centuries is vast, but I am tempted to think that Barth's reading of Anselm appears to be slightly more plausible; but let us explore a little further to see what Anselm's writing reveals to see how both of these readings are perhaps oversimplifications.

The element of Anselm's thought that has invited the heaviest attention, especially from Thomas Aquinas and Kant, is his Ontological Argument for the existence of God. This argument is described by Anselm himself as a proof; but in regards to a proof, we should keep in mind that Anselm uses the verb '*probare*', a form of inference that is not the same as the notion of a deductive, axiomatic mathematical proof as we would use the word 'proof' today. This point has not been well appreciated by Anselm's critics over the centuries, notably in modernity. Anselm's use of the word 'proof' is couched in terms of *quod dicitur* ('what is said' by himself, a believer). Hence, there is reason to suspect that he is not a straightforward rationalist. That is, Anselm is making an argument in language that is satisfying to him as a believer, the person who began by uttering the different words of the '*Credo*'.[18]

Does this mean that Anselm is just playing at what Wittgenstein calls different 'language games'? No, what it does indicate is that Anselm's reference to and argument for God is an argument that accepts the distinct roles played by reason and scripture/tradition. The claim for God has to be owned by the one making it; claiming God cannot proceed on the basis of pure speculation or abstraction. Anselm's 'proof' is an argument of reason, but it is a proof that makes most sense to the believer whose language of belief is shared by human reason for the purpose of understanding.

In the *Monologion*, the importance of reason is apparent in the prologue where Anselm announces that, under pressure from his fellow monks, he will provide a reasoned argument that does not possess a warrant in scripture. Though it seems that Anselm follows this way of arguing, his language is in fact constantly marked by the influence of scripture, although at least he avoids directly touching on the interpretation of scripture. In this respect, as Ian Logan has noted, we have here an example of theological method rooted in Augustine's *DDC*.[19] Yet, for contemporary theologians considering Anselm's contribution, notably *Cur Deus homo* ('Why the God-Man'), his thought seems barren, completely bereft of a description of God's saving power and the light of his presence.

In the *Proslogion*, Anselm tries to sum up the many arguments that he develops in the earlier *Monologion* about which he was likely dissatisfied for the many tangential points he makes there. In the *Proslogion* he makes a breakthrough, which is that God can be conceived as 'that than which nothing greater can be conceived'. Having been dissatisfied with the messiness of *Monologion*, Anselm develops his famous *unum Argumentum* in the *Proslogion*. The format of this one argument can be seen in terms of a syllogism, as follows. The concept 'that than which a greater cannot be conceived' is the middle term ('X') of the major premise 'X is in the [human] understanding (*in intellectu*) and in reality (*in re*)', which in turn assumes the Platonic doctrine that ideas are greater in reality than being merely in the mind. The starting minor premise is that 'God is X'.[20] Once one accepts the minor and major premises, the conclusion that 'God exists' follows logically as a truthful propositional statement according to Anselm. To be sure that he has been well understood, he recalls that if we can conceive of something that is greater than that which can be conceived as God, then we have not yet conceived of God. Moreover, in his reply to Gaunilo's response to the *Proslogion*, Anselm stands his ground: 'I insist . . . simply if it can be thought it is necessary that it exists.'[21]

Very simply, Anselm is arguing on the grounds of reason alone to corroborate what has been revealed and proposed doctrinally in a distinct way. The effect of Anselm's method of argument is to develop a systematic theology that draws on a dialectical exchange between himself and a figure who voices scepticism regarding the veracity of scripture and its historical interpretation. So, Anselm is credited with establishing a highly rational means for dealing with the idea of God under a separate heading altogether from a strictly theological account. But, a theological account is not abandoned to pure reason. Reading further on in the *Proslogion*, one sees Anselm breaking off to recount his prayers to God. The introductory chapter alone is filled with allusions to the Psalms. In his reply to Gaunilo, he begins by appealing to the faith and to the conscience of his detractor, not to reason *per se*, before nonetheless continuing with his highly rational response to Gaunilo's response. And in the *Proslogion* itself, otherwise one of the most rational reflections on God of the entire medieval period, we find the following:

> I strove to ascend to God's light and I have fallen back into my own darkness. Indeed, not only have I fallen back into it, but I feel myself enclosed within it. I fell before 'my mother conceived me' (Ps. 50.7). In that darkness indeed 'I was conceived' [ibid.] and I was born under its shadow. We all, in fact, at one time fell in him 'in whom all of us sinned [Rom. 5.12] . . .' Help me 'because of your goodness O Lord.[22]

Contextualizing truth claims in terms of the limits of human sinfulness lends a distinctly prayerful character to Anselm's portrait of rationality. This theological anthropology of fallen creaturehood would become a centrepiece in the theologies of

Luther and of Calvin himself during the Protestant Reformation and thereafter.

In *Cur Deus Homo* (*CDH*), which was written largely in exile from Canterbury during the years up until 1098, Anselm undertakes a similar method as that of the *Proslogion*. Written also in the format of a dialogue, it may have arisen in light of the Westminster abbot Crispin's disputation with a Jew, hence Anselm's felt need to argue for God's becoming a human person. His argument in *CDH* contains no recognizable theological reference to Christ as a historical or biblical figure, however, which gives it its highly metaphysical cast and which once again contributes to Anselm's reputation as a dialectician, though a dialectician who does not argue with primary reference to the scriptural account or the history of scriptural exegesis. The preface to this work includes an assertion that the argument will proceed as if Christ had never existed. This announcement of an argument '*remoto Christo*' and the execution of this argument on the basis of the feudal legal concept *satisfactio* (satisfaction) has been a highly contentious sore point for readers who see this as evidence of Anselm's unbiblical quest. But the critics may not have appreciated that Anselm's point is explicitly to show that without a God-man, no human being can be saved. Anselm's primary purpose is to buttress the doctrines of the Incarnation and the Atonement, not replace them. How he executes this defence is once again through the form of dialectic, this time with the monk Boso. But methodologically, there is at least one other significant move that Anselm makes concerning these doctrines, and this is best seen in Chapter Three of *CDH*. There, Anselm deploys the Latin verb *oportet* and other terms to designate the 'fittingness' of the plans of salvation and the beauty of God's redemption. It also connotes the moral necessity that must attend the redemption of humanity from sin. The criterion of beauty, what another translation terms the 'appropriate' way that God saves, is an argument of natural theology. Anselm does not hesitate in deploying the term 'appropriate'/'fittingness' in *CDH*; he uses it a total of 76 times.[23]

In *CDH*, 'will', 'power' and 'necessity' frame his thought, conceptually speaking. Because human sin has destroyed order and harmony in the universe, something had to be done to restore right order, *recto ordo*. Framing the problem, in metaphorical terms, of the feudal relationship between a lord and his subjects, Anselm sees God's sending of a God-man as the efforts of one who is able to restore a universal problem, the scope of which is completely beyond the power of human beings to restore on their own. The nuances of Anselm's argument are not the focus of our attention here. But in terms of his method, Anselm is drawing on the legal system of his time to corroborate a doctrinal affirmation about the Incarnation and the Atonement. Stretching things somewhat, we might say that Anselm's argument is a harbinger of modern-day correlationism.

God's mercy is judged to be exceptional in the sense that God is willing to restore justice and right order in a fitting way that conforms to the coherence and harmony of something like the legal system with which Anselm is familiar. The human need for a salvation from sin, which human beings cannot obtain in a strictly penitential worldview, is won, according to Anselm, in this more aesthetic view. Contemporary critics like Gustav Aulèn see in Anselm's novelty a flat contradiction of the Atonement theory of Irenaeus and other church fathers. The early churchmen thought that the rights of the Devil over humanity were perfectly in accord with the principles of justice set out at creation. But for Anselm, the Devil is subject to a new form of justice as is the very law itself. The Devil does not lie outside justice as an agent free of the demands of justice. So, Anselm reinterprets the law and the Devil in light of true justice.[24]

What this suggests, methodologically, is that Anselm is reformulating a foundational category as it pertains to God. In this case, Anselm wants to alter the meaning of justice, and he reinterprets justice in light of how the doctrines of the Incarnation and the Atonement corroborate the granting of mercy within the medieval feudal system. It is a brilliant move. Anselm thus develops the implications of two doctrines as a systematic theologian. These doctrines are rendered in accord with the necessity of God's justice. They are transformed into theories or explanations of divine agency, which is deeply harmonic and denuded of the drama of conflict with the Devil which had characterized the early church's 'ransom theory'.

In most of his works, despite his commitment to reason, dialectics and the propositional content of doctrine, we see Anselm strongly dedicated to the integration of theology with the practice of prayer. We should not underestimate the significance of Anselm's move to make this connection explicit in his theology. One modern scholar suggests that Anselm prefigures contemporary hermeneutics by virtue of his exhortation of the practical context of prayer within which to make sense of his words.[25] In fact, Anselm wrote with the intention of training the emotions and the virtues of his students and readers according to a tradition that goes back to the Benedictine rule. So, in Anselm's method, reason takes its shape within a keenly doxological framework.

Given his preference for the dialogue format in his work, one might think of Anselm's method as dialectical. But, I think it is more accurate to say that Anselm is going over the dialectical background that systematically contributes towards Christian foundations and doctrine. Anselm provides the classic formulation of a systematic theology that goes beyond the explanatory function of doctrine while maintaining a close connection to doctrine and the dialectical stage that precedes doctrine. For Anselm, the Christian must do theology in order to understand what is to be believed.

Anselm's theological method can be characterized in other ways as well. One of the most important novelties of his approach is his proceeding from the world to God in a manner distinct from what scripture and doctrine teach. Systematic theology proceeds thus in order to meet the *logical* demands of what is explanatory in doctrine. Anselm is one of the first to express a systematic theology as a fully developed natural theology, with the help of dialectic. In the *Monologion*, he recommends to his monk students that they consider God by beginning with a consideration of the good and proceed by considering higher and higher forms of the good until conceptually, the good is beyond human comprehension. It is therefore but a short jump from this method to the famous formulation of the ontological proof or the existence of God that is outlined in the *Proslogion*. Another example lies in his work titled *On the Procession of the Holy Spirit*, where Anselm responds to the controversy over the *filioque*. Not knowing the history of the dispute, he writes about it from the perspective of reason, specifically to establish its symmetry:

> Only the Son has a Father; only the Father has a Son; only the Spirit does not have a Spirit proceeding from himself. But both the Father and the Spirit do not have a Father; both the Spirit and the Son do not have a Son; and both the Father and the Son have a Spirit proceeding from themselves.[26]

The logic of a doctrine never escapes Anselm's notice. In this case, the controversial Western claim for the Spirit's distinct procession from both Father and Son receives support. Anselm wrestles with the problem of free will and its reconciliation with divine foreknowledge in an interesting way.

It is always the case that there is a link between one's conception of human nature and theological method. In Anselm's case, the picture he paints of human reason is a very specific one, so that, as we have already seen, human reason is a form of cooperation with God, not an autonomous activity. Consistent with his rational procedure in the *Monologion*, Anselm contends that 'every rational being exists for this [purpose]: to love or refuse things to the extent that, by rational discernment, it judges them to be more or less good or not good'.[27] What this suggests, as Aquinas would later confirm in a much more elaborate fashion, is that the sum total of human searching for truth is really a search for God. If one loves God, one will understand much more readily. The search for truth and goodness will be much more satisfactorily resolved as a consequence. Anselm's greatest impact immediately following his death was in his spiritual writings, not in his more speculative theology. Subsequently, as we have mentioned in regards to the different views of Gilson and Barth, Anselm's notoriety pertains chiefly to the logic and reason that marks out his systematic theology. However, if we take seriously the spiritual writings and his numerous invocations of God in his work, we see that Anselm does indeed develop a systematic theology, not a philosophy of God. His reliance on doctrine and his use of dialectic in that context ensure his legacy as a theological one. The dialectical and even the foundational issues, such as the one concerning divine justice in *CDH*, are resolved retroactively as a re-tracing of steps that seem reasonably necessary in corroborating theological doctrine with medieval notions of justice. But never does Anselm keep the work of reason separate from the spiritual concerns of a monk turned bishop.

Thomas Aquinas

Regarded by the Roman Catholic Church as 'sacred doctor' for his magisterial presentation of theology in dialogue with philosophy and the secular arts, Thomas Aquinas is a formidable commentator on scripture and a systematician *par excellence*. Born in 1225 in Roccasecca, on the outskirts of Aquino, midway between Rome and Naples, he entered the Domincan 'Order of Preachers', and after some preliminary studies under the direction of Albert the Great in Cologne, he came to the University of Paris in 1252. It is there that Aquinas completed his exhaustive studies of the Bible and began his intensive writing, beginning with a commentary on Peter Lombard's *Sentences*, which was a mainstay of thirteenth-century theological education.

No one has shaped the discipline of theology more than Aquinas, except perhaps Augustine, and for Protestants, Calvin. Aquinas is best known for his *Summa Theologiae*, literally titled a 'summary of theology'. This work is the key to understanding Aquinas's theological method, although we ought to be careful not to underestimate his many scriptural commentaries. The *Summa* summarizes Christian doctrine and engages in a significant number of logical analyses of systematic theology. These analyses add understanding to the truth of doctrines with considerable reference to scripture and philosophical sources. The *Summa* probably originates with a felt inadequacy over the scope of the theology texts available to the communities of Dominican friars at the time.

His rather abstract synthetic writing style masks two things that are vital for understanding the theological method of Aquinas: the priority he places on revelation and the variety of theological tasks he undertakes. First, Aquinas accords a high place for the authority of revelation. The very first article of the *Summa* defines theology as *doctrina quadem secundum revelationem divinam* – 'doctrine that springs from divine revelation'. This reference to revelation does not, alas, actually define it. In fact, revelation and the response of faith and sacred doctrine are so crucial to theology that he criticizes rational or natural theology as it was known in its Platonic form.[28] For Aquinas, revelation is a form of knowledge that arises in the response of faith with a cognitive locus. As inspired, it can take several forms. Prophecy, for instance, is one form of revelation that is discussed quite often in the *Summa*. This by itself is interesting, because since prophecy is a genre of biblical literature, he is pointing to the kinds of person (prophets) who make up revelatory acts in history, rather than to the texts themselves as if they were composed apart from inspired persons.

But regardless of the form it takes, revelation is the basis for sacred doctrine, the teachings of faith. Revelation is not opposed to reason. It is a form of knowledge that responds specifically to the human need for salvation, as the first article of the *Summa* also states. Thus, as a form of knowledge necessitated by our need for salvation, it is knowledge about God that is made possible through God's grace, which instigates internal conversion. Interestingly, Aquinas does not go the extra step to say that revelation is a form of knowledge deemed necessary due to a *lack* of knowledge on account of sin. As with his Franciscan counterpart, Bonaventure (1217–74), Aquinas sees revelation as a reference to a cluster of things. It is the contents of divine communication, the source for human transformation, the historical events in which the revealing takes place and the transformation itself. Aquinas explains why scripture is possible to conceive as a source for theological reflection. He does not assume its authority, as earlier medieval theologians did. Unlike earlier interpreters who presuppose in scripture a qualitatively reified historical situation giving rise to the biblical texts, Aquinas conceives of scripture as attestation to God's grace, universally offered to all, to actors biblical and non-biblical. As such, it is the gift character of revelatory divine communication that is the key, not the form which it takes. Doctrine plays a key role in mediating the revelatory witness of scripture and factors external to scripture.

As such, sacred doctrine is a science, *scientia*, or true knowledge. Here is the text of Article 2 in the first question of the treatise on sacred doctrine in the *Summa*, where Aquinas deals with this issue of doctrine as knowledge:

Whether sacred doctrine is a science?

Objection 1: It seems that sacred doctrine is not a science. For every science proceeds from self-evident principles. But sacred doctrine proceeds from articles of faith which are not self-evident, since their truth is not admitted by all: 'For all men have not faith' (2 Thess. 3.2). Therefore sacred doctrine is not a science.

Objection 2: Further, no science deals with individual facts. But this sacred science treats of individual facts, such as the deeds of Abraham, Isaac and Jacob and such like. Therefore sacred doctrine is not a science.

On the contrary, Augustine says (*De Trinitate.* xiv, 1) 'to this science alone belongs that whereby saving faith is begotten, nourished, protected and strengthened.' But this can be said of no science except sacred doctrine. Therefore sacred doctrine is a science.

I answer that, Sacred doctrine is a science. We must bear in mind that there are two kinds of sciences. There are some which proceed from a principle known by the natural light of intelligence, such as arithmetic and geometry and the like. There are some which proceed from principles known by the light of a higher science: thus the science of perspective proceeds from principles established by geometry, and music from principles established by arithmetic. So it is that sacred doctrine is a science because it proceeds from principles established by the light of a higher science, namely, the science of God and the blessed. Hence, just as the musician accepts on authority the principles taught him by the mathematician, so sacred science is established on principles revealed by God.

Reply to Objection 1: The principles of any science are either in themselves self-evident, or reducible to the conclusions of a higher science; and such, as we have said, are the principles of sacred doctrine.

Reply to Objection 2: Individual facts are treated of in sacred doctrine, not because it is concerned with them principally, but they are introduced rather both as examples to be followed in our lives (as in moral sciences) and in order to establish the authority of those men through whom the divine revelation, on which this sacred scripture or doctrine is based, has come down to us.[29]

Theology, as a reflection on sacred doctrine, is thus attached to doctrine completely. It does follow an order, although *not* an Aristotelian demonstrative science of syllogisms and proofs. Aquinas was greatly influenced by Aristotle, but he does not reduce theology to a merely logical form of inference. As Chenu famously said in the 1940s, for Aquinas, sacred doctrine is a science, but only in an attenuated sense. Sacred doctrine is not a discipline of proofs, as though it were a demonstrative science of necessary causes and effects. Neither is it the kind of science that Aristotle describes in his *Posterior Analytics*. Nevertheless, Aquinas manages to smuggle certain ideas about what constitutes a *scientia* into his account of theology that resemble Aristotle's ideal.

The key element that is conveyed in this article early in the *Summa* is the idea of a discipline as 'subaltern'. Sacred doctrine is analogous to that knowledge possessed by angels and the saints, as the principles of music are related to the propositions of arithmetic. Music depends for its very existence on the principles of arithmetic, and this dependence is analogously reflected in theology's subaltern dependence on those who already 'behold the divine essence'.[30] Additionally, theology's 'scientific character' is even more evident in his Five Ways for accounting for God's existence from the effects of God's acting in creation. By arguing according to reason, not authority, and from effect to cause, Aquinas indicates a particular kind of scientific thrust to his theological synthesis.

On the contemplation of God from effects, Aquinas anticipates an objection that this scientific description may not fit theology. A scientific approach may describe a form of metaphysics and therefore is not to be regarded as theology.

Whether God is the subject matter of this science?

Objection 1: It seems that God is not the subject matter of this science. For, according to the Philosopher, in every science, the essence of its subject is presupposed. But this science cannot presuppose the essence of God, for Damascene says (*De Fide Orth.* i, iv): 'It is impossible to express the essence of God.' Therefore God is not the subject matter of this science.

Objection 2: Further, whatever conclusions are reached in any science must be comprehended under the subject-matter of the science. But in Holy Scripture we reach conclusions not only concerning God, but concerning many other things, such as creatures and human morality. Therefore God is not the subject-matter of this science.

On the contrary, The subject-matter of the science is that of which it principally treats. But in this science, the treatment is mainly about God; for it is called theology, as treating of God. Therefore God is the subject-matter of this science.

I answer that, God is the subject-matter of this science. The relation between a science and its subject-matter is the same as that between a habit or faculty and its object. Now properly speaking, the object of a power or habit is that under whose formality all things are referred to that power or habit, as man and stone are referred to sight in that they are coloured. Hence the coloured is the proper object of sight. But in sacred doctrine, all things are treated of under the aspect of God, either because they are God Himself or because they refer to God as their beginning and end. Hence it follows that God is in very truth the subject-matter of this science. This is made clear also from the principles of this science, namely, the articles of faith, for faith is about God. The subject-matter of the principles and of the whole science must be the same, since the whole science is contained virtually in its principles.

Some, however, looking to what is treated in this science, and not to the aspect under which it is treated, have asserted the subject-matter of this science to be something other than God—that is, either things and signs, or the works of salvation, or the whole Christ, that is, the head and members. Of all these things, in truth, we treat in this science, but so far as they are ordered to God.

Reply to Objection 1: Although we cannot know in what consists the essence of God, nevertheless in this science we make use of His effects, either of nature or of grace, in the place of a definition, in regard to whatever is treated in this doctrine concerning God; even as in some philosophical sciences we demonstrate something about a cause from its effect, by taking the effect in place of a definition of the cause.

Reply to Objection 2: Whatever other conclusions are reached in this sacred science are comprehended under God, not as parts or species or accidents but as in some way related to Him.'[31]

Revelation marks out theology from the other sciences according to Aquinas, and the accent on effects as the proper starting point for knowing causes is an emblematic feature of Aquinas's theology that witnesses a parallel between theology and the other true sciences. It is a kind of knowledge received by God, judged and interpreted through the capacities of our study of the effects of God's creation and salvation through grace. Thus, the sources of revelation are scripture and tradition, whose origins are divine, not human. He writes in Article 5 of the first question that:

> other sciences derive their certitude from the natural light of human reason, which can err; whereas this derives its certitude from the light of the divine science, which cannot err; in point of the higher dignity of its subject-matter because this science treats chiefly of those things which by their sublimity transcend human reason; while other sciences consider only those things which are within reason's grasp.[32]

Other disciplines, according to Aquinas, are like handmaidens for theology, and in this sense, theology 'can in a sense depend upon the philosophical sciences, not as though it stood in need of them, but only in order to make its teaching clearer'.[33] Those who are involved in the revelatory process, notably the biblical writers, are participants in divine wisdom. Rejecting an either/or choice between objective information and subjective experience, Aquinas's notion of revelation contains an insight into the dynamic way we may speak about God which has eluded some followers and critics. Thus, on the premise that such an abstract expression of doctrine and theology might not bear on the issue of biblical interpretation, many readers of the *Summa* miss Aquinas's explicit intention to write it as an aid to reading scripture. But that is what the *Summa* is.

The second matter that can be obscured by the dialectical style of Aquinas's writing is the range of theological inquiries that he values. His method of tackling individual issues is fourfold. He (i) poses a *quaestio*, (ii) supplies an initial objection or set of objections, with reasons (*videtur quod*, 'it seems that'), (iii) outlines the argument to be defended (*sed contra*, 'on the contrary') and (iv) details the *responsio*, incorporating a detailed refutation of the initial answer and the replies to the objections. This dialectical style is increasingly common from the late twelfth century onwards. And while he is clearly dealing with theological and philosophical opponents, overall, Aquinas is seeking a synthesis, a resolution and explanation.

As such, Aquinas provides much more than Peter Lombard's open-ended *Sic et non*. That twelfth-century work expressed a dialectical presentation of contentious theological issues without resolving them. Aquinas writes a theology that is fully engaged with scripture, often in terms of its literal sense one must concede. He is not adventurous in the way that Origen was, yet Aquinas sees developments in truth that can elaborate on what is contained in scripture far beyond what the intended sense of scripture entails. To that extent, Aquinas may even be said to be open to the idea of the 'development of doctrine', a concept that did not emerge fully until the nineteenth century.[34]

However, given the dogmatic breadth of the *Summa* and his other theological works, we would do better to describe Aquinas's thought as a systematic theology, oriented to revelation in scripture and sacred doctrine. This systematic theology anticipates a broad range of theological tasks which operate in the foreground and background of theological practice. Like Anselm, he is doing much more than engaging in logical argument or dialectics, appearances to the contrary. Buried in most of the arguments of the *Summa* are the statements, positions and themes of scripture and the Fathers of the Church, especially Augustine. So, the *Summa* is both an explanation of foundational principles that bind together a variety of sources, as well as a project of immense magnitude detailing an organic, metaphysical structure for supporting doctrine. Jean-Pierre Torrell calls this presentation a 'synthetic doctrine', always dovetailing on the significance of biblical texts, which are cited repeatedly.[35]

This systematic doctrine is also conveyed apologetically, especially in *Summa contra Gentiles*, another work devoted to explaining the grounds for belief. There, Aquinas follows a method that for the first time weaves the distinction between doctrine and systematics in a manner that is explicit. As Lonergan comments:

> '[In] the fourth book of *Summa contra Gentiles* . . . [C]hapters Two to Nine are concerned with the existence of God the Son, Chapters Fifteen to Eighteen with the existence of the Holy Spirit, Chapters Twenty-seven to Thirty-nine with the existence of the Incarnation. But Chapters Ten to Fourteen center in the question of the manner in which a divine generation is to be conceived. Similarly, Chapters Nineteeen to Twenty-five

have to do with the manner of conceiving the Holy Spirit, and
Chapters Forty to Forty-nine have to do with the systematics of
the Incarnation.[36]

So, Aquinas sees the need to make a distinction between a theology
of revelation that is mediated by the church (a theology via
authority) and a theology that springs forth from the heuristic
power of questions, the 'manner of conceiving' things in the
first place. This dual 'back-and-forth' appeal to authority on the
one hand, and to reason on the other hand, is classic Aquinas. It
would be transformed at the hands of later scholastic thinkers into
a dualism of thought, and later still, into a dualism of doctrinal
and natural theology proper. It is this dualism that would provide
Luther with one of his grounds of protest. In Aquinas, however,
we ought to say that there is still an organic link between two
ways of theological reflection, the distinction between the doctrine
as explained and the doctrine as conceived through language and
reason, as understood. And, these two ways conform roughly with
what Lonergan means by the two functional specialties of doctrine
and systematics.

   This distinction in fact upends prior theological methodology.
Up until the thirteenth century, in the Christian tradition, we
see the deployment of philosophical categories that serve to
interpret scripture in light of tradition and formulated in doctrinal
explanations. Anselm begins to break free from this approach by
going back over the dialectical and foundational steps in theology,
as if scripture and doctrine were either unavailable or in need of
advance proof. Aquinas boldly sets out to develop a system of
theological elements that assist the reading of scripture through
constructing a given structure in advance of that reading and
interpretation – a kind of *prolegomena*. An apparent autonomy
thus obtains for a metaphysical theology. Aquinas makes explicit
the distinction between two basic characteristics in theology: the
practical and the speculative. But whereas some see in Aquinas a
separation of theologies, Aquinas himself only sees a distinction
according to the order of questioning.

   There are several ongoing debates over Thomas Aquinas that
continue to mark the reception of his theology, and these debates
have a great deal to do with methodology. The first debate concerns
whether he yields too much to the Greek, philosophical account of

God instead of relying on specifically Christian sources to articulate who God is. For instance, as has already been alluded to, near the beginning of his great *Summa Theologiae*, Aquinas speaks of God as simple, perfect, immutable, infinite and wholly good. These divine attributes do indeed look more akin to those of Greek philosophy than the Christian Trinity. But on closer examination and in the context of the *Summa* as a whole, we should see Aquinas's starting point in a different light.

These attributes do not so much serve to simply describe God. Rather, these words serve to adumbrate the grammar of speech about God. What is the difference? Taking his cue from the negative theology of Dionysius, Aquinas intends our speech about God to avoid all forms of idolatry. In Question 11 of the *Summa Theologiae*, Aquinas directly links his accent on monotheism to the invocation of Deut. 6.4: 'Hear O Israel, The Lord our God is one Lord', which is followed by directly addressing the relationship of divine unity to the Trinity. So, Aquinas is still dealing directly with the biblical witness and that of the tradition by beginning with the simple attributes for God. Also, by not adopting the Trinitarian attributes for analysis from the beginning, he avoids giving the impression that revealed categories are the only categories available for speaking of God. Methodologically speaking though, what Aquinas is doing in mapping the terrain this way is settling the difference between systematic and doctrinal theology proper. Contrary to what Jurgen Moltmann and Karl Barth say in the twentieth century, Aquinas is not abandoning the Trinity in order to settle for a Greek philosophical notion of God.

Systematic theology is well suited to elaborate on the doctrine of analogy, the basis for all theological systems, according to Aquinas. Bearing in mind the Dionysian background to this insight, the idea is to avoid speaking of the infinite and eternal as if they are straightforward extensions of the finite and temporal. For Aquinas, one cannot know God in terms of 'what he is', but only in terms of 'what he is not'.[37] This means that theological language, for all its intended precision, is inherently limited. The result is the famous doctrine of analogy. To be specific, the great doctrine regulating theological language is known as the *analogia entis* – the 'analogy of being', which was formalized in relation to the doctrines of the church at the Fourth Lateran Council in 1215. There, it was affirmed that for every similarity between the creature and God, there is always a much greater dissimilarity.

According to Aquinas, we can affirm God analogously from certain features of the natural created world. Analogy has the dual benefit of describing both the similarities and differences between the feature of the created world and those attributes of God being compared. Effectively, Aquinas is developing a twofold approach to God. One is negative in the sense that Aquinas limits the directness of linguistic reference. Nevertheless, Aquinas affirms the ability of analogical language to positively address God from the created effects of this world to their creator and cause. Analogically, God is like certain aspects of the created world. From this 'natural knowledge of God', theology proceeds from below upwards as well, and so it is that Aquinas's name has become associated so closely with the genre of natural theology.

Before he raises the topic of analogies in the *Summa*, in the prologue, Aquinas uses the term '*ordo disciplinae*' to refer to the order by which he plans to summarize his entire theology. This means that Aquinas orders his theology methodically, with priority given to meaning and pedagogy, the 'manner of conceiving'. A pedagogical obligation also underlies his decision to begin with the simple attributes for God, rather than with God as three persons. The order of his theology is intended to reflect the movement of revelation and faith: from God to creation and back to God through Christ's saving grace. Aquinas also proceeds by moving from what is more known or well appreciated to that which is less known. The metaphysical vision is captured in the *exitus et reditus* pattern that we reviewed in Dionysius. In Aquinas's case, however, it also resembles a circular vision of reality as he received it from Aristotle. That said, what is most noticeable in the organization of the *Summa* is the progression of agency from God to human beings to Christ: three parts with three distinct actors.

Both the metaphysical horizon and a pedagogical outlook help explain why the first part of the *Summa* deals with the nature of theology and God. The second part of the *Summa* is second because its treatment of human morality, sin and Christian faith, hope and love can only be understood in terms of the reason why human beings seek purpose and goodness; namely, God. The third part of the *Summa*, which deals with Christ, comes last, since Christ can only be understood in light of the conceptual apparatus regarding God erected at the start and the predicament of sin and the offer of salvation in Christ which are raised by considering morality and human purpose in the second part.

For Aquinas, the fact that the world is created by God is the basis for adapting Dionysius' 'negative' approach associated with the naming of God. And this explains why he famously develops his five ways (*quinque viae*) to prove the existence of God. We must take note of the order of Aquinas's reasoning, however: the five ways are intended as ways to employ philosophical reason in the service of adducing proofs for God's existence. Indeed, these five ways appear in the second article of the first part of the *Summa*. These five ways have been assumed to be directed against forms of atheism, real or imagined. However, this section has in fact more to do with establishing the *raison d'être* of theology, a discipline that is able to incorporate reasons for establishing God's existence rather than simply proceed on the assumption that God exists. Again, what is significant here is the methodological point. Systematic theology can explain the manner of conceiving what doctrine might be, known as it is from revelation. The position that God's existence is self-evident was known in the medieval period as ontologism, and it is against this view that Aquinas writes.

By seeking to provide reasons on God's existence, however, Aquinas has been misunderstood. When the *ordo disciplinae* and the context of medieval debate are ignored, we should not be surprised to see that since the early modern period, Aquinas has been interpreted by both 'Thomist' followers and his Protestant detractors as authorizing a form of 'foundationalism'. Especially problematic for postmodern thinkers who resist any grand narratives stemming from particular statements, Aquinas is accused of articulating the existence of God on the basis of several foundational philosophical propositions alone, separate from theological considerations. How could Aquinas be perceived this way?

It is essential to recall once again that Thomas Aquinas is a theologian who sees the virtue of asking different questions about God. The *Summa Theologiae* takes up two questions that straddle the border between natural or systematic theology and doctrinal theology in the Christian tradition. These two questions are, in fact, the emphases of Anselm and Dionysius, respectively;

but Aquinas handles these questions in different ways. The first question concerns whether God exists (Anselm's *an sit* in his ontological argument, which Aquinas critiques in the *Summa*'s first part, Question 2) and second, the question of what God is (Dionysius' *quid sit*, which Aquinas references in terms of scripture and doctrine to a much higher degree than Dionysius).

Furthermore, in the *Summa*, the five 'proofs' concerning God's existence appear immediately following a quotation from the Bible (q.2, a.3) in which Aquinas recalls that God reveals Himself to Moses as an existing reality (Exod. 3.14).[38] From this admittedly Dionysian starting point, Aquinas goes on to explore the intelligibility inherent in the being of God, taking up the revelation to Moses that God is 'I am who I am'. If the recourse to reason in the Five Ways and elsewhere in Aquinas's writings seems too indebted to the Greek philosophical tradition, recall that, for Aquinas, there is no such thing as secular reason as we would understand that term today. Reason, for Aquinas, is a participation in the light with which God sees things. Holding on to this aspect of Neo-Platonism, reason is conceived as spiritually constituted because it is a gift from God.

It is impossible to summarize the breadth and depth of Aquinas's theology in a short space; but there is sufficient evidence here to indicate several important turns in theological method that develop in the Middle Ages generally, and which are exemplified in his theology. Above all, the distinction between systematic theology and doctrine which is already operative in a number of earlier theologians, including Origen and Anselm, comes to a full flourishing in Aquinas. But Aquinas should not be understood as the only medieval theologian worthy of mention in the context of theological method. It is significant that the theologies of all three theologians mentioned in this chapter have been revived in the recent century for one reason or another. The revival of Aquinas after the 1879 papal encyclical *Aeterni patris* turned out to be a less successful prelude to the more recent revival of interest in Aquinas of the past twenty years. Anselm has been the subject of a revival of theological interest in the modern period, particularly among so-called analytic theologians, but beginning with Karl Barth's 1960 monograph which is subtitled, *Fides quarens intellectum*. Dionysius continues to provide a subtle and energetic voice to revived Eastern orthodox theology as well as the Radical Orthodoxy group, which endorses his more poetic conception of the theology-philosophy relationship.

Hence, it is vital, if the contemporary retrieval of medieval theology is any indication, to be aware of the different conceptions of theological method in medieval theology, for that diversity is profound and significant. It is important to see, among other things, that the metaphysical gloss on medieval theology is not proposed in the absence of scripture and tradition. At a time when church doctrines become more numerous and complex, the forging of a distinct language of systematic theology is crucial for the development of theological method. To be sure, the Protestant Reformation and the retention of traditional theology in Eastern Orthodoxy represent counterparts to the more stifling scholasticisms that grew out of the medieval theological mindset. What is also significant, nonetheless, is that medieval theology is expressed with methodological novelty thanks to the infusion of philosophical tools. New concepts introduced at that time are still with us because of the creative thrust of these theologies which sharpened the dialectical procedure of theology in response to the rise of the university academy and specialized knowledge. In short, the concept of theology's task and its procedures became more distinct during the medieval period, especially in Dionysius, Anselm and Aquinas.

CHAPTER FIVE

The meaning of
sola scriptura

The Cross alone is our theology.[1]

With the rise of Reforming movements in the fourteenth century and a revival of Augustinian theology through the *via moderna* in the fifteenth century, a decisive shift in theological method began to take hold. Until this point in time, the ways of doing theology are referenced to a recurring set of multiple sources, chiefly scripture, but with increasing attention to reason over the medieval period. Despite the differences between the metaphysical apophaticism of those like Dionysius and the anti-speculative bent of those like Irenaeus, theological method is arguably coherent from the patristic period through to the fifteenth century. The range of sources, criteria, procedure, types of prolegomena and reliance on philosophy, while divergent, are not so wildly different.

With the onset of Reformation theology, we detect a keener explicit interest in scripture. The motto 'scripture alone', or *sola scriptura*, becomes the calling card for the Protestant Reformers in their struggle to whittle away the undue influence of reason and tradition in the church and in the theological academy. Thus, in theological method, a chasm opens up between the scriptural *foci* of the Reformers in contrast to the scriptural, traditional and rational character of Catholic theology. This change is obviously a function of the dialectical pressures of Protestant and Catholic traditions, each of which was anxious to build up a theological pedigree that could attain maximum leverage over the intellectual and cultural life of Western Europe. Beneath the historical contingencies of this period lie the gripping division over method in theology. The divisions within Christendom, even though they are mainly political, are also deeply methodological.

The Protestant Reformation, like other methodological revolutions which would follow in the modern period, forces the theologian to reflect more attentively on the nature of theological reflection that precedes the revolution. Standing back from the melee of Christian history, some contemporary theologians have taken the diversity of methods before, during and after the sixteenth century as well as their consequent theologies to indicate a 'paradigmatic' character to Christian theology. Following the development of the paradigm concept by the historian of science Thomas Kuhn (1922–66), theologians like Hans Küng and George Lindbeck have adapted its use for understanding the way theologians deploy concepts and use languages over time, according to their own respective theological commitments. Though such a concept can be overused to understand the history of theology, such theologians take the new theological method of events like the Protestant Reformation to imply that the language of individual traditions are rather impervious to neutral evaluations from outside those traditions. Yet the traditions break down when critics from within such traditions begin to test auxiliary or secondary hypotheses that end up stretching the paradigm beyond what it can contain within itself.

The Reformation principle of *sola scriptura* is an appropriate example of a paradigm emerging from the strain of a medieval theological practice that had grown diffuse. *Sola scriptura* is, in truth, a methodological emphasis that stems from medieval Augustinianism, yet the slogan itself does not adequately spell out what precisely the 'new' theological method meant, since it was bandied about by theologians with a very different command of sources and hermeneutical styles. Take Martin Luther's approach towards reason, for instance. In various places, his characterization of reason is hostile to say the least: 'Reason is a "beast", an "enemy of God", a "source of mischief". It is "carnal" and "stupid".'[2] We know from a perusal of Luther's writings that his overriding intent is to disabuse his audience of any positive perspective towards medieval scholastic theology and its assumed basis in Aristotle. At times, Luther communicates a substitute for this specific attack with an attack on reason as a whole. Ironically, however, Luther demonstrates great familiarity, respect and learning in the tradition of Renaissance humanism and the academic approach towards scripture. We must be extremely careful to distinguish what the theologians of this period say in some of their polemics with what their theological method actually consists, especially given certain similarities with the medieval period. In this chapter, we will summarize and briefly assess some of the most important Protestant theologians of the period 1500–60 and render several cursory conclusions about how the theology of this period was carried out.

Martin Luther

Born in 1483, Martin Luther became the voice of what is later known as the Protestant Reformation. To the extent that he was chased, accused and tried as a heretic by his Catholic opponents, Luther served as a lightning rod for developments and conflicts that both preceded him and which engulfed the church thereafter throughout Germany and the rest of Europe. The symbolism of his nailing 95 theses to the door of the church in Wittenberg tends to over-signify Luther's own standing in relation to the unfolding controversies of the 1520–60 period. The 1521 Diet of Worms would likely have issued a litany of complaints against abuses on the part of several Catholic rulers without his provocations. Indeed, Luther's fellow faculty members at Wittenberg were fully involved in precipitating the confrontation with Rome that eventually ensued. Despite the matter of historical contingencies, however, Luther's theology is testimony to a retrieval of Augustinian theology, especially its accent on grace, with the result of instigating a precedent-setting cascade of theological insights and ecclesial reforms.

To this day, assessments of Martin Luther vary to the extent that different criteria are employed to evaluate his theological significance. To the extent that Luther articulates a distinct theology, we can characterize it as partly medieval and partly modern.

Luther remains very much an enigmatic figure from the standpoint of theological method, because, like Paul and most patristic theologians, Luther did not present a full systematic theology or a dogmatics (to use the term of Reformed thinkers). Still, as one modern scholar has claimed, Luther's thought is an early, emblematic form of 'anthropocentric theology', a label intended to be critical.[3] One biographer, Roland Bainton, remarks that 'his faith may be called the last great flowering of the religion of the Middle Ages'.[4] True, Luther railed against speculative theology, especially in the form of scholastic theology; and he was familiar with scholastics (such as William of Ockham) and he was a follower of Gabriel Biel, who was associated with the *via moderna*, a late medieval movement that encouraged renaissance learning in the church. Luther criticized the use of logical syllogisms in theology by noting that such inferences belonged to the realm of philosophy. And, like other Renaissance humanists, he was strongly opposed to what he saw as the dialectical absurdities of medieval scholastic theology. Still, he is not considered a Renaissance thinker, in the mode of the Italians and other Europeans who fit that moniker.

As with the theologians of the early church in particular, Luther's theological writing was occasional. Luther's approach contrasts with the work of Calvin, the pre-eminent sixteenth-century Reformed theologian whose biblical commentaries, especially the *Institutes*, exude systematic coherence. Bernhard Lohse compares Luther's output to that of Calvin and Luther's devotee Philipp Melanchthon by stating: 'It seems that if there had been a dogmatics from Luther's hand, it would not have differed from others in structure and composition, but indeed in its treatment of individual doctrines.'[5] Like his Reformation colleagues, and despite his medieval frame of mind, Luther sets the tone for Protestant theology by presupposing so much that is fresh. One of the important, yet too often unacknowledged, ways in which Luther re-conceives theology is his steadfast commitment to overcome the false opposition between theory and practice in theology. He sees theology instead as essentially a *vita passiva*, a passive life, in contrast with both the *vita activa* and the *vita contemplativa* of late medieval academic theology. For Luther, the twin pitfalls of a works-based faith, especially that of the monks and clergy, as well as the abstract speculations of scholastic theology, conspired against the relational priority of Christian faith.[6]

Because of Luther's arguments with Rome and with other Reformers, such as Zwingli, and with representatives of the 'Radical Reformation', we have plenty of material evidence for his theological views. What is not so clear is whether the episodic nature of Luther's writing hides or reveals anything like a coherent theological method, an awareness of the tasks that make up the work of a theologian. Understanding Luther's theological method is much harder than understanding theological method in Aquinas because Aquinas has addressed the question explicitly. There are obvious resemblances between Luther, Paul and some of the patristic theologians in their occasional style of theology. With Luther, the question of context becomes paramount – more than for the other theologians we have studied thus far, because the cultural, theological and intellectual forces that were in play during the early sixteenth century were more intense and pluralistic than even a century earlier.

Luther's 'Reformation discovery', his insight into the nature of the righteousness of God, is so important in the history of theology that it deserves close attention. It is an event, the context of which Luther himself relays as follows:

I had conceived a most unusual, burning desire to understand Paul in his letter to the Romans; thus far there had stood in my way not a cold heart but one single word that is written in the first chapter: 'In it the justice of God is revealed' (Rom. 1.17) because I hated that word 'justice of God.' By the use and custom of all my teachers I had been taught to understand it philosophically as referring to so-called formal or active justice, that is, justice by which God is just and by which he punishes sinners and the unjust. – But I, impeccable monk that I was, stood before God as a sinner with an extremely troubled conscience and I could not be sure that my merit would assuage him. I did not love, no, rather I hated the just God who punishes sinners. In silence if I did not blaspheme against God, then certainly I grumbled with vehement anger against him. As if it isn't enough that we miserable sinners, lost for all eternity because of original sin, are oppressed by every kind of calamity through the Ten Commandments. Why does God heap sorrow upon sorrow through the gospel and through the gospel threatens us with his justice and wrath? This was how I was raging with wild and disturbed conscience. Thus

I continued badgering Paul about that spot in Romans 1 seeking anxiously to know what it meant.[7]

What interests us about this passage are its ramifications for Luther's method in theology. It is clear that Luther's interest in justice and the theological doctrine of justification implies a conflict with lesser doctrines concerning, for example, how to practice penance (the power of the absolution of sins, for instance, belonging to clergy and laity alike) and, of course, the practice of indulgences in the Catholic Church. Luther's other contribution, with respect to justification, is his upholding of this doctrine as primary. It is, he said the 'ruler and judge over all other Christian doctrines',[8] something that the twentieth-century theologian Paul Tillich has resoundingly confirmed. Luther's claim that soteriology be so prominent, relative to other doctrines is an unusual emphasis. It is unusual when we consider the fact that the ancient creeds prioritize those doctrines pertaining to Christ and the Trinity. We are right to conjecture then, methodologically speaking, that Luther thinks inadvertently in the way of the systematic theologian by distinguishing one doctrine over others. Alas, this is not how we should think of Luther ultimately. What he is most concerned about is the foundational reality that is indicated by the sacrament of penance, and the deep-rooted mistake regarding the nature of God's justice that lies behind the practice of indulgences. The medieval theology of penance is indeed the problem that spawns his inquiry into justification. In this context, Luther establishes a new foundation for thinking about signs. In the case of penance, the shift Luther inaugurates is the shift from priestly absolution as a sign of justification towards thinking about the reality of justification unfolding as a speech-act. Oswald Bayer remarks on Luther's thought:

> the sentence 'I absolve you of your sins!' is no judgment which only ascertains what already exists, therefore assuming an inner, divine, proper absolution. Rather, the word of absolution is a speech-act that first establishes a state of affairs, first creates a relationship – between the one in whose name it is spoken, and the one to whom it is spoken and who believes the promise.[9]

For Luther, a dialectical engagement with his Catholic opponents is not resolved by establishing a new foundational category in addition to those of the Bible and the early church. Rather, Luther's dialectical theology means to shift the meaning and reason for repentance of sin. He wants to revise the semantic framework for thinking about divine justice. The shift, for Luther, is from a metaphysical ontology of God's being and God's abstract attributes, to a foundational ontology of relationality. Luther prefers to think of our relations with God through the prism of repentance and justification, an outlook or horizon of our personal becoming. It is, to put it perhaps a bit crudely, a transition from an impersonal to a personal foundation of theological logic. The consequence, among other things, is to a paradoxical anthropology: we are simultaneously sinners and justified before God: Luther's famous *simul justus et peccator* (simultaneously justified and a sinner).

Such a shift in perspective is massive and explains why Luther can argue for the priority of the doctrine of justification over other doctrines, on the latter of which there is accepted agreement with Catholics. Luther recasts the category of divine justice, the *iustitia dei*, to make it the measure by which other doctrines are measured. The classical doctrines of the ancient church dealing with Christology and the Trinity are not up for revision. Yet he revisits the foundational grounds on which these doctrines are formulated in a way that few late medieval theologians do, apart from William of Ockham's nominalist philosophy, which did penetrate the theological academy during the fourteenth century.

Luther's formulation of justification contains the idea that God is not answerable to the way that reason formulates justice, and he criticizes Aristotle's *Ethics* heavily for its leading idea of the judge who dispenses justice according to the merits or demerits of the accused individual. For Luther, on the other hand, our status as sinners means that God's justice must mean something different. As in a flash, upon reading Rom. 1.17 where Paul says 'For the righteous [or 'just', 'to employ an alternative translation for the Greek *dikaios*] shall live by faith', Luther comes to think of whole swaths of medieval soteriology and moral theology as semi-Pelagian. For Luther, too much medieval thought contains accounts of justice, virtue and merit that are opposed to the righteousness of God as announced through Christ.

For Luther, it is necessary to overturn the medieval synthesis of faith and reason and break it down, at least on those issues that matter to him, on grounds established by a reading of scripture and on account of the gospel in particular. Thus, Luther engages not in a piecemeal re-interpretation of this or that particular passage, but confronts an entire historical tradition of theological exegesis. His re-founding of the category of the justice of God means that he re-reads scripture in order to establish a new tradition of scriptural interpretation. Methodologically, by articulating the justice of God, on the basis of Rom. 1.17, as a *sui generis* form of justice, Luther forecloses certain possibilities, in principle, of a systematic theology that would aim to weave theology with philosophical insights.

This leads, naturally enough, to the methodological slogan '*sola scriptura*', which Luther made his own in the various disputes that ensued. *Sola scriptura* is not merely intended to indicate a source from which speech about God must begin and end. It indicates also a derivative and second *principle* of scriptural interpretation at the same time. This second principle is summarized in the famous Latin expression '*scriptura sui ipsius interpres*' – 'Scripture is its own interpreter'. This means, for Luther, that each scriptural passage needs to be interpreted in light of the entire biblical message. This is far from the first time that this principle is advocated in Christian theology, since we see it in Origen and in Augustine, in nuanced form. The hermeneutical breadth of this second interpretive principle can hide the fact that in coming to convey the biblical message entire, Luther really needs an extra-biblical doctrine about scripture, a shorthand rule, a canon about the canon. As an applied doctrine about scripture, the rule concerning scripture being its own interpreter comes to mean that the role of the individual interpreter is all-important. It is insufficient, on Luther's terms, to declare that scripture alone tells us of God's works of salvation. It is necessary that interpreting scripture be a scriptural matter for the theologian to work out, apart from what the tradition might say.

On the phrase 'justification by faith', Luther selects a third principle that allows scripture to be interpreted in terms of theological criteria. As we saw in dealing with Paul's exegesis of Jewish scriptures for a Gentile context, tensions emerge with Paul's different realms of meaning. Paul himself takes certain aspects of the Hebrew Bible literally and other parts non-literally, in light of Christ's gospel. The difference between letter and spirit, based on Paul's experience of salvation in Christ, comes to dominate his view of scripture. In Luther, a similar tension takes shape, which is the contrast between the law and the gospel. For him, either scripture refers ultimately to Christ or it is not scripture.

Luther's distrust of the Epistle of James is indicative, perhaps, that he is less committed to the idea that scripture interprets itself than he says elsewhere. Since that epistle contains the admonition to do good works as necessary for salvation ('faith by itself, if it has no works, is dead', Jas 2.17), Luther has to develop a criterion for dealing with those biblical books which flout the doctrine of justification by faith alone. This obliges him to go beyond *sola scriptura*. To the extent that he sees tremendous tension between James's letter and the doctrine of justification by faith, Luther uses the doctrine as the measure of the scriptural canon, or at least the Epistle to James along with Hebrews and portions of Revelation too. Of course, to seek the removal of the Epistle of James from the New Testament would be plainly inconsistent. Its separation from other New Testament books would mean trouble for a Reformer who is supposed to uphold scripture. For that reason, James was consigned as an appendix in his German translation of the New Testament.

What Luther also had in mind concerning scripture, was the problem of allegory. By the time of the Reformation, with the newfound awareness of ancient history and languages, Luther was able to perceive a certain arbitrariness in allegory. He thought of it as opposed to the literal sense of scripture, which he wanted to explore through attention to grammar and the original texts. Despite his rough exchanges with Erasmus, the leading Rotterdam humanist and Bible translator, Luther took keen interest in ancient languages. By 1517, he had already helped introduce new courses in languages while he let go older courses on Aristotle at the University of Wittenberg where he taught.

In terms of Lonergan's functional specialties, Luther is engaging in a multi-pronged theological enterprise. The new experience of freedom he feels in his employment of dialectic against an old meaning for the foundational category of divine justice suggests that he is aware of a historical trajectory in the meaning of God's justice. He is aware of the ways that this history is at odds with Paul's meaning of it in Rom. 1.17. Luther is thus freely working to interpret scripture anew, obviously while critiquing the Catholic tradition's way of treating scripture. He also frames the resulting perspective in a dialectical way, which provides the foundational categories that germinate Luther's theology.

Luther's theological method is thus a largely interpretive and dialectical matter with glimpses of history and foundations emerging from his writing. This is one way to describe the procedural landscape of Luther's work. It is easier and clearer to frame Luther's theology not as an amalgam of tasks, but in light of the foundational fruit that he provides in his preaching and for his readers. For example, in his disputation with his fellow Augustinians in 1518 at Heidelberg, Luther formulated two theses which are important for understanding his overall approach, even as it evolved in his later mature theology. In Theses 19 and 20, he writes:

19 The man [sic] who looks upon the invisible things of God as they are perceived in created things does not deserve to be called a theologian.
20 The man [sic] who perceives the visible rearward parts of God as seen in suffering and the cross does, however, deserve to be called a theologian.[10]

There are, in fact, several typical Lutheran theological emphases found in these theses, beginning with the strongly dialectical nature of his argument. In Thesis 20, Luther makes an allusion via the 'rearward parts of God' to Exod. 33.23, where God tells Moses that 'you shall see my back; but my face shall not be seen'. This passage itself speaks to the *Deus abscondicus*, the God who is concealed while paradoxically revealing himself. Thesis 19 reads as a broadside against the scholastic tradition with which Luther was both familiar and critical. Another key emphasis mentioned here is the *theologia crucis*, the theology of the cross. This is Luther's way of speaking of the power and even non-rational way that God is revealed to the world in the dreadful form of Christ's weakened humiliation on the cross. The paradox of Christ is duplicated in the paradox concerning the critical role of faith in doing theology. As McGrath says, for Luther, 'In that it is God who is made known in the passion and death of Christ, it is revelation; in that this revelation can only be discerned by the eye of faith, it is concealed'.[11] Luther's theology of the cross is thus a lens or framework that presents, in a direct way, what God wants to reveal. Another way that Luther articulates this category is through his reference in his *Large Catechism* to Christ as the 'mirror of the eternal'. Such metaphors are important for understanding Luther's theological language in contrast to the metaphysical language of Christ as the second person of the Trinity, divine procession and so forth. In leaving metaphysics behind, Luther embraces the dramatic and the poetic, and he makes this language a part of his argument with the tradition, its interpretation, its categories and some of its doctrines.

Where Luther's theological method may be distinct is in regards to the connection he wants to draw between paradox (once again) and its scriptural support. Statements such as the following, which is based on 1 Cor. 9.19, are splendidly paradoxical:

> A Christian is a perfectly free Lord of all, subject to none.
> A Christian is a perfectly dutiful servant of all, subject to all.[12]

Like the Pauline expression of faith, dialectic in a Lutheran vein is blunt. It is coarse, rugged and not given to systematic exposition. For his followers, Luther provided the *'reine Lehrer'* or 'pure doctrine' of the gospel of justification through faith. Pure doctrine suggests a ready account of faith in the context of its dialectical tension, between law and gospel most obviously. The dialectic becomes positively divisive when Luther turns to individuals who challenge the paradigm of grace. Of Moses, Luther comments: 'his rule ended when Christ came'. Moses is a proto-Christian, 'the fountainhead out of which all good works must flow'.[13] Such contrasts underscore Luther's alternative historiography of biblical interpretation. It clarifies his opposition to the history of Catholic interpretation which he believes subsumed faith to works. For Luther, works flow from faith, and that ordering is central to his theology.

Luther's way of engaging dialectics is complex and, as we have seen, is also couched in terms of key foundational categories. One of these general categories is that of paradox, an ontologizing of dialectic in fact. Epistemically, the paradoxical nature of theology flies in the face of Aristotelian logic, which is what Luther intends. His basic conception of theology is that of a *sapientia experimentalis*, a wisdom that comes from the experience of 'prayer, meditation and trial'. Theology is not *scientia* as Aquinas envisioned it; instead, theology is 'an infinite wisdom because it can never be completely learned'.[14]

The embrace of a methodology of *sola scriptura* is clearly central to Luther's humanist instincts. Yet his attention to scripture should not blind us to the ways that he employs hermeneutical strategies

to frame biblical interpretation through dialectical argument
and the proposing of foundational categories. Luther is not only
interested in scripture; he is also keen on principles that guide
a correct understanding of scripture in the first place. Nor is he
just alluding to scripture in ways that are more direct; he is aware
that the recourse to scripture results in a different theology. He is
also more than aware of the need for new soteriological criteria
to shape theology, inversely proportional to the receding role of
philosophy in theology he envisions. However, partly because of the
revolutionary spirit with which he lodges his theological protest, he
remains somewhat unaware of the different ways *he* uses scripture
in constructing that theology.

Melanchthon

Philipp Melanchthon was Luther's younger protégé and a University
of Wittenberg teacher of Greek (1497–1560). He is widely credited
with rendering Lutheran theology more comprehensive and systematic. Hence, he is implicated in the question of theological method.
He was one of a number of theologians who are collectively
dubbed the 'Wittenberg Circle', and Melanchthon himself was never
ordained. Without his efforts at preserving and communicating
Luther's theological corpus to wider audiences, Lutheran theology
itself would not have had such a wide impact. What is so arresting
about the thought of Melanchthon is his interest in natural philosophy, inspired in large part by the humanist movement. Thus, almost
from the beginning, the Protestant Reformation's range of available
sources in its application of theological method was not reducible
to interpreting scripture. As one who cherished linguistic clarity and
classical literature, Melanchthon would go on to write two works
on natural philosophy. He interpreted Aristotle, Galen and other
ancient sources in a way that scholars today have identified as specifically 'Lutheran'. Thus, as Erasmus alleged, Melanchthon 'was
more Lutheran than Luther himself'.[15]

One of the key contributions that Melanchthon made was
in the area of educational reform, for which he has been given
the title of *Praeceptor Germinae*, schoolmaster of Germany.
With Luther, Melanchthon initially advocated the curtailment of

Aristotle's *Physics* and *Ethics* in education. Yet by 1527 he was ready to teach the moral philosophy of Aristotle's *Ethics*, partly in response to the social crises which were by then spiralling out of control. As he later put it, moral philosophy 'is a part of divine law'.[16] In 1540, Melanchthon wrote a commentary on the soul, in which he accepted a large part of what Aristotle contributed while inserting his own emphases, such as the role of conscience. As splits emerged among the Reformers, Melanchthon's expertise in languages and the arts curriculum became indispensible components of an approach to disciplines ancillary to theology. With Luther, his approach suggested a return to natural philosophy and arts education managed by bureaucracy and formal supervision by state personnel in what has become known as the 'Magisterial Reformation' in German education.[17] But, this meant that he would have to defer to Luther in seizing the nub of theological matters. He perhaps felt insufficiently theologically oriented, despite his willingness to employ rhetorical skills at the service of Luther's theology.

Melanchthon is best known for treating scripture as a source book for Christian doctrine – the Bible as a *doctrinae Christianae compendium*. His first major theological contribution came in a work entitled *Loci communes*, an exposition of Lutheran theology that was instigated by Luther's enthusiasm for Melanchthon's lectures on the Letter to the Romans. In the *Loci*, Melanchthon takes certain ideas already associated with Luther and interprets these ideas in a much stronger way through an ordering of key theological themes following the way those themes are developed in the Book of Romans. The *Loci* thus constitute a hybrid between a scriptural commentary and a Book of Reformation Dogmatics. Dogmatics would become the tradition for this style of doctrinal exposition in the church. In the *Loci*, Melancthon merely makes assertions that connect and extend Luther's thought. On the issue of the human will, for example, he argues for the power of the affections in limiting our freedom. He goes further by rejecting a sizable portion of the anti-Manichean Augustine by declaring: 'Since all things that happen, happen necessarily according to divine predestination, our will has no liberty.'[18]

This work was followed up in the course of Luther's conflict with the Pope in 1520 by a work on the relationship between faith and philosophy in which Melanchthon strikes a distinctly Lutheran tone:

> Many men adore philosophy because it puts man before his own eyes, and the ancients regarded the fruit and end of philosophy thus: to know oneself. But how much more felicitously has Paul surpassed this, in whom it is to discern, as in a mirror, whatever was placed in the inner recesses of man! Nowhere could you contemplate more completely about the grounds of imperfections and nowhere more precisely about the power and founts of virtue.[19]

Yet, despite this broadside against philosophy, philosophy is later praised as useful:

> When Paul said 'Beware lest any man spoil you through philosophy', it should not be understood thus: that that philosophy which teaches us to speak well and teaches the natures of remedies and of bodies, is empty: for Paul permits us to use that very judgment of reason like clothing or provision . . . you should all the more respect this philosophy which God gave for the sake of the procurement of necessities of life.[20]

And, in a supporting echo of Luther's doctrine of two Kingdoms regarding church and society, Melanchthon carves out, for philosophy, a jurisdiction in the corporeal realm thus:

> the Gospel is the teaching of spiritual life and of justification in the eyes of God; but philosophy is the teaching of the corporeal life (*doctrina vitae corporalis*), just as you see that medicine serves health . . . The use of philosophy in this way is very necessary and approved of by God; as Paul says in many places, that creatures of God may use it with thanksgiving (1 Tim. 4.4).[21]

For Melanchthon, the *sola scriptura* principle is far from a complete way of summarizing the theological method of the Lutheran Reformation. The complex relationship that existed between Luther and Melanchthon in part turns on the different assessments each man had of the role of reason in theology. Melanchthon's more positive interpretation of reason within the faith-reason relationship largely prevailed, yet it is for his doctrinal work *per se* that he is best known.

The single most significant document Melanchthon produced, albeit in consultation with his Wittenberg colleagues, is the *Augsburg Confession*, a collection of cautious doctrinal statements made at the behest of the Catholic Emperor Charles V, who had called a meeting (*diet*) of the German nobility in 1530 in order to reconcile differences among Catholics and various Protestants in the face of external threats to the empire. This document is a collection of twenty-one statements that purport to concern largely shared agreement with Catholics. It is followed by seven claims concerning contested statements. It is clearly a rhetorical effort designed to communicate theology concisely in a setting marked by considerable political tension and social strife. The Confession was also written with the Zwinglians in mind, against whom Melanchthon wanted to distinguish the Lutheran tradition as theologically credible and stable.

In his efforts to explicate Lutheran theology, the very structure of the Augsburg Confession gives the impression of a theology that is ecumenically driven rather than the confrontational style that was typical of Luther. That is, Melanchthon and his colleagues go out of their way to propose twenty-one claims with which they believe Catholics might agree. The ordering of theological claims also gives the reader a sense of what is more valued and what is less valued. Among the claims that Melanchthon cites as important are those clauses dealing with God (citing the Council of Nicaea), sin (citing Augustine's rejection of Pelagianism), the Incarnation (citing the Apostles' Creed) and justification (the fourth article, citing Romans). What is largely missing from this text is the virulent thrust of Luther's original protest. Most of the sections begin with the expository phrase 'It is taught among us', followed by a summary of the particular topic being reviewed. A Christian view results, offering a condensed assessment of what is believed and, accompanied by some ecumenical gestures, it constitutes an ordered statement of what Lutherans hold. The irenic tone is meant to entice Catholics as well, though Melanchthon explains the differences among Catholics and Lutherans in the last seven sections of the statement.

The Augsburg Confession is a summary of theology which asserts the creedal belief in a form which emphasizes the evangelical calling of the Christian believer. Like other confessional documents of the Protestant Reformation, it draws upon various sources, interpretations, categories, church tradition, doctrines and arguments that attempt to relate faith to moral and social realities. But unlike some of the other statements, the Augsburg Confession reflects Melanchthon's desire to characterize Lutheran Christianity in a Catholic vein. This is not so much the case with the stronger Apology for the Augsburg Confession that he wrote later in 1531 after the negotiations with the Emperor broke down and the refutation of the Augsburg Confession by the Catholic Church had been received.

In this later document, Melanchthon explicitly draws on a variety of sources in making dialectical statements, some of which begin with 'It is false'. This pattern of thinking leads him to make the typical claim that proof for this or that position can be derived not only from scripture, but also from the Fathers, going so far as to cite the medieval Dominic and Francis in his Apology (Article V). Citing Augustine's doctrine of grace against what he terms the Pelagian position of the Catholic Church, Melanchthon roots Luther's dialectical theology within patristic and more broadly based biblical warrants. Perhaps the closest to a systematic approach comes in this *Apology* where Melanchthon defends 'justifying faith' as follows:

> We must remember that these three elements always belong together: the promise itself, the fact that the promise is free, and the merits of Christ as the price and propitiation. The promise is accepted by faith; the fact that it is free excludes our merits and sows that the blessing is offered only by mercy; the merits of Christ are the price because there must be a certain propitiation for our sins.[22]

What Melanchthon brings together are not only the doctrines of justification and the atonement, but also the way these cohere with the biblical (and foundational) category of God's promise, which is akin to Luther's 'Reformation discovery'. In accord with Luther's theology, while there is an effort to forge coherence among Christian doctrines, we see in Melancthon the work of a theologian whose systematic forays presage centuries-long efforts at systematizing the Protestant theology of the anti-systematic Luther.

Calvin

Of John Calvin, Karl Barth has written:

> Unlike Luther, Calvin was not a genius, but a conscientious exegete, a strict and tenacious thinker and at the same time a theologian who was indefatigably concerned with the practice of Christian life, and life in the church.'[23]

Regarded as a figure of formidable skill and possessing a taciturn character, of equal parts medieval and modern, John (or Jean) Calvin is one of the most influential Christian theologians in history. Born in 1509, Calvin, a Frenchman, was greatly influenced by the humanist movement, especially during his five years spent at the Collège de Montaigu in Paris where he earned an MA in the liberal arts and later in law at Orléans and ancient languages back in Paris. Hounded out of Paris after becoming associated with the Reformist views of Nicholas Cop, the rector of the University of Paris, Calvin returned home to Noyon, where he wrote his first volume in theology, *Psychopannychia*, before fleeing to Basel in Switzerland due to a rise in the persecution of Protestants. Later, he would be invited to Geneva by the Reformer Guillaume Farel.

After a 1537 quarrel with Pierre Caroli, a Lausanne minister, Calvin was again forced to flee, this time to Strasbourg, whereupon he began his serious theological writing, including the all-important *Institutes* in their first of three editions, as well as a commentary on the Book of Romans. One of the first methodological decisions that Calvin takes is to distinguish the writing that aims to understand scripture from the writing which contains more elaborate accounts of doctrinal matters. The doctrinal texts include details that, were they contained in the exegetical commentary, would distract the reader from the scriptural text. About the *Institutes*, Calvin claimed that they were designed to help people know what to look for in scripture. Echoing Augustine's *De Doctrina Christiana*, Calvin's work is a major step forward in the self-conscious awareness of theological method in the Protestant understanding of theology and its communication.

No summary of Calvin's theological method will suffice if it does not allude to the first section of his massive systematic theology, the *Institutes*, where he states: 'Nearly all the wisdom we possess, that is to say, true and sound wisdom, consists of two parts: The knowledge of God and of ourselves.'[24] The French translation (from the Latin) underlines the strong epistemological point being made here: 'In knowing God, each of us also knows himself.'[25] That is to say, for Calvin, there is no neutral epistemological starting point that stands outside of the search for *true* knowledge that isn't already guided by God. God is the author of true knowledge, with the implication being that the scholastic distinction between theology and philosophy, which, on many accounts, became a full blown separation of two ways to know God, is misguided as far as Calvin is concerned.

This first sentence of Calvin's *Institutes* stands out because of the reference to knowledge. Unlike the tomes of Aquinas and the other scholastics, Calvin does not emphasize 'being' or 'existence'. Rather, he emphasizes knowledge ('cognitio' in the first sentence and 'notitia' thereafter), a category which is linked to God's revelation. In turn, this suggests a limit on the role that natural knowledge or natural theology can play. The title of Book I is 'The Knowledge of God the Creator'. God is the creator on Calvin's terms, which, ironically, include an interpretation of themes in natural theology. Yet, God is not the abstract God of the philosophers, as Pascal termed it, but the God of the Christian Bible. Calvin wants to be specific in how he claims this knowledge is possible. As with Luther, there exists for Calvin a shift towards the use of categories that are primarily soteriological in nature rather than categories which pertain to the creation as an existing reality. Knowledge, moreover, is rendered serviceable for the understanding of faith itself. In 3.2.14 of the *Institutes*, Calvin writes:

> When we call faith 'knowledge' we do not mean the comprehension of the sort that is commonly concerned with those things which fall under human sense perception. For faith is so far above sense that man's mind has to go beyond and rise above itself in order to attain it . . . From this we conclude that the knowledge of faith consists in assurance rather than in comprehension.[26]

Shorn of the scholastic metaphysical language which accounted for the supernatural end of faith alongside the natural ends of knowledge, Calvin's way of describing faith makes the epistemological point that theological doctrine is a distinct form of knowledge. As such, Calvin is buttressing doctrine from a perspective in foundational theology and systematic theology. Arguably, without the medieval apparatus of theology conceived as a full *scientia*, the foundational and systematic scope of Calvin's theology is more limited, and his method is arguably truncated. Thinking in terms of Lonergan's functional specialty of foundational theology momentarily, Calvin supplies the category of revelation with solid soteriological meaning. Assurance is an eschatological and future orientation to the kind of knowledge that faith promises. From the perspective of systematic theology, faith is the basis for theology, conceived as a form of knowledge distinct from other kinds of human knowledge. This can be described in terms of the respective present/future orientations of each.

For revelation to count as a soteriological form of divine communication, Calvin needs only to turn to the Reformation principle of *sola scriptura* in order to clarify the means and purpose of God's speech. In the first book of the *Institutes*, Calvin links the essence of scriptural inspiration to the category of the Word, a strong way of providing conceptual weight to the scriptures themselves. How do the Word and scripture relate to each other? In a deft appropriation of Augustinian hermeneutics, Calvin expands on the idea that God accommodates human weakness, through the action of the Holy Spirit, with stories and other forms of narrative that we can understand. And what we will understand there is Christ, of which we will say more shortly. For now, another aspect of God's accommodation of the human condition is relevant to the question of method. As Calvin says in Book I, in a section that discusses Plato and Plutarch:

> There is within the human mind, and indeed by natural instinct, an awareness of divinity . . . To prevent anyone from taking refuge in the pretense of ignorance, God himself has implanted in all men a certain understanding of his divine majesty. Ever renewing its memory, he repeatedly sheds fresh drops.[27]

So, Calvin, despite the profound and heavy distinction he makes between prelapsarian and postlapsarian humanity, is not bereft of a kind of natural theology in which God is, in principle, knowable by virtue of our created reason. But more important for our knowledge of God, according to Calvin, given our sinful state, is the knowledge that comes from reading scripture. Calvin's theological method is thus different in principle from prominent patristic and medieval theologians. With Calvin, moreover, difficulties with scriptural interpretation do not centre on the textual ambiguities, as with Origen. Rather, the perversity of the human mind is responsible for our problems in understanding correctly what scripture teaches.[28]

Calvin advances scriptural interpretation in a way that is consistent with the spirit of Renaissance humanism, especially through his insistence on the correct understanding of the Greek and Hebrew language in which the Bible is originally written. Calvin's focus on scripture's original language is a part of a broader theological outlook which places a priority upon the intended meaning of the writer. The truth of revelation is not so much hidden in the biblical text as it is waiting to be discovered by converted minds and hearts. It is therefore important, according to Calvin, to exposit scripture with 'lucid brevity', while bearing in mind the hearers of scripture and their cognitive limitations. Calvin feels that it is also obligatory to call upon the authority of the church fathers, the figures of ancient tradition whose extensive scriptural commentaries Calvin believes serve the Reformation cause. This is a hermeneutical strategy that comes to the fore later in his career. Exegesis, for Calvin, is thus neither opposed to rhetorical approaches of the Renaissance nor opposed to the doctrinal purpose of scripture.[29] Calvin is opposed to the overly fanciful ways of scriptural interpretation associated with the (over)use of allegory, by Origen and other church fathers.

It is the principle of Accommodation that renders Calvin's approach to scripture distinct and fairly Augustinian. The goal which motivates his commentaries of providing 'lucid brevity' in explaining scripture is guided by Augustine's idea that the reader of scripture is confused. Whereas Augustine resolves this issue through recourse to the distinction between sign and thing, Calvin turns to the original intended meaning of scripture as discovered through language studies in order to alight upon the teachings contained in scripture. Implicitly, we can see in Calvin, through his nod to Renaissance learning, an acceptance of the intellectual advances being made in the world of his time. Like his guarded acknowledgement of the knowledge of God that is possible through the observation of nature, there is an aspect of Calvin's theology that is predisposed towards reason. Nevertheless, Calvin's anthropological presupposition is simply that the 'fresh drops' of divine revelation are the direct grounds on which our knowledge of

God is actually based. He goes on to make the conceptual link to epistemological assurance of doctrine:

> whether God became known to the patriarchs through oracles and visions or by the work and ministry of men, he put into their minds what they should then hand down to their posterity . . . there is no doubt that firm certainty of doctrine was engraved in their hearts, so that they were convinced and understood that what they had learned proceeded from God.[30]

Of course, Calvin is concerned to root scripture in the experience of God, in response to what he perceives to be the Catholic position that scripture comes from the church. The role of experience, for all of Calvin's insistence on the centrality of scripture, should not be played down. Calvin refers to his own conversion on at least one occasion, in a preface to his commentary on the Psalms. But, of course, conversion is a divinely ordered event through the action of the Holy Spirit. This point is affirmed in the following lines from the *Institutes*:

> [T]he Scriptures obtain full authority among believers only when men regard them as having sprung from heaven, as if there the living words of God were heard . . . But a most pernicious error widely prevails that Scripture has only so much weight as is conceded to it by the consent of the church. As if the eternal and inviolable truth of God depended upon the decision of men![31]

A reading of the *Institutes* reveals a theologian who resembles Melanchthon in relation to his concern to put the Christian faith into a systematic theological form, yet a theologian who contrasts with Luther the dialectician. Nevertheless, Calvin's procedure in the early 1536 edition of the *Institutes* parallels that of Luther's Catechism, by beginning with law and moving on to creed, the Lord's Prayer and sacraments with two appendices attacking the additional five Catholic sacraments and a discussion of Christian liberty in Chapter Six. By the time Calvin revised the definitive 1559 edition of the *Institutes*, the theological procedure had changed dramatically to a systematic presentation of God and revelation in eighty chapters, contained in four books: God, Christ, Holy Spirit and Church. The famous doctrine of election is presented in the third book, but despite its importance in the history of Calvinism, it does not occupy more than four out of twenty-five chapters of that book. It is contained within a large book entitled 'The Mode of Obtaining the Grace of Christ. The Benefits it Confers and the Effects Resulting From it'. More poignantly still, the number of references to scripture and the church fathers had multiplied by the 1559 edition. For Calvin, evidently, the impulse to provide a systematic basis for doctrine had solidified around the central argument over God and the knowledge of God as a Trinity. The systematic thrust of Calvin's theology is paradigmatic by beginning with the criterion of Trinitarian doctrine. It sets the standard for future systematic theology, though arguably it is betrayed by some of the Reformed Dogmatics which took Calvin's doctrine of election and made it the cornerstone of his legacy.

Of course, the dialectical elements are present in Calvin's thought. This is particularly noticeable in the fourth book of the *Institutes* where he rails against 'popish masses' and advocates for the proper form of church governance, in contrast to that of the papacy. But, theological method for Calvin is something determined by the mind, in spite of its frailty occasioned by Adam's fall into sin, a condition inherited by all of humanity. The gospel, for Calvin, is intended to lead us to the knowledge of God that, as he says in the *Institutes*, is 'naturally implanted in the human mind' yet subjugated by sin. The interesting part about Calvin's reference to the gospel is the way he renders it as the only basis for doctrine itself:

> [T]he Spirit, promised to us, has not the task of inventing new and unheard-of revelations, or of forging a new kind of doctrine, to lead us away from the received doctrine of the gospel, but of sealing our minds with that very doctrine which is commended by the gospel.[32]

Here, *sola scriptura* takes on new life as a revelation of not just particular doctrines of salvation, justification or election, but as a doctrine in itself, a gospel of 'truths'. Citing 2 Tim. 3.16, Calvin affirms that the gospel is 'profitable for doctrine or teaching . . . for instruction in righteousness'.[33] Righteousness arises from sanctification, which is responsible for the kind of mind that is necessary for a proper knowledge of God. Thus, for a theologian to expound the doctrine of the gospel, he or she must be grounded in a basic anthropological understanding about the proper conditions of righteousness that are prerequisites for knowledge of God.

By framing the human mind in this way, Calvin clears the way for a theology that can justly employ reason and experience in addition to scripture in its procedure. For instance, in Book III, Calvin argues for the role of the Spirit in procuring faith. Faith cannot arise in the mind by itself. After making this assertion, Calvin then turns to making 'proofs' for it by turning to an analogy to the way in which Christ taught disciples, thus engaging in a twin recourse to logic and scripture at the same time.[34]

Discipleship itself is crucial to Calvin's theology and is implicit to his theological method, which hinges so greatly on the revelation of the gospel. His theology of the church flows from the doctrinal implications of *sola scriptura*, and is well known from the following passage from the *Institutes*:

> Wherever we see the Word of God preached and heard, and the sacraments administered according to God's institution, there, it is not to be doubted a church of God exists [cf. Eph. 2.20]. For his promise cannot fail: 'Wherever two or three are gathered in my name, there I am in the midst of them.'[35]

The theological task is a task of the church, as Karl Barth would later affirm in equally explicit terms. The bond which unites the church is the bond of doctrinal religion, despite the presence in the church of what Calvin calls strangers:

> But that we may clearly grasp the sum of this matter, we must proceed by the following steps: the church universal is a multitude gathered from all the nations; it is divided and dispersed in separate places, but agrees on the one truth of divine doctrine, and is bound by the bond of the same religion. Under it are thus included individual churches, disposed in towns and villages according to human need, so that each rightly has the name and authority of the church. Individual men who, by their profession of religion, are reckoned within such churches, even though they may actually be strangers to the church, still in a sense belong to it until they have been rejected by public judgment.[36]

Calvin's ecclesiology thus contains the constant possibility that we have erred in regards to God's will and God's justifying grace. Our knowledge of the composition of the church is as imperfect as our knowledge of God, despite the illumination made available to our minds by the Spirit of Christ through the gospel. This is the well-known idea of the invisible church, but what is of note is Calvin's procedure, which hinges on making a correlation between two scriptural passages (from Ephesians and Matthew). He compares the scriptural testimony with descriptions of current churches that presently fulfil the conditions that Calvin believes are set out in the biblical texts. Besides preaching and sacraments, Calvin is interested in seeing the composition of the church framed by the promise of Christ, a way of arguing theologically that contains vestiges of medieval voluntarism, the stress on God's will active in the world. In this case, a link is established between Christ's words and the intentions of those gathered in his name 'in separate places'.

The procedure of Calvin's theology, as I have already said, is thoroughly systematic though not logically unassailable. Later Reformed Dogmatics would render Calvin's systematic theology in scholastic form, which is ironic considering Calvin's clear and resolute opposition to scholasticism. Calvin aspires to systematic breadth by referring early on in the *Institutes* to the vanity of trying to fortify scripture with arguments that do not point back to scripture itself, in all its plain beauty. The order of scripture defies mere human attempts at elegance, according to Calvin. Thus, in its ordering, the *Institutes* follow the doctrine of scripture and the revelation of God's triune nature, leading us to conclude that, for Calvin, the systematic nature of theology is derived through an imitation of God's revealing Word. A systematic or beautiful account of the knowledge of God cannot be something created by a theologian.

Still, Calvin's theology is arguably structured like its medieval Catholic forebears. For example, though obviously different in its content, Calvin's theological procedure somewhat resembles the way of Aquinas's *Summa*: the following of the creed's affirmations, the citations from scripture followed by an inductive procedure of relevant elements that contribute to an understanding of the topic at hand. Usually, Calvin's theology and method are characterized in contrast with that of medieval theology, especially with that of Thomas Aquinas over the issue of natural theology. I am not convinced that this contrast is as stark as the evidence suggests. One way this matter is contested can be seen in the 1930s when Karl Barth and his fellow Reformed theologian Emil Brunner engaged in a heated exchange over whether we can know something of God from nature, without revelation. Both claimed Calvin in their defence of diametrically opposed viewpoints, and the question has not been solved on historical grounds. But, Calvin's commendation of the witness to God from the perspective of God's creation suggests that he can serve as the basis for a natural theology. Calvin's specific claim that human beings are innately religious buttresses this idea. This kind of verdict may be surprising to those who are accustomed to depictions of Calvin as essentially hostile to the role of reason or nature in theology.

One of the more peculiar attributes of Calvin's writing, notably in the *Institutes*, is the frequent reference to religion, not theology. While the usage may seem accidental or even arbitrary, commentators indicate differently. In speaking of religion, Calvin stresses the directly catechetical role of theology. The first edition of the *Institutes* is prefaced by a letter to the King of France, Francis I, in which Calvin comments: 'My purpose was solely to transmit certain rudiments by which those who are touched with any zeal for religion might be shaped to true godliness.'[37] We see here further evidence of methodological diversity in Calvin. There is a distinct missiological purpose of the *Institutes*. Calvin's systematic theology is also an evangelizing tool. Calvin's concern for theological precision is guided by his overriding concern for righteousness and correct worship. So, Lonergan's understanding that communication (admittedly a broader term than evangelization) is a distinct theological functional specialty would describe an important aspect of Calvin's theology. In Calvin's mind, that distinction is not explicitly present, yet by raising the need for inspiring godliness, or what is elsewhere termed 'piety', Calvin is indicating a wider intended audience for his systematic theology.

Conclusion

Traditionally, the Protestant Reformation and the theology of the leading Reformers has been seen as the shift from tradition to scripture as the basis for doctrine and church practice. While nothing to the contrary is being claimed here, I suggest that attention to the procedures by which theologians of the Reformation do their theology gives us a more nuanced picture of this historical period and Protestant theology as well. Looking back at this period, we can see theology practised not in one uniform Protestant way, but in different ways, each with somewhat different aims and procedures in mind, despite their shared Protestant (Luther, Reformed) identity.

Avery Dulles, a modern Catholic theologian has identified no less than ten approaches or ways to use scripture in theology in the contemporary world.[38] A number of these ways are traceable to the Protestant Reformation. What those differences suggest is a broad diversity in method that is based on the more subtle differences present in the theological writing of the sixteenth century. We certainly see traces of this diversity between Luther, Melanchthon and Calvin and also within the work of these theologians too. This is not to suggest that medieval theology, by contrast, was not diverse. Surely, the metaphysical frameworks of Aquinas and Anselm were significantly different. But the import of that diversity is not as noteworthy. For reasons of historical contingency and owing to the particular retrieval of scripture by Reformation and humanist scholars, the theological diversity of the Reformation means something much more than it did a century or two earlier. The criterion of scriptural warrant is certainly the greatest attribute of Protestant theological method that fosters new directions in theology.

As we have seen, John Calvin's theology not only rivals the comprehensive scope of Aquinas's theology, it also retains and deepens the differentiated character of theology. By distinguishing theologically and rhetorically the interpretation of scripture from the judgements of doctrine that lie at the heart of the *Institutes*, Calvin's theological methodology marks a major achievement for Reformation thought. It is one of the foremost pre-modern examples of a differentiated theological method. In that sense, Calvin in particular represents a leap forwards in sophistication, at least in comparison with Luther and Melanchthon. Of course, Calvin's boldness and incisive doctrinal theology could not have succeeded without the important methodological leads made by the other Protestant Reformers.

CHAPTER SIX

Early modern theology – The rise of explicit methodology

As a Protestant theologian, I shall let no one curtail my right of development.

Friedrich Schleiermacher[1]

Turning to the modern period, we see noticeable divergences that the Protestant Reformation implied for theological method and several other developments that arose somewhat independently of the Reformation. The methodological variety in Christian theology becomes more entrenched and self-aware by the nineteenth century. While this variety is not as serious as the differences over scripture and tradition which emerged in the sixteenth century between Protestants and Catholics, the methodological differences tended to reinforce church division. Ironically, however, while methodological differences were reinforced during the nineteenth century, the seeds for an ecumenical movement were also sown. Differences between Christian theological methods open up within church traditions, and the secular beachheads of Enlightenment thought spread their influence. As theological problems deepened with respect to the sciences, and as churches grappled with the prospect of sweeping social change, theological faculties and seminaries, as well as individual theologians, began to reel from the effects. The nineteenth century was a time of great theological unrest – and theological renewal.

The intellectual ferment in theology is especially marked when it comes to considering the two greatest theologians of the nineteenth century, Friedrich Schleiermacher and John Henry Newman, whose lives and work bookend the century respectively. Schleiermacher was a Reformed minister and philosopher who died in 1834, while Newman was a convert to Catholicism halfway through his life, which spanned almost the entire century itself. He died in Birmingham, England, in 1890 at the age of 90 and was canonized a saint by the Catholic Church in 2010. Because these two theologians are so influential for the development of twentieth-century theology, it is vital that we appreciate the elements of their work specifically. This makes the task of understanding theological method in the subsequent century that much easier. As with the other periods examined in this book thus far, we shall analyse a representative sampling of their work and the main themes which each man covered in the course of his writing. What will make this assessment of theological method more representative will be a brief consideration of the thought of Albrecht Ritschl and Adolf von Harnack. Their approaches to the topic of doctrinal development tracked along different lines from that of Newman yet their influence is equally important, methodologically speaking.

Friedrich Schleiermacher

Still unknown to many outside the discipline of theology and beyond the confines of hermeneutical philosophy, Friedrich Schleiermacher is one of the most important figures in modern theology. Indeed, he is known as the 'father of modern theology' for his role in inaugurating the practice of theological hermeneutics with respect to the experience of the biblical interpreter and church historian. Born in 1768 in lower Silesia, Schleiermacher is known as one of Germany's most revered academic scholars. He was a Berlin Reformed Church hospital chaplain at one point, and at another point, a practising philosopher. He met the challenge of writing a theological dogmatics and, in the process, overturned what the word 'dogmatics' meant. His theology has been highly influential among a number of theological movements, beginning with the Lutheran School at Erlangen, whose nineteenth-century exponents Franz H. R. von Frank and Johann Christian von Hoffman promoted a theology the contents of which would be derived from the experience of the regenerated Christian. Thus, Schleiermacher is connected with what George Lindbeck calls the 'experiential-expressive' approach to theology. This is a category that Lindbeck means to encompass quite an array of theological influences, including the work of Catholic theologians of the twentieth century, such as Karl Rahner. More significantly though, from the vantage point of theological method, his most well appreciated and genuine breakthrough concerns the need to reflect on experience and his hermeneutical theory.

After writing the apologetical work *On Religion: Speeches to its Cultured Despisers* in 1799, Schleiermacher faced suspicion on all sides, especially from rationalist sceptics who were disappointed in his recommendation of Christian religion. As a defender of the role of experience in the formation and expression of Christian faith, Schleiermacher represents a prominent Romanticist-inspired reaction to Enlightenment thought. At the same time, some of his fellow theologians and pastors also expressed unease at what they evidently felt was the odour of pantheism in his thought.

With respect to his later dogmatic or systematic theology, he is an exponent of high Pietism, a tradition of Christian expression that was frequently hostile to academic theology. Thus, his theology is markedly distant from the tradition of Lutheran and Reformed Dogmatics that followed in the wake of Melanchthon and Calvin. Yet, with those traditions, Schleiermacher constructs a Christology that is much more than the barren Enlightenment portrait of Jesus as a moral, humane teacher. Also key to Schleiermacher's theology is the life of the church and especially his praise of earliest Christianity. On these and quite a number of issues, he differs from the Enlightenment critics of Christianity. Schleiermacher's admiration of the early church would herald a trend in nineteenth- and twentieth-century theology. These are important considerations in assessing his legacy and place in Christian theology, since it is often remarked that Schleiermacher paved the way for a stripped-down edifice of theological doctrine, one that is more pleasing to the modern eye. But I think it is fairer, based on an examination of his three main works – *A Brief Outline of the Study of Theology*, the *Speeches* and *The Christian Faith*, which is subtitled *Presented Systematically According to the Principles of the Evangelical Church* – to view Schleiermacher's work more positively, at least from a methodological perspective. While his theology has defects, we ought not to assume the correctness of the well known, negative critique levelled against him by Karl Barth.

Schleiermacher is regarded as one of the foremost representatives of a style of theological foundationalism, a way of thinking about theology on the basis of claims that stem, directly or indirectly, from a core 'essence' of Christian faith. The idea of a core essence of Christianity is rooted in nineteenth-century thinking about the task of apologetics in an age of rationality and progress. It is an idea that would culminate in Hegel's philosophical synthesis of Christian doctrine, though Hegel's way of articulating a Christian essence is very distinct from Schleiermacher's. The label of foundationalism is applied because Schleiermacher conceptualizes religious experience rather than particular ideas or doctrines as the basis for constructing theological claims. For Schleiermacher, religious experience is comprised of a certain 'feeling' (*Gefühl* in the *Speeches*). This feeling of Christian consciousness is not a notion of the self in action, but rather a realization of the self's inability to be at one with the world. Schleiermacher's choice to determine theology – including the selfhood of Jesus – on an anthropology of feeling, would have widespread consequences, one of which is a renewed methodological debate over starting points in theology. Barth's reaction to Schleiermacher a century later is in large measure a reaction against an anthropological starting point for theology. In the second speech, Schleiermacher comments on religious consciousness this way:

> The contemplation of the pious is the immediate consciousness of the universal existence of all finite things, in and through the Infinite, and of all temporal things in and through the Eternal.

Religion is to seek this and find it in all that lives and moves, in all growth and change, in all doing and suffering . . . Where this is found religion is satisfied . . . Wherefore it is a life in the infinite nature of the Whole, in the One and in the All.[2]

The whiff of pantheism, possibly as a result of the influence of the philosopher Schelling, can certainly be inferred from passages such as this. Such passages seem to confirm the impression that Schleiermacher's thought is distant from the doctrinal and scriptural concerns of sixteenth-century theology. Yet he regarded himself as a Protestant theologian of the church confessions. He 'moves between past and present', as Bruce McCormack says of his dialectical method, between scripture and the evangelical church confessions.[3]

In *The Christian Faith* itself, Schleiermacher is fully aware of writing a work in dogmatics. But, he comments there on the subjective possibility of such discourse from the standpoint of religious self-consciousness or piety, 'a state in which Knowing, Feeling, and Doing are combined'.[4] In constructing God as the object of theology from the standpoint of self-consciousness, Schleiermacher makes the famous connection between the human feeling of absolute dependence and God:

In self-consciousness, there are only two elements: the one expresses the existence of the subject for itself, the other its co-existence with an Other. Now to these two elements, as they exist together in the temporal self-consciousness, correspond in the subject its *Receptivity* and its (spontaneous) *Activity* . . . The common element in all those determinations of self-consciousness which predominantly express a receptivity affected from some outside quarter is the *feeling of Dependence*. On the other hand, the common element in all those determinations which predominantly express spontaneous movement and activity is the *feeling of Freedom* . . . As regards the identification of absolute dependence with 'relation to God' in our proposition: this is to be understood in the sense that the *Whence* of our receptive and active existence, as implied in this self-consciousness is to be designated by the word 'God', and that this is for us the really original signification of that word.[5]

While this is certainly not a natural theology, much less a proof for the existence of God, Schleiermacher directs us to God through the feeling of dependence that arises in self-consciousness. The method of such argumentation is from the world of experience to God, without the immediate recourse to scripture or tradition that marks the theology of earlier periods. Deep religious feeling, *Gefühl*, animates Schleiermacher's truly theological epistemology and this 'sense of God' or 'God-consciousness' is related to *Heilandsliebe*, God's redeeming love. Notwithstanding this shift, the doctrine of the redemption of Christ still exerts a control over the way that theology, and in Schleiermacher's case, his dogmatics, function. With Schleiermacher, anything other than a theological worldview conceived on a Christian basis is impossible. Yet critics see his adverting to the categories of experience and apologetics as part of a slippery slope from an established framework for theological method to something much more amorphous.

What about Christ? Schleiermacher is explicit about Christ's role in redemption. He states that the dogmatic system 'elaborates how the redemption is effected by Christ and comes to consciousness within the Christian communion'. Yet that communion and its 'Founder' are announced in a different key: 'Jesus is Founder of a religious communion simply in the sense that its members become conscious of redemption through him.' Also, Jesus is absorbed into serving the human need for redemption: 'all religious moments, so far as they are free expressions of the feeling of absolute dependence, are set down as having come into existence through that redemption'.[6] Thus, George Hunsinger has termed Schleiermacher's theology and, by implication, most of nineteenth-century theology as 'formally but not substantively christocentric'.[7] *The Christian Faith* corroborates this assessment because of the anthropological parameters set out for theological claims. The form of Christ is reached through a human filter, but the substance of Christological doctrine recedes somewhat from view.

Schleiermacher's *Brief Outline of Theology* (*Kurze Darstellung*) was first written in 1811 and revised in 1830, and it is the first of his books to be translated into English. The first striking claim in the *Brief Outline* is Schleiermacher's characterization of theology as a positive science, alongside medicine and jurisprudence. Positive science is contrasted to the 'real' sciences that are themselves either empirical or speculative. On the other hand, a 'positive' science is one that is rooted primarily in a historical or cultural institution, which for theology would be the church. Such a characterization supports the impression of Schleiermacher as the first great theological pragmatist. As Christine Helmer puts it, for Schleiermacher, the underlying assumption must have been that 'Medicine serves human health, jurisprudence serves inter-personal health, and religious communities serve spiritual health. The task of theology is to support the thriving of the human person in religious community with others'.[8] In the *Brief Outline*, we find his clearest methodological indicators for theology. This work is Schleiermacher's 'theological encyclopedia', to borrow a term that refers to the early nineteenth-century practice of publishing concise texts for particular disciplines around a core philosophical idea. In this work, we see three things going on.

First, we read about theology in a way that serves as a backdrop to the contents of *The Christian Faith*. Second, we also see him coming to some startling conclusions in a work that is intended to be an introduction to theology for beginners. Third, and most importantly, Schleiermacher is able to distinguish within theology three types or genres, namely: philosophical theology, historical theology and practical theology. This tripartite division contrasts with the typical divisions of his day, which were the four disciplines of exegetical, historical, systematic and practical theology.[9] For Schleiermacher, since historical development is the expression of ongoing acts of theological interpretation in the church, theological method must be dynamic. It must be served by and for the service of theological judgements, which are historically contingent cognitional acts. While philosophical theology serves a critical goal, historical theology is institutional, while practical theology is described as the 'technical' implementation of thought to practice. Surprisingly, what Schleiermacher terms, along with his Reformed and Lutheran colleagues, 'dogmatics', lies within the bounds of historical theology. It lies alongside the disciplines of exegesis and church history. Dogmatics is a historically shaped enterprise that is subsequent to the study of 'primitive Christianity'. And, in most respects, it is what would later come to be called 'systematic theology'.

This organization of theological material is confusing, at first glance, because it purports to mix different theological tasks together in a way that is out of kilter with both traditional and more recent theology. Contrasting with Schleiermacher's presentation of theology, we are more accustomed to think that the formulation of doctrine properly belongs in closer relationship with systematic theology than with exegesis or church history. Schleiermacher sticks with the term 'dogmatics', since he is convinced that systematic theology possesses the capacity to 'conceal, to the detriment of the subject, not only the historical character of the discipline but also its aim in relation to church leadership'.[10] In effect, Schleiermacher is articulating the insight that doctrine and systematics are two distinct theological ways of knowing and that dogmatics retains its locus in ecclesial judgements made in the midst of history. Despite the systematic nature of *The Christian Faith*, which is divided into two parts that deal with the development of religious self-consciousness and the facts which result from religious self-consciousness in terms of 'the antithesis of sin and grace', respectively, Schleiermacher argues for the historical, 'positive' character of dogmatics. Schleiermacher's category for guiding his terminological choice is Christianity and the church. Contrary to Barth's allegation, he does not make theological claims for pre-determined philosophical reasons. Philosophy's role is heightened in his thought, however, a step that is a vital development in theological method. Schleiermacher retains a distinct role for philosophical theology, the main function of which is apologetics (see *Brief Outline* § 43–53). Schleiermacher also lauds the role of dialectic and hermeneutics as key to theological method. For Schleiermacher, hermeneutics, the art (the German word used is '*Kunstlehre*') of interpretation, takes into full consideration the views and priorities of the interpreter. Hermeneutics in theology means, for Schleiermacher, an attention to the grammatical and contextual nature of literature, an essential element for understanding not just the historically situated meaning, but also the intention of the writer of a text. Thus, for Schleiermacher, there is no pure experience apart from language. This point is important to appreciate, since this aspect of his method has been misunderstood.[11] And, the importance of hermeneutics is due to the practical demands of pastoral ministry, the demand for adequate preaching for instance. Thus, it is impossible to understand Schleiermacher correctly without taking seriously his own emphasis on ministry as a necessary complement to hermeneutics.

What is important for Schleiermacher is the unity of the theological enterprise, another emphasis often missed by his modern critics. At the outset of the *Brief Outline*, Schleiermacher places the emphasis on experience in contrast to the 'rational theologies' which purport to describe a speculative science 'entirely different' from the one he wants to advocate.[12] Experience is filtered through the adoption of faith, which is the key to transforming a mere report of church doctrine into a coherent dogmatics, a way of connecting the believer with the theology of the past. For Schleiermacher, experience is a more universal grounding for the theological enterprise. It can be justly said that Schleiermacher anticipates the postmodern reaction to rationalism and scientific dominance which separate fact from value. For him, there are no historical studies in theology that are 'wholly divested from the scholar's own particular viewpoints and opinions', a paradigmatic hermeneutical insight.[13]

Being so explicit about the distinctions and divisions that are proper to theology, Schleiermacher anticipates, though not directly, a number of key features of modern theological method, including the programme of Lonergan. One of these elements is the understanding of historical studies at the heart of the theological enterprise, studies which make use of historical criticism and the philosophy of religion. Lonergan and Schleiermacher share the presupposition that human beings are naturally religious, and both men also cherish the anthropological portrait that frames theology, including the idea that the converted theologian is historically guided yet mindful of the church's responsibility to formulate and reformulate doctrine.

The question which has dogged modern readers of Schleiermacher, however, is whether his theological method allows him to make any substantive claims about God. Beginning with Johann Adam Möhler's criticism of Schleiermacher, which turned on the charge of Sabellianism, and in light of later critiques such as Robert Jenson's charge that Schleiermacher is an Arian, there is a question mark about the theological harvest that Schleiermacher's method has reaped. Barth's broadside against Schleiermacher's placement of the Trinity in the conclusion of *The Christian Faith* is the most trenchant and well-known criticism. It is emblematic, too, of the popular idea that the greater preoccupation one has with theological method, the less vigorous is one's theological doctrine. And yet, as with Thomas Aquinas's decision to leave the Trinity until the end of the *Summa*, Schleiermacher's decision to forestall discussion of the Trinity until the end of his book dealing with doctrine neither indicates a fatal application of method nor an occlusion of Christian tradition – not in itself, at least.

Schleiermacher's theology, even his limited Trinitarian reflections, should not be read only through the prism of later liberal Protestantism, even though there are plausible grounds for seeing in his theology the origins of later efforts to water down Christian thought. We therefore ought to assess Schleiermacher in terms of his own proposals in *Christian Faith*, which is intended as a book on the doctrine *of* faith, not doctrines *about* God. This is not to suggest that he is immune from critique, but what Schleiermacher provides is tailored as a response that is best seen in terms of the culture and *zeitgeist* of his time. Beginning, as he does, with the anthropological triad of knowing, feeling and doing, the organization of *The Christian Faith* is clear evidence of his beginning with the experience of human living and the related philosophical problem of epistemology followed by the need for faith expressed in piety or *Frömmigkeit*.

In the second main part of the book, Schleiermacher deals with the experience of God through sin and redemption, the latter being described in terms of the attainment of God-consciousness. It is through the human experience of sin that God's reality can come into clearer focus through the redemptive reality of grace, received as the gifts of wisdom and love and ultimately clarified in the concept of the Trinity. Theology, for Schleiermacher, is adequate if it can begin with theological anthropology. He is careful to avoid extremes and he is explicit about the character of the alternatives on offer in the proper understanding of our feeling of absolute dependence on God in a situation of tension between sin and grace (rather than a simplistic feeling of dependence *per se*): 'there is no general God-consciousness which has not bound up with it a relation to Christ, and no relationship with the Redeemer which has no bearing on the general God-consciousness.'[14] Indeed, the pivotal role that Christ plays in Schleiermacher's theology ensures that his theological method is not reducible to an exalted anthropology. The central role played by Christ as Redeemer means that for Schleiermacher, notwithstanding the impossibility of proving the satisfaction of Christ's redemption, it is the fact of Christ's redemption that is experienced through faith as supplying the redemption that we seek (*Christian Faith* §14-1,2). Schleiermacher's Christ is wholly different from the Christ of the Enlightenment rationalists. And human beings are ever in need of grace from within the state of sin in which they are found. Such is Schleiermacher's framework for doing theology, and yet this is not the Schleiermacher that is taught and described in some theological texts. Schleiermacher's Christ is the one who confirms Protestant church dogmatics in place of any would-be philosophical stand-in: the church feels that 'the distinctive form of its propositions does not depend on any form or school of philosophy, and had not proceeded at all from a speculative interest, but simply from the interest of satisfying the immediate self-consciousness solely through the means ordained by Christ' (*Christian Faith* §16.3). Later efforts by twentieth-century theologians would clarify what Schleiermacher claimed – for instance, what C.S. Lewis called the 'God-shaped hole' in life – being the basis for arguing in favour of a personal, redeeming God. The 'modern', Schleiermachian way of speaking about God from the experience of human faith is not just a foreshadowing of the development of phenomenology in philosophy. Neither is it merely a critical, historically based alternative to the complex Hegelian metaphysic which collapsed theological categories into abstract philosophical concepts. It is the basis for a hermeneutical way of doing theology that knows few serious rivals in our time.

It is Schleiermacher's consciousness-based approach to theology that has earned him a reputation as a modernizer. What Schleiermacher's hermeneutical dogmatics makes possible, however, is a genuinely dialectical role for the individual theologian in the church. It also suggests that theology be carried out in terms of specific tasks that bear on the personal appropriation of faith in constructing a foundational theology.[15] Whether this justifies the epithet of 'foundationalist', lodged against him by Lindbeck and others in the 'Yale school', is disputable. In the meantime, we must consider a very different framework – one proposed by John Henry Newman – for understanding the theological task in nineteenth-century modern culture.

John Henry Newman

John Henry Newman was an establishment figure, an English priest in the Church of England whose conversion to Catholicism rocked a significant part of British society when it was announced in the autumn of 1845. It was all the more shocking, for it marked a dramatic shift of allegiance socially, as well as ecclesially, into a church that was poor and largely influenced by Irish immigrants. While he had authored some little-known books such as *Arians of the Fourth Century* prior to his conversion, it was Newman's thinking on the development of doctrine that was already well developed. It was the sheer logic of his thought in the development of doctrine that compelled Newman to reconsider his life in the *via media* of the Church of England. In the same year as his conversion, the sweeping and dramatic *Essay on the Development of Christian Doctrine* was published, a piece of writing that helped to deflate the Oxford movement with which Newman had previously been the central figure in promoting the traditional liturgy in opposition to the liberal tendencies current in the Church of England.

In this essay, Newman articulated what was seen as a scandalous distinction between an orthodox Roman church and Anglican heterodoxy. Newman recognized the formidable power of liberal thought in church and theology and reacted by turning to the Catholic Church. Yet, his entry into the Catholic Church cannot be seen as a strictly conservative reaction. As Robert Pattison comments, 'Newman was the creature of the liberalism he despised'.[16] This is especially apposite when it comes to assessing the way Newman thinks about theological method. His embrace of patristic doctrine, notably the writings of Origen and Athanasius, alongside his plain admission of contingent, historical forces that he claimed altered the terms and function of Christian doctrine over time, make Newman's thought a harbinger of later theological method. Newman is a figure who prefigures contemporary fusions of liberal and conservative instincts in Christian theology, such as the recent post-liberalism of the Yale School and the fusion of traditional with postmodern thought in the Radical Orthodoxy of John Milbank.

Comparable to Schleiermacher's focus, Newman's theological method does not grapple with the complexities of scriptural commentary, but rather with the understanding of the church's tradition and doctrine. Schleiermacher's concern is to relate the Christian tradition with the reality of human consciousness. Newman, however, is deeply interested in patristic theology and other historical theology; for it is there that he senses the deep roots of church tradition that are the bedrock of the faith. This predilection for the church fathers is partly what led him into the

Catholic Church. As he says, 'To be deep in history is to cease to be a Protestant'.[17] For Newman, the question that pervades all theology is ultimately addressed by asking 'What is it that distinguishes Christianity from alternatives?', to which he responds by nuancing the historical answer of Vincent of Lerins, whose 'canon' of true doctrine is '*quod simper, quod ubique, quod ab omnibus*'. For Vincent, true or valid doctrine is that which has been 'held always, everywhere and by everybody'. For Newman, this saying provides cover for the (mostly) seventeenth-century 'Anglican divines', who erroneously wanted to ignore the Pope while retaining the authority of the church fathers. As Newman points out, in particular cases of doctrinal dispute, it is much easier in principle than in practice to separate valid historical authority from valid contemporary church authority:

> if it be narrowed for the purpose of disproving the catholicity of Pope Pius, it becomes also an objection to the Athanasian; and if it be relaxed to admit the doctrines retained by the English Church, it no longer excludes certain doctrines of Rome which that Church denies.[18]

Thus, for Newman, what became impossible to hold on to was the dream of a *via media* between Catholicism and Protestantism. The consensus imagined by the Anglican admirers of Vincent of Lerins's formula for valid church tradition in order to exclude certain historical churches could also be used to exclude central Christian doctrines as the Trinity, about which there was not a consensus in the first centuries of the church's existence. Newman notes: 'Tertullian is heterodox on the doctrine of our Lord's divinity . . . Origen is, at the very least, suspected, and must be defended and explained rather than cited.'[19] The myriad disputes over Sabellian (modal) and other seemingly viable alternatives to Trinitarian orthodoxy should, according to Newman, spur us on to find better criteria for the authentic development of doctrine. The search for authenticity in development will prevent us from falsely conceiving of concise definitions of true doctrine that end up denying historical development.

Development, as Newman sees it, is what Christians should expect of a faith that is not decipherable from scriptural texts alone, but in the 'ideas . . . in the writer and reader of the revelation' and existing as a universal religion that is suited 'not simply to one locality or period, but to all times and places'.[20] Scripture does not contain propositional doctrines, and so

> The question, then, is not whether this or that proposition of the Catholic doctrine is *in terminis* in Scripture, unless we would be slaves to the letter, but whether that one view of the Mystery, of which all such are the exponents, be not there.[21]

Newman's focus is on the coherence of all doctrines, which tend to cluster into themes. What Newman is suggesting is that the question of doctrine's authority does not turn on a scriptural proof-text, but on whether any and all doctrines pertain to God, as attested by scripture but not reducible to such attestations. Newman asserts, beginning in his Anglican period in the 1830s, that if theology were based on scripture alone, as it is for dissenting (non-Anglican) Protestants, then truth would be a matter of private opinion, since every theologian would interpret scripture in his or her own way. Yet scripture does not contain its own interpretation. This suggests that Newman is contradicting rather than straightforwardly invoking the patristic sense of interpretation.

By the time of his later writings, in which Newman's idea of the church had been brought into some coherence with his early reverence for the church fathers, Newman argues that there is an essential difference between mere change and authentic development. Nevertheless, he asserts the dialectical reality that Schleiermacher diplomatically skirts: 'all parties argue . . . from scripture; but argument implies deduction, that is, development.' On the divinity of Christ, he asks, in an allusion to the 'Word became flesh' of Jn 1.14:

> What is meant by 'the Word', and what by 'became'? The answers to these involve a process of investigation and are developments. Moreover, when they will have been made, they will suggest a series of secondary questions; and thus at length a multitude of propositions will result.[22]

From the vantage point of his concern with development springs Newman's interest in the question of authority in the church. This is a topic with which his name is most closely associated, especially since it is so contentious in Catholic-Anglican relations. For

Newman, authority in the church has to be grounded theologically, a link he establishes by the 1870s in a preface to the re-publication of his early Anglican work *The Via Media*. Here, Newman correlates the threefold ministry of Christ as prophet, priest and king with the threefold ministry of the church, expressed as 'teaching, rule and sacred ministry'.[23] The church, then, is itself a dialectical activity of teaching, ruling and worshipping, in which teacher theologians have the obligation to correct and restrain the ruling activities of bishops, whose human frailty can lead to error. However, the authority that is invested in the church is an authority that renders the Christian faith coherent. True doctrine is protected from false interpretation if it is reliant on more than a vague sense of tradition. Tradition needs to be personified by figures of authority that can develop the tradition authentically for each historical period. From those controversial events surrounding the role of the Bishop of Rome in connection with episcopal councils in the early church, Newman defends a moderate account of papal supremacy. In his *Essay on the Development of Christian Doctrine*, this emphasis on papal authority even includes a restriction of the role of individual bishops, in order to avoid the polarizing and debilitating effects on the church of theological disputation.

Newman assumes something that is far from granted in the contemporary theological academy; namely, the presupposition that Christian theology is not a guild of erudite autonomous scholarship. Rather, theology is but a fostering of theological excellence for the church, akin to the role of medieval theological schools. Theological dialectics is, for Newman, a dialectics that is within and for the church. This accent on the church returns in the twentieth century, albeit in a different way in Barth and others.

In contrast with Schleiermacher, Newman's theological method is not determined solely by the priorities of faith or personal experience. The opposite perception might be the case if one were looking only at his book *An Essay in Aid of A Grammar of Assent*, written in 1870. What is crucial for Newman all along is the metaphysical scope of Christian faith, which comes from his sympathetic study of the Fathers and philosophy. From that study, he latches on to the Platonic way of thinking about the Trinity. For Newman, like Athanasius and the other Alexandrians, Christian faith, pursued to its fullest, is a participation in the life of God made possible by Christ and guided by the Holy Spirit.

This perspective of Newman, while containing an implied systematic worldview, does not lead him into writing what we would call a systematic theology. Unlike Schleiermacher, whose theology of experience leads to the comprehensive theology of consciousness, sin and grace in *The Christian Faith*, Newman considers a narrower range of subjects in terms of specific historical and doctrinal judgements. His writing, in fact, mirrors the occasional style of many of the patristic fathers whom he so admired. And, whereas Schleiermacher dwells on the meaning of salvation in the light of a notion of consciousness, Newman interprets consciousness in a completely different key by retrieving the patristic reality of divinization. While both nineteenth-century theologians tackle the newly problematic terrain of epistemology from an anti-rationalist perspective, they do so in remarkably distinct ways, and these ways are affected by their respective church traditions and academic cultures.

One of the most vital reference points in Newman's theological procedure is his focus on cognition, though not in the abstract German view of consciousness. What Newman calls the 'illative sense' in *Grammar of Assent*, or what we refer to as judgement, is a cornerstone for Newman's view of historical development and the progressive evolution of doctrinal forms. The human act of judgement makes all the difference in Newman's theological method. Clarifying its inevitable role and positive function in the history of theology, Newman endeavours to go one step further than Schleiermacher's experiential hermeneutics. He promises his readers something with greater epistemological depth than the lone theologian hermeneut who interprets a text's authorial intent. Newman wants to set the authority of individual hermeneutical interpretations within the framework of corporate assent, the judgement of the church. History and doctrine are two forms of theological judgement for Newman. History serves as the basis for settling a proper framework by which we interpret the Christian past and, more distantly, Christian texts. Doctrine centres on the authoritative role played by the Catholic Church, dramatically centred upon the Bishop of Rome, the Pope. Struggling as he did with Anglican antipathy towards the Catholic Church, on the one hand, and the ultra-montanism of more extreme partisans within Catholicism on the other hand, Newman was in a perpetual state of flux over how to reckon with the tension of history and doctrinal differences.

The locus of cognition, and especially of individual conscience, is prominent in his struggle over the scope of authority exercised by the Catholic Church, and specifically by the Pope, after the formulation of the Doctrine of iInfallibility in 1870. The formulation was one with which he disagreed on grounds of prudence, though privately he did not see as problematic the idea that the Pope should be credited with being protected from error on matters of faith. But on the question of morality, Newman insists on the role of an individual's conscience. His stance is a plea for human dignity, a call for reflection on a key to Christian humanism. As an advocate for the liberal arts and the mission of the university in the building of civilizing culture, Newman's famous saying that he would certainly be willing to 'toast the Pope, but conscience first . . . that "aboriginal Vicar of Christ"' expresses his view concisely.[24] That he possessed such a liberal-minded view on authority is indicative of the complex texture of his thought, characterized as it was by various aesthetic, moral and philosophical considerations too numerous to describe here.

What should bear mentioning, however briefly, is Newman's explication of the term 'conscience' to include within its purview a view of natural religion, a way of speaking about God and the human capacity to ascertain God. This is Newman's natural theology, something which concurs with Schleiermacher's way of talking about the revelation of God from a universal anthropological viewpoint. Whereas Schleiermacher places his trust in the sense of absolute dependence, Newman articulates a sense of moral compunction that is simultaneously our access to God as 'supreme Governor, a Judge, holy, just, powerful, all-seeing, retributive'.[25] Newman's dependence is not about the feeling of consciousness but rather a sense of deference to God's almighty providence. Overall, it is difficult to attribute to Newman a single view of theological method. Yet he supplies new elements and retrieves older elements that would become vital to the explicit theological methods of twentieth-century systematic theologians, notably on the historical development of doctrine and the relationship between the individual theologian and the church. These strong criteria for guiding theological work and his modest philosophical awareness are strengths that more than offset his disinterest in the technicalities of theological procedure.

Albrecht Ritschl

The nineteenth century saw other theological strides being taken in directions that entrenched both Catholic and Protestant impulses of the previous three centuries. Albrecht Ritschl (1822–89), for instance, inaugurated a programme of theological pragmatics under the influence of a revival of Kantian thought. Believing that theology is pre-eminently a practical discipline, Ritschl proclaimed 'No metaphysics in theology!' and 'no mysticism in theology!'[26] Taking Schleiermacher to task for his mystical bent, Ritschl claimed that Schleiermacher placed too much primacy on individual experience rather than the communal experience of the church and the biblical faith of Luther and the other Reformers. Central to Ritschl's critique here is his interpretation of the source of experience in Christian theology. Against Schleiermacher's view of it as a feeling of 'absolute dependence', Ritschl prioritizes the theological reality of the historically situated gospel of the New Testament, the self-disclosure of God in Christ. In response to this historically situated revelation, Christians set out, in faith, to understand what is intended for the living of life. Mindful of the legacy of the philosopher G. W. F. Hegel and his theological disciple, F. C. Baur, Ritschl seeks to avoid two opposing tendencies that were prominent in the nineteenth century: the Hegelian rationalization of God, on the one hand, and the mystical style advocated by Schleiermacher on the other hand. The problem with both of these styles of theology is their assumption that we can know God in Himself. For Ritschl, as for the Kantian-inspired theology of the twentieth century, the inner life of God is beyond our awareness. We can only understand it through the soteriological effects God has upon us. Christ cannot be known apart from the faith of the early Christians. Alongside the sexteenth-century Reformers, he focuses on the God who reconciles and redeems humanity. The focus of his main study is the doctrine of justification. Mindful of our epistemic limits, which such a focus on justification presupposes, as opposed to the metaphysical abstractions of natural theology and Hegelian theory, Ritschl prioritizes a certain perspective in soteriology through doctrinal criticism. He also sees profound dangers at play in a naive historical approach to Jesus:

> It is no mere accident that the subversion of Jesus' religious importance has been undertaken under the guise of writing

His life, for this very undertaking implies the surrender of the conviction that Jesus, as the Founder of the perfect moral and spiritual religion, belongs to a higher order than all other Men. But for that reason it is likewise vain to attempt to re-establish the importance of Christ by the same biographical expedient.[27]

As with Newman, though with an eye on the Protestant priority of biblical faith, Ritschl wants to counter the rising tide of historical positivism. Theology must be safeguarded from simplistic narratives of the fact of Jesus' existence. Yet it is with the historical Jesus that he wants to begin and, by doing so, he downplays the relevance and knowledge of later doctrinal developments as false attempts to be scientific. This is what is meant by doctrinal criticism. He emphatically embraces Luther on this point:

> while assuming the formula of the two natures, Luther really connects the religious estimate of Christ as God with the significance which Christ's work has for the Christian community . . . According to Luther, the Godhead of Christ is not exhausted by maintaining the existence in Christ of the Divine nature; the chief point is that in his exertions as man His Godhead is manifest and savingly effective.[28]

Ritschl's anti-speculative attitude extends to certain accretions in Christological doctrine, such as (medieval) satisfaction theory, which insufficiently regards Jesus' humanity:

> it is not accurate theology to limit God – to the satisfaction He receives or to the propitiation of His wrath – the direct saving efficacy of the action and passion of Christ: and to deduce the forgiveness of men's sins, or their reconciliation with God, merely as consequences from that result, and so to make the saving efficacy of the action and passion of Christ's work as regards man dependent only indirectly or secondarily upon His doing and suffering.[29]

Underlying this embrace of methodological Lutheranism is Ritschl's association of Christ and Christian community with the moral or ethical vocation. In this regard too, Ritschl's theology, expressed in his reflections on the Kingdom of God, are highly influential and not entirely deserving of the criticisms that were directed against him and other nineteenth-century German theologians – criticisms which centred on his alleged bourgeoisification of Christian theology. In summary, through his emphasis on the ethical features of the Kingdom of God, a foundational category derived from the importance that he attaches to the historical Jesus as apprehended by early Christians, Ritschl wants to promote a practical faith purged of speculation. Ritschl's theology is one that accentuates the historical task of Christian theology in the service of faith and the Kingdom of God, a theology that seeks to communicate the meaning of the gospel. In doing so, there is a focus on making doctrinal theology soteriologically coherent. His references to culture and the ethical dimension of Jesus' life suggest a dedication to the essence of Christianity rather than these more abstract ways of articulating Christian theology. His influence has been remarkable over the succeeding century, beginning with the theology of Adolf von Harnack, about whom we should say a few words as well.

Adolf von Harnack

Like Ritschl, Adolf von Harnack aspired to further a coherent yet unmetaphysical approach to Christian theology until his death in 1930. Born in 1851 in Estonia into a strict Pietist Lutheran family, Harnack was the son of a theology professor, and his own doctorate was in church history. Harnack's *History of Dogma* (*Lehrbuch der Dogmengeschichte*) is one of the most impressive historical treatments of doctrine. As with Ritschl, he provides a perspective on theology that is shorn of explicit philosophy, although there are plenty of implicit philosophical assumptions that determine how Harnack argues his case with the one obvious influence being that of Hegel. A crucial presupposition underlying Harnack's theology is that explicit philosophy prevents theology from communicating the reality of Christ and faith. Philosophy does not and cannot aid in this task. The resulting theological method is thereby philosophically thin, although it is arguably stronger because Harnack fully endorses historical method, which he appreciates as the true method that one would expect to use in relation to Christianity, which is itself a historical phenomenon.

Harnack's theology, because of its historical gravitas, echoes the thought of Ernst Troeltsch in that:

> We study history in order to intervene in the course of history . . . with respect to the past, the historian assumes the royal function of a judge for in order to decide what of the past shall continue to be effective and what must be done away with or transformed, the historian must judge like a king.[30]

As with Newman, Harnack advocates a sharp distinction between the core of a doctrinal tradition and its numerous expressions. For Harnack, the core essence of Christianity is simply 'the gospel' or the 'gospel of Jesus Christ'. It comes laden in 'historically changing forms'. Dogma, on the other hand, is the product of the Greek mind toiling on the soil of the gospel. Harnack's view does not necessarily lead to the view that dogma is dispensable. The gospel is not dependent on doctrines, but the reverse is certainly true. The development of dogma is not progressive, however; and in this respect, Harnack differs from Newman, since Harnack's historical method turns on the affirmation that in its history, the church has become authoritarian in its ecclesiastical and institutional forms.

Once again, Luther is the hero who registers a bold resistance to authoritarian patterns of thinking. Yet, and here is something remarkable about Harnack's train of thought, Luther's boldness did not go far enough. Luther's later conservatism has a strong pedigree in Christian thought; and for good reason – in the beginning, Christian thought had to shield itself from attack. Thus, for example, Marcion's rejection of the Old Testament was itself rejected by the church, which was praiseworthy; but in arguing for the plausibility of later opportunities to rid the Christian Bible of the Old Testament, Harnack leaves the reader with the impression that prudence is the ultimate governing criterion of theological method:

> The rejection of the Old Testament in the second century was a mistake which the Great Church rightly refused to commit; its retention in the sixteenth century was due to the power of a fateful heritage from which the Reformers were not yet able to withdraw; but its conservation as a canonical book in modern Protestantism is the result of a paralysis of religion and of the church.[31]

Of course, it is also possible to see in this remark a distinctly ominous foreshadowing of twentieth-century anti-Semitic theology. Marcion's theology, after all, turned on the proposal to remove the Old Testament entirely from the biblical canon. And, anti-Judaism would become institutionalized in the pro-Nazi sentiments of the German national church of the 1930s. Harnack's musings about the shape of the canon in this context is thus disturbing. Nevertheless, his thought cannot be reduced to future uses of pro-Marcionite interpretations of Christian history. Other elements in Harnack's theology are distinctive, plausible and authentically focused on Christ. He cannot be dismissed either for his ardent support of Germany in World War I, something which triggered Karl Barth's vehement opposition.

As the essence of the gospel, Harnack's Christ is understood according to three registers specifically: 'Firstly, the kingdom of God and its coming. Secondly, God the Father and the infinite value of the human soul. Thirdly, the higher righteousness and the commandment of love.'[32] Each of these registers carries a certain imprint of methodological value. Clearly, they reflect a certain interpretive endeavour with regards to the New Testament. Second, they reflect a certain unrecognized retrieval of the Jewish basis for Christian theology, especially the second theme of God's fatherliness, understood as Jesus' perfect knowledge of God. Third, the ethical imperative as reflected in the third theme is a typically Lutheran and Protestant interpretation of the moral life, with its centre being ethical deliberation and the occasional trials of the person engaged in such deliberation.

Harnack's greatest relevance appears through his direct appeal to biblical sources as pertinent to a communicative theology, a theology that is aware of contemporary culture and the theological significance of modern questions. There is a highly personal approach to theology, and a highly individualistic approach as well, with an apparent distaste for the institutional rubrics of church life as seen in his assessment of Catholicism, about which Harnack writes that 'the whole outward and visible institution of a Church *claiming divine dignity* has no foundation whatsoever in the Gospel'.[33] The elevation of the category of 'the Gospel', therefore, is the priority of the Church, in order to overcome the obstacles of historical developments that stand in the way between the believer and the original Jesus.

For Harnack, there is a basic opposition and struggle between doctrine, on the one hand, and history on the other hand. History allows the theologian to discern where, when and how the corruption process entered into the development of doctrine. For Harnack, the development process is invariably regressive. It is a movement that persists in substituting Greek metaphysical ideas for the pure gospel. According to Harack, 'recovery' thus becomes the *modus operandi* for theologians, the urgency in retrieving what has been lost. Doing theology must not be reducible to doing the philosophy of religion. Unfortunately, given the estimable pedigree of the liberal Protestant ethos Harnack represented, his opposition between history and dogma became a chasm that saturated much of twentieth-century theology. Whereas Lonergan articulates a distinction between history and doctrine as two forms of judgement set within a multi-faceted theological set of tasks, Harnack and his theological descendants foresaw only tension. Through their Kantian perspective, they could only imagine that Greek metaphysics had done harm to the theological enterprise. Lonergan, on the other hand, sees history as a distinct task that brings the critical enterprise to bear upon scripture and tradition, for the purpose of determining what is of value from the past for the present and what is of disvalue. For Lonergan, no closure on metaphysical categories can be announded a priori. Doctrine, having been shaped by the conversion of the theologian in light of what is indeed valuable, is also a judgement that tries to constructively explain what the past has brought forwards. For Lonergan, the patristic and medieval recourse to philosophy and metaphysics is a vital part of the past that needs to be retained in the doctrinal task. This last point has also been taken up recently by theologians such as Joseph Ratzinger and the theologians of the Radical Orthodoxy movement, as we shall see in Chapter Eight, but the legacy of Harnack's zero-sum game between history and dogma is, nevertheless, with us still.

Conclusion

The nineteenth century witnessed important developments in the understanding of theological method, with Schleiermacher and Newman being the most important figures in this regards. For Schleiermacher, the importance of history mandated a hermeneutical way of interpreting texts, as well as the displacement of authority away from tradition and towards personal religious experience. Ritschl and Harnack took Schleiermacher's historical approach seriously but avoided the emphasis on human consciousness by downplaying the constructive aspects of doctrine altogether. In doing so, they go substantially beyond Schleiermacher's incorporation of doctrine into historical theology. The tension that we see in these thinkers between various theological tasks, a tension arising from the new historical awareness, is missing in Newman's more organic thinking. His theological method takes historical awareness seriously but interprets it as a development of insight that is basically progressive. Newman keeps the central threads of spiritual insight and core judgements of doctrine as the key to continuity in tradition and authority that is derived from tradition. As we shall now see, this basic difference over the meaning and role of history and doctrine in theology has tremendous spill-over effects in the twentieth century, which is the century of division and pluralism in theological method.

CHAPTER SEVEN

Modern theological methods – Correlation and anti-correlation

Methodological awareness always follows the application of a method; it never precedes it.

Paul Tillich[1]

Twentieth-century Christian theology has moved decisively yet sporadically in a number of contradictory directions. The sporadic character of theology is most deeply felt in terms of theological method. As theological scholarship widened to include a global scope of cultures and traditions to which the academy and churches were previously indifferent, theology took on a vastly more pluralistic tone. Participation within the academy has grown to include newcomers who were historically marginalized, and theologians have come to adopt widely different hermeneutical positions on how theological inquiry should proceed. Of course, much of this new diversity has been inherently refreshing and exhilarating. For others, diversity brings with it a distraction from the central theological task of inquiring into the nature and attributes of God and the means of God's revelation. As forms of New Testament criticism broadened to diagnose ever new kinds of textual difficulties, the biblical exegesis on which theology had previously depended migrated away from theology. This situation has left historical, practical and systematic theologians bereft of biblical scholars with whom to discuss biblical theology. A heightened attention to language in philosophy and an increasing egalitarian impulse in world politics have also made significant impacts on twentieth-century theology, its presuppositions, procedures and principles.

Theologians have reacted to such developments with a mixture of irenicism and criticism. Twentieth-century theology has, by and large, adapted the theological developments of the nineteenth century to a culture that is no longer habitually Christian. The rise of Protestant liberalism in the nineteenth century, exemplified in the work of Schleiermacher and Troeltsch in Germany, as well as in lesser English-speaking figures, has deeply influenced early twentieth-century theology. It is arguable whether it is philosophy, theological criteria or the interpretation of certain sources which most distinguish the types of theology that have emerged in modernity. Hans Frei in his book *The Five Types of Theology* makes the distinction among theological types largely on the basis of whether various theologians believe that theology requires philosophy. For instance, theological types can be differentiated by whether theology can be substituted by philosophy in one type or whether it is autonomous from philosophy in another type.[2] Philosophy undoubtedly remains vital to distinguishing theological methods; but perhaps the question that matters most in making sense of theological method pertaining to this century is the question of how the theological task is perceived and carried out. Both of these issues, and the other problems of procedure, criteria and the differing emphases on sources, make up the nature of the inquiry into twentieth-century theological method. We should begin with the theological method of Rudolf Bultmann, whose shadow looms over all theology from the 1930s onwards.

Rudolf Bultmann

The figure of Rudolf Bultmann in theology can be compared with that of Charles Darwin in biology without too much exaggeration. It is fitting that we begin this chapter on the twentieth-century approaches to theological method with a section devoted to the thought of Rudolf Bultmann. His theological instincts are complex and even contradictory, but they have shaped the entire trajectory of Western theology since, especially Protestant theology since the 1930s and Catholic theology after the 1960s. Of all twentieth-century theologians, moreover, Bultmann has been the most assiduous in absorbing the lessons and insights of nineteenth-century theology. Schubert Ogden calls him the 'the methodological conscience of his theological generation' for probing more deeply than other theologians the chasm which opened up in the nineteenth century between Enlightenment modernity and the classical formulations of faith and doctrine.[3] Bultmann's theology is usually associated with dense terms such as ' 'de-mythologization'. But his assessment of theological method and his willingness to go to the roots of the Christian tradition, to distinguish the important aspects of liberal theology from the less important and to separate the authentic from the inauthentic, signals a striking boldness of theological inquiry which goes beyond a familiarity with the significance of the de-mythologization concept. Moreover, his outlook is one of the first explicit attempts to correlate the core insights and themes of Christian theology with that of modern learning and modern science. While Paul Tillich's name is most associated with the expression 'critical correlationism' as a methodological strategy for organizing theological claims, it is Bultmann who forges this path with originality, because of the sweeping changes that he recommends for theology in the face of modern science especially.

What marks out Bultmann for special attention is the degree to which he absorbs the vast successes of modern science and interprets that edifice of knowledge as a foil against which he justifies taking controversial yet influential theological positions. In Bultmann's work, we see a clear enunciation of features of modern theology that are now taken for granted. The distinction between the Jesus of history and the Christ of faith, for instance, is largely a product of Bultmann's separation between faith and history. Another such stance is his view of the resurrection ('not an event of past history'[4]), meaning that for Bultmann, the resurrection is better suited to describe the rise of faith among Christ's disciples. On that issue, he remarks, in a criticism of Karl Barth, that 'the resurrection of Jesus cannot be a miraculous proof by which the skeptic might be compelled to believe in Christ'.[5] While seeking to couch his view of the resurrection in terms that Karl Barth might admit, the real intent of Bultmann's theological programme emerges on a number of fronts. Faith and historical facts are seen by Bultmann to be of different orders, something adopted from one of his teachers in particular, Wilhelm Herrmann, who in turn adopted a neo-Kantian approach to faith. As with other theologians since, Bultmann made full use of another Marburg thinker, existentialist philosopher Martin Heidegger. Faith, for Bultmann, is conceived in a way that is fundamentally in line with Luther and Schleiermacher too, yet divergent from those theological forebears in the sense that he situates faith as a perspective of self-understanding of (one's) existence (*Selbstverständnis*), rather than merely the understanding of God.

Bultmann does not want to expel myth from the New Testament as is so frequently supposed. Rather, he wants to explicate the intention from behind the text which is obscured by a mythical presentation. To a limited extent, his aim in this regards is that of Augustine. A mythical presentation of the gospel expresses 'man's understanding of himself in the world in which he lives'.[6] As such, myths are necessary, but as such, they invite the kind of criticism that he feels is warranted because of the inconsistencies and contradictions that plague the text. His concern is with the elusive intent of the authors of the biblical books, an intent that is shrouded by mythical language. Myth is a necessarily mundane, this-worldly language that he believes modern science has now shown to be obscure.

In terms of the theological method in Bultmann's thought, there is undoubtedly a concern for proper biblical interpretation in his work, according to a particular philosophy and worldview. Interpretation, on Bultmann's terms, involves ensuring a clear distinction between the personal subject and objective history:

> the 'most subjective' *[subjectivste]* interpretation is the 'most objective' *[objectivste]*, that is, only those who are stirred by the question of their own existence *[Existenz]* can hear the claim which the text makes.[7]

Theology is, then, a task of restatement of what lies in the text. Interpretation or re-interpretation also applies to doctrine, but this is so that doctrine renders universally (existentially) significant what it previously claimed only in relation to the Christian story. One feature of Bultmann's claim that seems radical is the implication that the New Testament is nothing other than an attempt to re-state the identity of God. Akin to the earlier analysis that we made in Chapter One concerning Paul, Bultmann sees the existential thrust of interpretation driving theology within the biblical canon as well as beyond it. Of course, such an impression carries with it the associated idea that the biblical canon may not really be authoritative. That is one implication, among many others, which critics of Bultmann have claimed stems from his method. But as for the biblical text and its mythological framework, Bultmann is simply making the straightforward point that the literary presentation of a theological claim is never the same as the faith that motivates the making of that claim. Furthermore, faith must not be objectivized or else it turns into something else:

> The restatement of mythology is a requirement of faith itself. For faith needs to be emancipated from its association with every world-view expressed in objective terms . . . Our radical attempt to demythologise the New Testament is in fact a perfect parallel to St Paul's and Luther's doctrine of justification by faith alone . . . It destroys every false security . . . security can be found only by abandoning all security.[8]

Consistent with both Schleiermacher and modern existentialism, Bultmann resists and rejects a metaphysical apparatus to theology. Faith is something willed; a cast of mind that issues from personal decision. Whether through his campaign to divest the mythical language of the New Testament of its theological significance or his re-stating Christology within the human desire for a meaningful soteriology, Bultmann recasts the scope of theology inwards and makes it an existential encounter. It is shorn of the salvation history that arises from the Old Testament and Judaism, apart from his judicious use of the prophets. Methodically speaking, for Bultmann, theology can be seen as a way of interpreting scripture. Systematic theology does not play the central role it does in the wider theological traditions of Protestant and Catholic thought. For this reason,

Bultmann's theology is regarded as thoroughly hermeneutical, to the point that, as Thomas Torrance says, God becomes a 'cipher for our *relations* with God'.[9]

One important current in his New Testament theology is the significance he attributes to Gnosticism, the ancient movement that permeated the Middle-Eastern cultures of the early centuries during which Christianity emerged. Bultmann is far more willing to grant Gnosticism a role in forging the conceptual framework of early Christian belief, particularly as exemplified in the Gospel of John. For Bultmann, 'Gnosticism is the only possible source of the idea of the absolute Logos' and 'the idea of the incarnation of the redeemer is itself originally Gnostic, and was taken over at a very early stage by Christianity, and made fruitful for Christology'.[10] The recognition that he gives to Gnosticism is taken back, however, when it comes to substantive issues such as the value of the body and physical nature in general. It is true that Bultmann distinguishes between faith and psychic phenomena, for instance, a crucial insight to deciphering the difference between early orthodox Christianity and Gnosticism. However, one cannot help notice that he sometimes fails to draw that distinction as sharply as historical theologians have done. Bultmann's stress on personal illumination as the event of Easter faith is a case in point. Bultmann's emphasis on individualism in his view of Paul also resembles a certain distrust of ecclesial form:

> God's grace is not an historical phenomenon. It is not the possession of a historical nation, membership of which guarantees the security of the individual . . . In the Christian church there is neither male nor female, for all are 'one in Christ Jesus' (Gal. 3.28, 1 Cor. 12.13; Col. 3.11). This also means that man is absolutely alone before God. Of course, in belonging to Christ he is a member of his body, and is therefore bound to the other members in the unity of the Church. But before God he stands, in the first place at any rate, in utter loneliness, extricated from his natural ties. The fundamental question which is asked of man, 'Are you ready to believe in the word of God's grace?' can only be answered individually. The individualizing of man's relation to God has its roots in the psalms and Wisdom literature, and above all in Jeremiah. But its full implications were never realized until the time of Paul with his radical conception of the grace of God.[11]

For Bultmann, God's grace is an interior state that contradicts the demands of external knowledge about God and the world. In this respect, the focus on God and grace are assets in Bultmann's theological instincts that should assuage some of his critics. But, God is heard from but is not historically visible. From the Old Testament prophets onwards, for Bultmann, the life of faith in a covenant strongly suggests the gift of wisdom in contrast to the Greeks' attempt to acquire propositional knowledge. Wisdom, as Bultmann sees it through the prism of existentialism, emerges in a thoroughgoing demythologization approach. The process of understanding the New Testament according to the way of demythologization involves, for Bultmann, the contrasting of faith and works, where 'to press for [myth]'s acceptance as an article of faith would be to reduce faith to works'.[12] The core of faith lies behind what he refers to as the 'biblical doctrine'. The biblical doctrine is what Bultmann famously terms the 'kerygma', a term which substitutes for doctrine in identifying the core of Christian thought that is in constant need of recovery in every historical situation. The succession of historical situations is, for Bultmann, decisive when considering theological method as a whole:

> there can be no normative Christian dogmatics ... it is not possible to accomplish the theological task once for all – the task which consists of unfolding that understanding of God, and hence of the world and man, which arises from faith, for this task permits only ever-repeated solutions, or attempts at solution, each in its particular historical situation.[13]

Considering Bultmann's focus is on the New Testament, interpretation is the most obvious task of a theologian, a task that must consider the foundation of faith adopted by the individual and the historical trajectory of previous interpretations. The criterion of theology is, above all, the kerygmatic function of the biblical text, hidden beneath mythical form. Bultmann suspects that other ways of dealing with faith are, in the end, invalid, because of the verdict handed down on such attempts by historical changes in doctrinal expression. Newman and Lonergan take a vastly different view, of course. Whereas Bultmann sees change, they see development, from one stage of meaning to another, from a more descriptive to a more explanatory point of view and from a common sense appreciation to a theoretical formulation. For Lonergan, the growth of autonomous sciences, such as the social sciences, bears on the meaning of the kerygma, with the result that a wide incorporation of philosophy is required. Existentialism alone will not do since, for Lonergan, a foundational theology that accepts the total horizon of the theologian is what underlies the theological task. Thus, a variety of philosophical tools may be called upon to remedy a theological problem in principle. Fidelity to a particular philosophy or school of thought inevitably dates the theology that is expressed, despite the best methical intentions of the theologian. As we shall now see, Karl Barth proposes a view that contrasts with the views of both Lonergan and Bultmann concerning whether God needs any methical help in being properly described.

Karl Barth

Of far-reaching significance for the entire scope of the twentieth century theology is the thought of Karl Barth, the reception of whom continues apace. Christian theology, not only in the Reformed and wider Protestant tradition, but also beyond it, takes him increasingly seriously. Starkly in opposition to the entire legacy of the Enlightenment's impact on Christian theology and the approaches of Friedrich Schleiermacher and Rudolf Bultmann, Barth takes a firm and contrarian stance by narrating a seemingly anti-methodological stance. Barth's theology is not a theology of correlation; it is, in fact, anti-correlational. Theology is not analogous to anything of this world or any inquiry that speaks of world realities. Barth revels in the incoherence of human thought, precisely because that points up the distance that lies between human speech and the speech of an eternal God. Theology concerns the Word of God, revealed in scripture and the person of Christ, mediated through the Holy Spirit and the Church. It must be admitted that in setting out these theological priorities, Barth is not wholly at odds with the liberalism of nineteenth-century Protestantism. There is, after all, a certain consistency between Barth's Christological frame of reference and the concept of the gospel put forwards by Ritschl and Harnack. But, contrary to Bultmann's implicit premise, for Barth, theology is not dependent upon any existentialist worldview (*weltanschauung*).[14] The criterion for good theology is not epistemological *per se*, but strictly in terms of whether it allows God's own revelation to be clarified. The criterion for theology is the event of the Word of God.

Barth's earlier theology is a somewhat more obscure matter however. Drawing on the work of Søren Kierkegaard, Barth establishes a negative 'dialectical' theology, which is predicated on the utter difference between time and eternity, between crucifixion and resurrection. Partly in the light of his realization during World War I that Christendom was at an end, and in recognition of the fact that his theological mentors such as von Harnack had no way of crafting a theology that took this seriously, Barth reacted. Displaying a kind of Lutheran pessimism, Barth stressed the incomprehensible nature of the transcendent God. He stressed the paradox of faith and the uniqueness of Christ. This outlook won and lost him admirers in perhaps equal measure. The two editions of his blockbuster *Epistle to the Romans* published in 1919 and 1922 witness a shift to a more determined outlook on the Word of God, particularly in relation to the biblical narrative itself. Beginning in the mid-1920s, while his position in the German theological academy was still fairly shaky, Barth drifted into a theological position that took much more seriously the genre of dogmatics, the predominant genre against which liberal Protestantism had, up until this point, been in reaction. Meanwhile, his break with other theologians in the group of 'dialectical theologians' solidified as he denounced what he took to be various anthropomorphizing attempts to speak of God from a perspective other than the Word of God.

By the time of his writing of the *Church Dogmatics*, theology is described as a science (*wissenschaften*). The shift is important for all kinds of reasons having to do with the contents of Barth's theology. It marks a shift away from a purely dialectical, negative theology, and away from a depiction of God as incomprehensible. But, in terms of method per se, there is less of a shift than one might imagine. It is correct to say that Barth cannot do his theology without making certain claims that are steeped in methodological presuppositions, involving certain deductive and inductive inferences. Another characteristic of his theology that suggests inevitable attention to method is his indebtedness to other theologians who endorse procedure, Ulrich Zwingli (1484–1531) to some extent, but more importantly, John Calvin.

Calvin, it should be remembered, follows to a large extent Melanchthon's choice to think theologically in terms of *loci communes*. Calvin thinks of the various loci of theological statements as a hierarchy of statements of greater and lesser significance. Barth is notably enthusiastic about such a procedure in *CD* I/2: 'the only true scholarly method in dogmatics.'[15] By this, he refers to the presence of themes in the Bible, the theologically credible *Sache* contained in biblical books. Barth is not endorsing Melanchthon's way of engaging in theological dogmatics specifically, which Barth describes as merely 'assembling, repeating and defining' biblical teaching points;[16] however, Barth does want to engage in a *sachexegesis* of the Bible - a focus on the Bible's subject matter - as opposed to Bultmann's *sachekritik*, the critical de-mythologization of biblical formulations about God. Barth cannot imagine trying to rid theology of the biblical conceptual framework without neutering and destroying what theology is supposed to do. And, according to Barth, the Bible is quite distinct from revelation.[17] While his theology dons the mantle of an uncritical approach, this is not the same thing as a theology that is biblically literalist or naive. For Barth, the Bible even possesses a nature, in true Augustinian fashion, which is to be a sign 'to that which it signifies'.[18] And here is why Barth's theology comes to be known as neo-orthodox.

The issue which pinpoints Barth's ambivalence over certain methodical questions is his treatment of prolegomena at the beginning of his *Church Dogmatics*. The question of prolegomena is one of the most vexing for Barth, since by speaking words that come prior to the words of Christian Dogmatics, one can give the impression that what really matters are the human conceptual frameworks that must contextualize reflection on the Word of God. As Barth says:

> If there is involved a statement of what dogmatics is, from outside dogmatics, this is correct, only to the extent that the statement is made outside a specific dogmatics, namely Reformation and Evangelical, or indeed Roman Catholic dogmatics.[19]

This statement is classic Barth, in terms of capturing the specificity and yet the inadequacy of Christian speech. All speech is affected by the sin and division of the Christian church. Theological speech can nevertheless encompass Christ despite its entanglements in disunity and pride. What does this mean for prolegomena in Dogmatics? After relating an account of what he feels are the inadequacies of the Catholic organization of doctrine, such as its proposal (as Barth sees it) that Christ be incorporated into the church rather than vice versa, Barth states:

> prolegomena to dogmatics are only possible as part of dogmatics itself. The prefix *pro* in prolegomena is to be understood loosely to signify the first part of dogmatics rather than that which is prior to it.[20]

In Barth's thinking, a method that does not orient theology to a submission in the act of faith in a God who acts is a theology that will lead theologians astray. For Barth, who cites Calvin's inclusion of a prolegomena to the 1559 edition of the *Institutes*, dogmatics should only begin with words that aim to spell out what the defence of faith and the error of heresy implies. It must spell out that dogmatics seeks to understand who God is and what God has done through Christ. Anything that confuses the dialectic between God 'in heaven' and humanity 'on earth', between God's Word and the human word, as Barth puts it in his early theology, is inadequate theological dogmatics. Here, Barth is severely critical of Schleiermacher, whose vision of dogmatics in the introduction to *The Christian Faith* does not subscribe to this criterion.

So, it is in the way that Barth wants to follow the Reformers that his contention with method begins. Barth's objection to modern theological method is principled. He objects both to the formulae of fundamental theology that he perceives as overly abstract and unduly important in the tradition of Protestant Dogmatics from the seventeenth century onwards. He also objects, of course, to Catholic natural theology apologetics, as in his famous claim that the *analogia entis* is 'the invention of the antichrist'.[21] In fact, tacitly acknowledging Bultmann's criticism of his own selective approach to biblical themes, Barth's first and primary goal is to set out a theological method that rejects the historic Protestant bifurcation of theological statements into the categories of fundamental and non-fundamental. For Barth, the problem with such a structure for theology is that it grants theology an epistemological structure that resembles the other sciences, but which he does not believe theology possesses:

> Once the doctrine of the *articuli fundamentalis* was recognized, who or what was to stop the Pietists and Rationalists of the early 18th century from drawing the line of demarcation between fundamental and non-fundamental very differently from the older generation, in accordance with their different views?[22]

Whether Barth is being consistent with his Reformed heritage is a viable question. But, he is concerned with theological propositions properly speaking, not simply the first word of biblical exegesis.

Nevertheless, Bultmann criticizes Barth precisely for drawing conclusions between central and auxiliary themes of theological significance while foreswearing a method that explains why one would make such distinctions. Alluding to Barth's method of exegesis with specific reference to the re-interpretation of eschatology away from a chronological to a non-mythological variant, Bultmann critically remarks: 'the preacher must not leave his people in the dark about what he secretly eliminates, nor must he be in the dark about it himself.'[23] Is Barth deluded? Does he elide the mythological or conceptual apparatus of the New Testament and replace it with something else without realizing it or stating what he is up to? Partly for what he perceives as Barth's lack of method, Bultmann rejects the terms of systematic theology and opts decisively for a New Testament theology through the employment of a hermeneutical lens that reflects and correlates the philosophy of existentialism, especially that of Martin Heidegger. Barth wants to express the mirror-opposite view: he engages in the most systematic of dogmatic theology which prizes the testimony of scripture while rejecting the modernist critical hermeneutical enterprise as a whole. It is exceedingly difficult to detect any major philosophical influence in Barth's theology apart from an early fascination with Kierkegaard. Overall, he is resolutely hostile to the very idea of philosophical influence. Indeed, as a systematic theologian, Barth is suspicious of many grounds or presuppositions on which one might construct a theological system.

So, Barth's criticism of the idea of a hierarchy of theological propositions does not come off easily. True, he does reject epistemology in theology explicitly. Yet theology is still a science, as he himself says. A further complication in understanding Barth's thought is the distinction between theology and dogmatics. Theology is a general science, but dogmatics is one of the three disciplines of theology. He remarks that it is 'the self-examination of the Christian church in respect of the content of its distinctive talk about God. The true content which is sought is what we shall call dogma'.[24] Accompanying dogmatics are two other disciplines, which are interrelated as an abstract science: 'theology as biblical theology is the question of the basis, as practical theology the question of the goal and as dogmatic theology the question the content of the distinctive utterance of the church.'[25] In this respect, Barth's organization of theology resembles some nineteenth-century attempts, including that of Schleiermacher, ironically, to describe the variety of disciplines or fields contained within theology.

But, Barth's description of theology as a scientific discourse, carried on within ecclesial parameters, serves notice that, methodologically speaking, theology has a distinct objective and a distinct perspective. Theology, he says, 'confesses God as it talks about God'.[26] Barth's notion of theology is not simply the variety of formulations and emphases, but, more importantly, on who is the subject of theology. His argument is resoundingly about the proper criterion for theological reflection. As a science, after having styled theology's generalized speech to confession of God and of a particular way of conceiving of humanity, Barth reiterates that it is the church that produces theology. Theology, therefore, is a collective enterprise, one that is ecclesial in character and thrust. Moreover, the church engages in theological reflection in order to subject itself to self-examination.

Naturally, Barth's claim to be free of philosophy or worldview does not impress Bultmann. In correspondence, Bultmann writes:

It is right that dogmatics should have nothing whatever to do with a philosophy insofar as this is systematic; but it is also right that it must learn from a philosophy that is a critical (ontological) inquiry. For only then does it remain free and make use of philosophy as a helper of theology; otherwise it becomes the maid and philosophy the mistress. There is no alternative; it must be either maid or mistress. Your planned ignoring of philosophy is only apparent. Naturally lordship or servanthood applies to the forming of concepts. But if dogmatics is to be a science, it cannot avoid the question of appropriate concepts.[27]

But is the cost of holding on to this slippery slope argument too high? Does Barth's complaint over the efforts of nineteenth-century liberal Protestants to articulate an 'essence' of Christianity eliminate the raising of legitimate questions into the difference between fundamental and less vital aspects of Christian theology in the aftermath of the emergence of historical consciousness? There are good reasons to question whether Barth's protest is one that exercises as much force as his followers believe.

For instance, one of the enduring metaphors of Barth's theology is his image of the 'centre' of theology, what Stephen Sykes describes as Barth's implicit deference to a leading principle of the Romantic Movement.[28] The deference to a centre in theology actually constitutes an intriguing parallel between Barth and Bultmann because both theologians, each on the basis of completely different reasons, speaks of Christ as the centre. Bultmann speaks of the event of Christ 'as proclaimed'; Barth speaks of Christ as the subject of (our) election. The topic of a centre in theology also speaks to the radical difference between Bultmann and Barth, however. Whereas for Bultmann, the centre is Christ as a proclaimed answer to our existential quest, for Barth, the object of theology controls the method of theology.

As Barth comments, in response to a defence of critical-historical studies in theology by Adolf von Harnack, whose theology he characterized as a 'spectator theology':

> The reliability and communality of the knowledge of the person of Jesus Christ as the centre of the gospel can be none other than that of God-awakened *faith*. Critical-historical study signifies the deserved and necessary end of *those* 'foundations' of this knowledge which are no foundations at all since they have not been laid by God himself.[29]

Barth's fierce criticism of 'everything which flowed from the pens of the German theologians' from even before the World War I extends as far back to Schleiermacher. Barth is most concerned about him, due to Schleiermacher's decision to organize dogmatics around human religious consciousness.[30] In contrast, the *Church Dogmatics* is constructed around an almost medieval *exits/reditus* pattern of descent and ascent with God at the centre. In four parts, Barth structures a theology of the Word, first in reference to the Word of God, then to the Doctrines of God, Creation and Reconciliation. There are, indeed, parallels to be made with the *Summa* of Thomas Aquinas since the *Church Dogmatics* is a systematic theology that aims for a comprehensive scope of theological claims. Yet, as Barth himself knows, the attempt at a system is itself deeply problematic, in the sense that developing a system can be so logically tight that it leaves out what is most important. Regarding Schleiermacher's system, in its 'suspiciously brilliant' form, he says of Schleiermacher's efforts, 'there is no place for anything contingent, strange or indigestible in the statements of the Bible or the dogmas of the church'.[31] For Barth, what is more vital for dogmatics is not the structure of theological statements in their proper expression of human feelings about God, but their truth value. Whereas in Schleiermacher, who 'knows about the concept of *kerygma*, but [it is] a *kerygma* that only depicts and does not bring, that only states or expresses, but does not declare. Truth does not come in the spoken Word; it comes in speaking feeling.'[32] In contrast, of course, the *Church Dogmatics* posits that the form of revelation is inseparable from its content, a content that is given in stories not of our making and which are, as such, not determined by our methodological instincts. We see in Barth, then, the birth of what later theologians call 'narrative theology'. Much else could be said about Barth's theology and the increasing influence he held on theologians many years after his death in 1968. At least a sufficient amount has been said, however, so that we can move through the other twentieth-century theological giants to understand just how significantly Barth differed with most of his contemporaries on theological method.

Paul Tillich

Noted for being the most methodologically attentive theologian of the twentieth century, Paul Tillich (1886–1965) represents a crucial milestone in the story of theological method over the past hundred years. Although his critics have voiced vigorous defences of other theological options, Tillich's thinking is something of a benchmark against which much contemporary theological method is measured. Tillich is characteristic of twentieth-century theology's love affair with philosophy. Like Rahner in the Catholic world, Tillich's Protestant theology earned a large audience, partly because it reflects a shift in the intellectual framework of liberal Western thought in general. A philosophical vocabulary thus takes centre stage in Tillich's systematic theology, including the employment of terms like 'ground of being' for God, of 'ultimate concern' and of 'finitude'. And, to be sure, it is systematic theology that Tillich chiefly pursues, not a theology of historical tradition or biblical interpretation, despite his interest in both.

Tillich is the main figure in developing the theological method known as 'correlational theology' or 'correlational method'. For Tillich, the Christian kerygma and the human 'situation' stand in contrast and, as such, they are in need of harmonization, or 'critical correlation'. Existentialist thought is the underlying pattern to his theology, a trait he shares with Bultmann, although Tillich recognizes the limits of existentialist thought at a number of points. Nevertheless, he is aware of the pitfalls of a straightforward belief in 'methodological monism which includes chemistry as well as theology'.[33] As his thought matured, Tillich came to express theological method as the correlation of the questions of modern persons, on the one hand, and the answers of Christian revelation on the other hand. The goal is always to render the Christian faith meaningful to contemporary people:

> The method of correlation explains the contents of the Christian faith through existential questions and theological answers in mutual interdependence. Theology formulates the questions implied in human existence, and theology formulates the answers implied in divine self-manifestation under the guidance of the questions implied in human existence. This is a circle which drives man to a point where question and answer are not separated . . . The answers implied in the event of revelation are meaningful only so far as they are in correlation with questions concerning the whole of our existence, with existential questions.[34]

In an effort to bring forwards Schleiermacher's legacy with more precision, Tillich argues for the notion of encounter to complement that of experience as that which challenges us in our concepts and actions. The theological potential of one's encounter with reality is where one is 'existentially involved' with one's 'ultimate concern'. There are subtle overtones of dialectical theology in Tillich's language, and there is even a similarity with Karl Barth's early Kierkegaardian neo-orthodoxy in this respect. Tillich's early theology, too, is one of contrasting church and society, philosophy and theology, religion and culture. The philosophical character of his theology can be seen in the deep sense of dialectic that exists in the formulation of theological claims. He is thoroughly informed by the legacy of German (Hegelian) idealism. Yet Tillich is a theologian for the church. 'Theology, as a function of the church, must serve the needs of the church', as he says in the very first line of his *Systematic Theology*.[35] Indeed, Tillich was a brief participant with Barth in the German Confessing Church before he backed away from its 'supernaturalism', and before he was subsequently deported from Germany by the Nazis.

In advocating the method of correlation, Tillich charts a course which Barth refuses. Correlation for Tillich means three things:

> There is a correlation in the sense of correspondence between religious symbols and that which is symbolized by them. There is a correlation in the logical sense between concepts denoting the human and those denoting the divine. There is a correlation in the factual sense between man's ultimate concern and that about which he is ultimately concerned. The first meaning of correlation refers to the central problem of religious knowledge. The second meaning of correlation determines the statements about God and the world; for example, the correlation of the infinite and the finite. The third meaning of correlation qualifies the divine-human relationship with religious experience. The third use of correlative thinking in theology has evoked the protest of theologians such as Karl Barth.[36]

Tillich goes on to endorse the thought of Emil Brunner, another opponent of Barth's, on the topic of the third correlation, affirming the real relation between God and human beings, a relationship that means 'something real for both sides'. Mutual interdependence characterizes theology, because God is with us to the extent that we are for God.

The mutuality between anthropology and theology, strictly speaking, is Tillich's principled basis for theological method. The three kinds of correlation pertain to various sections of his important three-volume work, *Systematic Theology*, written in the later part of his life. So how does theology actually proceed? Again, this is a distinct question, since theological method is both a question of presuppositions or principles on the one hand, and the actual procedures of thinking on the other hand. Tillich states:

> Systematic theology proceeds in the following way: it makes an analysis of the human situation out of which the existential questions arise, and it demonstrates that the symbols used in the Christian message are the answers to these questions. The analysis of the human situation is done in terms which today are called 'existential.' Such analyses are older than existentialism . . . In the light of this message, he may make an analysis of existence which is more penetrating than that of most philosophers . . . The difference between the philosopher who is not a theologian and the theologian who works as a philosopher in analyzing human experience is only that the former tries to give an analysis which will be part of a broader philosophical work, while the latter tries to correlate the material of his analysis with the theological concepts he derives from the Christian faith.[37]

Tillich contends that this procedure comprises an alternative to three mistaken methods of theology: the 'supranaturalistic' ('the Christian message conceived as a sum of revealed truths'), the 'naturalistic' (the nineteenth-century mode of deriving the Christian message from 'man's natural state') and the 'dualistic' (the construction of a supranaturalistic structure of faith on a natural basis, such as is found in natural theology).[38]

The concept of ultimate concern is one of a number of such Tillichian terms with deep methodological significance, since it identifies the psychological framework of faith. Faith, or 'Absolute faith', as Tillich calls it on several occasions (to distinguish its meaning from that which other theologians speak about), is faith which encompasses tension, finitude and anxiety – the entire human condition. Especially in *The Courage to* Be, published in 1952, Tillich confronts the challenges of depth psychology and especially the influence of Freud. For Tillich, there is a lesson in thinking of God through a faith that embraces despair and negativity, since it refers to a God who is a 'God above the God of theism':

> 'The acceptance of the God above the God of theism makes us a part of that which is not also a part but is the ground of the whole. Therefore our self is not lost in a larger whole, which submerges it in the life of a limited group . . . This is why the Church, which stands for the power of being-itself or for the God who transcends the God of the religions, claims to be a mediator of the courage to be. A church which is based on the authority of the God of theism cannot make such a claim. It inescapably develops into a collectivist or semicollectivist system itself. But a church which raises itself in its message and its devotion to the God above the God of theism without sacrificing its concrete symbols can mediate a courage which takes doubt and meaninglessness into itself. It is the Church under the Cross which alone can do this, the Church which preaches the Crucified who cried to God who remained his God after the God of confidence had left him in the darkness of doubt and meaninglessness.[39]

Another methodological issue which distinguishes Tillich's theology is the primacy he places on symbols. Contrary to Barth, Tillich claims that 'The subject matter of theology . . . is the symbols given by the original revelatory experiences and by the traditions based on them'.[40] The 'direct object of theology is not God; the direct object of theology is . . . religious symbols'.[41] For Tillich, the Bible, and, more specifically, the 'picture' of Jesus Christ that is presented in the New Testament, comprises of texts with symbolic power. Their revelatory authority is due to their symbolic value. Theology's obligation is thus to elaborate on the power of the biblical symbols and, in particular, the symbol of Christ. Elaboration is itself a metaphysical task: 'Theology should not weaken concrete symbols, but it must analyse them and interpret them in abstract ontological terms.'[42] Thus, systematic theology is not an exercise of biblical interpretation. It is an effort, as Lonergan would presumably concur, to ensure that whatever understandings are present on the basis of the biblical text and made the revelatory basis of a decision of faith and symbolized at the conceptual level, are correlated with the questions and concerns of a particular culture.

Religious symbols, as Tillich calls them, are the basis of his theology of revelation. Also, as with the theology of Bonaventure and Joseph Ratzinger, revelation is an event; or, to be more exact, revelations are either original or dependent upon the original, with correlations occurring between what has taken place in reality with a new reality that has taken place in the mind. Revelation thus implies the involvement or participation of the person of faith who receives and engages it:

> The history of revelation indicates that there is a difference between original and dependent revelations. This is a consequence of the correlative character of revelation . . . Jesus is the Christ, both because he could become the Christ and because he was received as the Christ. Without both these sides he would not have been the Christ . . . This leads to a broader view of revelation in the life of the Christian. A dependent revelatory situation exists in every moment in which the divine Spirit grasps, shakes and moves the human spirit. Every prayer and meditation, if it fulfills its meaning, namely to reunite the creature with its creative ground, is revelatory in this sense.[43]

Tillich thus sees knowledge of revelation as the knowledge of God, albeit a knowledge that is analogous knowledge. Thus, there is agreement with the thrust of the classical *analogia entis* doctrine. For Tillich, according to David Kelsey, revelation *is* salvation. Whether or not that equivalence is justified depends on other factors that would require a more complex analysis, including an assessment of Tillich's high view of the Holy Spirit, God *in* history. For Kelsey, the disjunction that Tillich wants to promote between God's giving of revelation as an event in history and the religious experience of that revelation cannot be reconciled with Tillich's assurance that the giving is independent of the receiving of a revelatory occurrence.[44]

The main point in regards to Tillich's theological method is that we see a tight correlation between the dynamics of subject and object, of human and divine action, so tight as to force the reader to wonder, as with Bultmann's theology, whether Tillich is promoting a form of self-understanding in place of a more genuine notion of religious faith. What we do see in Tillich, notwithstanding an understanding of revelation that is ultimately quite weak, is a coherent grasp of the importance of method, in particular the need to clarify the philosophy that serves as his theological *prolegomena* and the notion of correlation that specifies the meaning of the field of systematic theology.

Hans Urs von Balthasar

Swiss theologian Hans Urs von Balthasar is regarded as one of the most profound Catholic theologians of the twentieth century. Born in 1905, he was a polymath as well as a student of German literature, music and culture, which shows itself in the immense amount of theological writing that he accomplished during his lifetime. Weeks before he died in 1988, Balthasar was made a Cardinal of the Catholic Church by Pope John Paul II, one his key admirers alongside Joseph Ratzinger (Pope Benedict XVI).

Balthasar's thought cuts in ways unfamiliar to many persons who are formed in the mode of critical theory and interdisciplinarity. While he joined the Jesuits in 1929, he left the order in 1950, partly because of his collaboration with a contemplative woman, Adrienne von Speyr, in establishing a lay, secular institute. It is her writings and mystical experiences which had a profound and lasting impact on his thought, an influence that he did much to corroborate. Also deeply influential on his thought were the philosophers of German idealism and the theologians of the *nouvelle théologie* in France and the Low countries, especially Henri de Lubac. The latter's influence probably accounts for his greater visibility after Vatican II, and his subsequent appointment to the Catholic Church's International Theological Commission. It is at this point that he gives voice to sharply anti-liberal theological views as well.

Balthasar was deeply influenced by the theology of Karl Barth in his approach to the Bible, but especially in regards to the centrality of Christ in the life of faith. In that regard, Balthasar's perspective on method is decidedly ensconced in the anti-Bultmann position that Barth constructed. Unlike Barth, however, Balthasar not only allows but positively celebrates the implicit theological significance of all human forms of the good, the true and the beautiful, what philosophers know and term the 'transcendentals'. Modelled on each one of the transcendentals, Balthasar's massive trilogy of multi-volume works (*The Glory of the* Lord, *Theo-drama* and *Theo-logic*) is testimony to the most learned theological absorption of European art, culture and philosophy in the twentieth century. It has even been said that Balthasar wrote more pages of theology than most theologians have read!

The shape of Balthasar's theology is impossible to delineate briefly. In continuity with Barth, it is steeped in an incarnational Christology. It is also a theology steeped in the practice of prayer, a 'kneeling theology', as he termed it. In contrast with Barth's theology, however, Balthasar takes the metaphysical categories of human thought and the reality of creation to be deeply informed by the power of God. He expresses a spiritual outlook that rejects de-mythologization, but not for the reasons that Barth rejected a gospel without dogma. Rather, Balthasar thinks that theology needs to retain philosophy as a partner in the great quest to speak of being and God. Theology needs myth and metaphysics, interpreted through philosophy and attached to faith. Christians are even 'called to be guardians of metaphysics' he says.[45] As the necessary context within which faith is nurtured and expressed, culture and myth are vital mediating languages of God's grace. So, Balthasar comes to reject the Bultmannian premise of de-mythologization. He also rejects thinking of faith solely as a personal decision. Otherwise, he argues, theology would 'serve only as a consolation for the existential subject'.[46]

Balthasar resented the (Suárezian) neo-scholasticism which he and his peers endured in their seminary formation. But a permanent theme running through his work is the need to emphasize the scholastic doctrine of *analogia entis*, the analogy of being inherited by Christianity to help speak of Christ through the presence of God in the whole world. Where Balthasar develops an almost wholly novel approach to analogy is with respect to its application to beauty, which he claims to be an underestimated analogue for divine glory. The *analogia entis* itself emanates from the medieval period in Aquinas's elaboration of the Fourth Lateran Council's holding to a greater dissimilarity between the Creator and the creature than exists in any similarity. For Balthasar, the theologian whose precise retrieval of analogy gives it the care and precision needed is the Jesuit theologian Erich Przywara (1889–1972).

Of course, Balthasar's reliance on analogy in his theology does not indicate a theological method *per se*, although it is an important criterion shaping his method. His entire corpus militates against an 'epistemological obsession' in theology, an obsession that assumes an individual subject cut off from the world in which humans were previously thought to participate. Method is one of those questions that, for Balthasar, as with Barth, tends to distract the theologian from the task at hand. So instead of subjecting theology to methodological constrictions, method is circumscribed by a single criterion for what makes a theological claim distinct. That criterion is analogy, as testified by such comments as the following:

> Without the notion of analogy nothing could be done with the question of the scientific structure of theology for it cannot possibly be placed univocally alongside other sciences (which argue from first principles evident to reason) . . . it can only then be called (analogously) a science, if what is accepted in faith can be appropriated intelligently in a genuine activity of reason. This implies two things: 1. It pertains to the essence of this and *only* this science, that its scientific objectivity rests upon the decision of faith. Therefore there can be (seen theologically) no neutral objectivity that deals with the object of faith without faith, or in other words, that prescinds from the issue of faith or lack of faith . . . 2. The apparently total isolation of theology from the rest of the sciences is being demolished in that the *Geisteswissenschaften* (human sciences-which only recently have become known in their true nature) are seen and accepted as the this-worldly proof of the analogy of the sciences. There is genuine science even of (relatively or completely) unique realities, even when these unique realities can be encompassed and expressed only with the instrumentality of a variety of analogies.[47]

Since Balthasar does not speak at length about interdisciplinarity, or of the structure of theology, or about the need to correlate theology methodologically with findings from the other sciences, we need to take these words seriously. And, from the kind of claim he makes here, we detect some profound agreement with Barth on the specific character of theology's scientific pedigree, as well as the priority of faith. Both thinkers give and take a great deal on this issue. Barth, as we have seen, wants to specify theology's scientific character with respect to the discipline of dogmatics, while Balthasar is not as specific. Yet, contrary to Barth's restriction of analogy to the analogy of faith, Balthasar offers a vigorous defence of the analogy of being. It is as strong as any defence of a specific kind of theological epistemology as one is likely to read in a twentieth-century theologian. Also unlike Barth, Balthasar is thinking of theology as a form of reflection that carries within it the need for a system. Whereas Barth thinks of dogmatic theology as propositions that follow in some sense as interpretations of the Word of God, Balthasar provides a much more elaborate account of the subjective mediations that attend such interpretations, such that the whole requires a systematic approach.

Balthasar offers a large number of surprising elements which suggest that, once again unlike Barth, he thinks of theology as not only systematic but also as a discipline that seeks correlations with forms of truth, goodness and beauty in the world. Balthasar thus agrees with Bultmann to some extent, in contrast to Barth's monistic reductionism, that:

> Theology has no choice but to make use of the concepts and categories fashioned by philosophy – how else could it think about revelation? But it must guard against simply equating the content of revelation with the content of philosophical concepts.[48]

In Balthasar's case, of course, it is Christ and the Word of God made real through the witness of the (Catholic) Church which measures whatever convergences and comparisons that can be made between theological truth claims and other truth claims. Balthasar himself gives the example of a 'fully developed Christology' that a theology which is bereft of philosophy would be unable to construct for this very reason.

He offers, as another instance, numerous references to salvation history as a drama. A more adequate understanding of salvation history is achieved when one understands, first, what makes for an adequate understanding of drama. Though God's entry into history through Christ is unique and stands as the measure of all human drama, nevertheless, as Dante and Virgil show, human drama historically takes on a particular form. This idea or general category of form is also crucial to an understanding of Balthasar's distinctive theology. Dante, for instance, is a crucial poet figure for extending what Balthasar calls the vocation of the 'lay theologian', conceived as the vocation of one who, like this poet, speaks about human existence from the perspective of hybrid thought forms. Balthasar notes that this 'lay' style involves, in the case of Dante, a mixture of elements 'scholastic and mystical, pagan-antique and Christian, sacral politics and spiritual Franciscanism, of courtly love and metaphysical wisdom, yet in such a way that "his work is not a sum total but an indivisible prime number"'.[49] Such is Balthasar's conception of mediation: an exchange of styles, purposes and languages, the interpenetration of the secular and eternal realms without the fear of weakening the singular message and meaning of Christ. The Word of God is not only revelation but a form of forms, a fulfilment of human longing which, while it cannot be anticipated by humanity, can nevertheless be understood in relation to human nature. Salvation history, as a super-drama, is the story into which all human action fits as drama. The super-drama operates to contextualize and comprehend the drama, but to be sure, human action within the drama plays a role in the workings of salvation history. Worldly dramas provide insight into salvation history, even if they are ultimately inadequate for a full understanding of it.

Perhaps Balthasar's theology of Holy Saturday and his understanding of God's victory over death illustrate his method most succinctly. His theology of Christ's descent into hell is among the most well known of his theological reflections. It has more recently come under more scrutiny as well. Nonetheless, Balthasar adapts a long-running Christological motif of descent and ascent in order to affirm what he thinks it means, dramatically speaking: 'It is for the sake of this day that the Son became man.'[50] Those familiar with Christian doctrine are accustomed to the famous soteriological principle attributed to Athanasius: 'Christ became man so that man could become God.'[51] Balthasar twists this around to restrain the soteriological reason for the Incarnation before affirming the dramatic reason for it. Thus, in this instance at least, Balthasar does not alter the Christological doctrine through his interpretation of it, but he does make a serious rearrangement of the categories by which the doctrine makes any sense to begin with.

Balthasar's focus on form (his *Gestalt* theology, as it has been called) leads to a typological reading of scripture too. His citations of scripture are enough to convince us that his systematic theology is, among other things, a theology for understanding the Bible in its wider dramatic context. Such a move begins with Balthasar's unsurprising emphasis on the integrity of the biblical text, written with a view not only to a theological drama into which the reader is invited to participate. But also, the biblical texts are, from a literary standpoint, creations that bear an integrity that do not merit mere historical-critical analysis, with its characteristic reductionism. These two points render Balthasar's approach distinct from more 'conventional' theological exegesis.

Echoing his enthusiastic attention for the church fathers, Balthasar articulates a fourfold type of saint, according to whether holy persons conform to the distinct ministry of Peter, Paul, James or John/Mary.[52] Mary herself is pure human form, due to the purity of her receptivity to God, modelled, according to Balthasar, on the perfect humility of Christ. Talk of form and type with respect to scripture brings us far beyond a mere employment of non-literal ways of reading scripture and towards a metaphysical theology that takes the material world, including human literary achievement, to be a sacramental sign of God's creation. It is no coincidence that Balthasar continually refers to the doctrine of creation in his theology, but as a doctrine, creation is the product of both an approach to scripture and of human spiritual experience. Again, as with Barth, Balthasar offers a systematic theology that is rooted in the doctrinal traditions of the church. Yet his systematic theology, through reference to the less predictable features of the biblical narrative and history, is articulated in a unique metaphysically shaped form.

Karl Rahner

A fixture of Catholic theology in the last half of the twentieth century, Karl Rahner was a Jesuit priest and theologian whose influence on the shape and contents of the Second Vatican Council was profound. He died in 1984. Rahner is best known and appreciated by many for offering a 'transcendental method', a way of articulating theological claims on the basis of an anthropological starting point and through attention to the human experience of asking questions. While the roots of his methodological outlook are Kantian and resemble Tillich's approach as well, his early scholarly work was indeed very philosophical and rooted in an interpretation of Aquinas. Yet Rahner's application of his method is distinctly different from the existentialist thrust of German theology of the twentieth century. The uniqueness of Rahner's theology is perhaps best glimpsed by a reading of the 23-volume *Theological Investigations* (*TI*), much of which takes up pastoral issues and church doctrines. Indeed, as Rahner said of his concern with 'practical theology', a term he proposed to replace the too-specific ministerial connotations of 'pastoral theology', it is 'the critical conscience of the other theological disciplines'.[53]

The density of Rahner's writing and his obvious interest in the ecclesiological concerns of the Catholic Church appear to be contradictory impulses. Indeed, this paradox threatens a coherent presentation of Rahner's theological method. What makes matters more complex is that Rahner did not explicitly discuss his theological method as Lonergan did. What he does offer his readers is a massive sprinkling of theological reflection on diverse topics that concatenate into an impression of a general scheme. Also, Rahner never wrote a series or a set of works in systematic theology. His way of speaking of system in theology as a system of 'what cannot be systematized' is testimony to his appreciation of the role of mystery as endpoint in the attainment of theological knowledge.[54] Thus, he treated many diverse topics in his occasional essays collected in the *TI* and elsewhere. In perhaps his most widely read book, *The Foundations of Christian Faith*, Rahner lays out an introduction to Christianity, beginning with some reflections on the way that theology and philosophy interact in the context of considering human beings as 'hearers of the word'. This phrase serves as the title of an earlier work in which Rahner considers the conditions for the possibility of receiving a revelation of God. This style of theology is probably the strongest methodological aspect of Rahner's work, and it is for this reason that his work is termed 'transcendental', a term which Canadian philosopher Charles Taylor defines as the following kind of argument: 'from an unquestionable feature of experience to a stronger thesis as the condition of its possibility.'[55]

Transcendental methodology, then, does not really comprise a set of definite procedures for Rahner, or even a particular starting principle; it is an epistemological clarification around what theological statements are. Rahner wants to evaluate the ultimate basis for a claim but not the steps taken to make it. He is not interested in the truth or falsehood of particular doctrinal claims by way of ordinary exegetical or historical analysis. This relative lack of interest in exegesis is rooted in the theology of revelation that he shares, more or less, with Tillich. Rahner thinks of revelation in terms of encounter, not as the reception of a body of propositions or exegetical statements.

Moreover, Rahner seeks an ontological ground for making the particular claims that are in fact associated with the Christian tradition, even very particular claims that make up the thrust of Catholic thinking. In his development of particular themes, however, his theology contains very few, if any, references to scripture. He acknowledges this paucity of references to scripture in the preface to *Foundations*. Even in his treatment of the relationship between scripture and tradition or biblical interpretation, he rarely addresses exegetical problems with regard to scripture. For these reasons and more, George Lindbeck, in his widely read book *The Nature of Doctrine*, criticizes Rahner for assuming that the language of Christian doctrine is a mere cultural imprint of generic human religious experience. This criticism comes with Lindbeck's label 'experiential-expressivism', the charge that Rahner posits some kind of pre-linguistic experience that ends up replacing God's revelation in Christ.

True, in setting up this enterprise of transcendental theology, Rahner allows, to a large extent, philosophy to express what he means to say theologically. Rahner had attended Martin Heidegger's lectures during the 1930s. And, the philosophical thrust of Rahner's writing contributes to the frustration experienced by those who find him difficult reading. His decision to employ philosophy to express theological ideas is a distinct strategy from that of Bultmann, however, despite their mutual reliance upon Heidegger and existentialism more broadly. For Rahner, existentialism carries metaphysical significance, and as such is bound up with the quest of faith, because the quest for knowledge is really a quest for mystery ('Absolute Mystery', as he calls it), which is actually a quest for God.

Influenced by his early exposure to the *Spiritual Exercises* of Ignatius Loyola, Rahner took to heart two Jesuit impulses: one, the fusion of the quest for knowledge and the quest for God; and two, the contention that the roots of any knowledge of God make up an experience of God. For Rahner, experience, or religious experience, is not a clearly defined matter. It is not completely separable from much of ordinary experience. Yet, the transcendental element of experience is essentially the mysterious aspect of human living, and it is mediated through what Rahner calls the categorical, finite realms of experience as that which is essentially mysterious. Without an experience of God, moreover, a Christian theology of grace breaks apart. The transcendent is also omnipresent and available to all, as a backdrop to all experience, the famous pre-apprehension of being (or *Vorgriff*) of Rahner's theological anthropology. Contrary to Lindbeck, however, Rahner is not saying that theology be *derived* from experience, nor even really that theology should always be *about* experience, but that it cannot ever be presented as fundamentally detached from us, as really having nothing to do with us'.[56] Thus, theology should be attached to human experience, though a philosophical expression of that experience may be called for.

Another methodological criterion which strongly conveys the thrust of Rahner's thinking is the conviction about the symbolic nature of things. Symbols, unlike signs, simultaneously represent and fulfil the reality being represented. An entity's identity is achieved in its expression, perhaps a vision rooted in Kant's distinction between the unknowable *noumena* and the knowable *phenomena*. The symbolic principle affects the way he carries out theology in a variety of contexts, whether in terms of the Trinity (the famous identity of the 'economic' and the 'immanent' Trinity) or sacraments.

One of Rahner's abiding concerns is the status and meaning of doctrine, Christology in particular. Again, his aim is ontological and foundational, with an eye on the insight into the development of doctrine so prized by Newman and the Catholic Reformers of Vatican II. Rahner wants to supply not simply a justification for the Chalcedonian dogma about Christ's person ('one person, two natures'), but also to reflect theologically on the systematic theological problems that are entailed by the Chalcedonian definition. For instance, in the article 'Chalcedon: End or Beginning?', Rahner revisits the council's use of the terms 'person' and 'nature' in light of the use of those terms in contemporary culture. The word 'person' is used by the council to refer to the entity of divine-human unity, whereas moderns think of 'person' in the psychological terms that the council reserved for the human nature of Christ. If the doctrine is to have plausibility, according to Rahner, basic terminological and systematic issues, such as this one, have to be resolved. Rahner asks:

how can the whole of Christological dogma be formulated so as to allow the Lord to appear as Messianic Mediator and so as true Man . . . ? who, standing before God on our side in free

human obedience, is Mediator, not only in virtue of the ontological union of two natures, but also through his activity, which
is directed to God (as obedience to the will of the Father) and
cannot simply be conceived of *simply* as God's activity in and
through a human nature thought of as purely instrumental, a
nature which in relation to the Logos would be, ontologically
and morally, purely passive?[57]

Accordingly, Rahner also interprets the Chalcedonian formula in
order to arrive at a different conception of the God-world relationship
than that expressed by neo-scholasticism. Rahner insists on a 'real
relation' between God and the world, whereas early twentieth-
century neo-scholastics took Aquinas to mean that God and the
world are two separate orders, the supernatural and the natural.
Here we have a major difference in the interpretation of creation
and Christ's saving grace. According to Rahner, the Chalcedonian
formula itself suggests a basically correlational dynamic between
human nature and grace, as in the medieval adage 'grace builds on
nature, it does not destroy it'. Rahner thus formulates his famous
'supernatural existential' to indicate his opposition to a notion of
'pure nature' in theology. The methodological point is that in order
to make these points in Christology and theological anthropology,
Rahner creatively interprets and begins from a point of traditional
doctrine. His strategy is essentially twofold: to uncover what are
sometimes hidden meanings in the terms, and to offer foundational
categories that underpin the formulation of doctrine before
correlating the newly transformed doctrine itself to some aspect of
contemporary culture and experience.

Before moving on, let us note one additional complexity that is
very important. What Rahner does by re-working the meaning of
Christian doctrine is, effectively, to operate in a way that Karl Barth
would have approved. Like Barth, Rahner begins with a doctrinal
tradition in order to explicate other aspects of reality in light of it.
Thus, his theology can be seen as apologetic. To be sure, Barth then
contrasts the reality of God's saving Word with the worldly rejection
of that Word. Rahner, on the other hand, while beginning with
doctrinal formulations on several occasions, proceeds to couch his
reflections on those formulations in relation to culturally relevant
foundational and systematic theology. This comparison simply
goes to show that for all the famous differences between Barth and

Rahner, as the exemplary Protestant and Catholic theologians of the twentieth century, there are still some basic methodological similarities. In the end, Barth and Rahner differ over whether theology and culture are to be contrasted or correlated, but they both begin their inquiries by considering doctrine.

Rahner and Barth also disagree on other matters in serious ways, such as the question of whether Christ's person is unique (Barth) or simply exemplary (Rahner), and whether salvation in Christ is exclusive of other narratives of salvation (Barth) or whether salvation in Christ is complemented by 'searching christologies' implied by our transcendental nature, thus leading to the possibility of anonymous Christians (Rahner). In the end, for Rahner, the effort to complement the doctrinal tradition suggests that his theology is the effort to relate the particular with the universal. Rahner is not engaging in a straightforward, explicitly correlationist theology, as in the case of Tillich. But, his reflections upon how the particular (tradition) is taken up in the universal is basically a correlationist method. It certainly provides grounds for his critics to see his treatment of doctrine as something more anthropological than theological, an extension of philosophy rather than a disjunction between philosophy and theology. It is also for this same reason that his admirers see in his vision of Christian existence something grand and accomplished.

Edward Schillebeeckx

One of the most creative Catholic theologians of the twentieth century, whose work spans two theological epochs before and after Vatican II, Edward Schillebeeckx died in late 2009. Born in 1914, he was a Flemish Dominican priest who spent the bulk of his theological career at the Catholic University of Nijmegen (now Radboud University) in the Netherlands. Inspired, first, by the life and work of Marie-Dominique Chenu, one of the great Dominican proponents of the *nouvelle théologie* in the decade leading up to Vatican II, Schillebeeckx himself went on to become one of the most learned and well-respected advisors to the Dutch bishops at the Second Vatican Council, although he was not an official advisor, formally speaking. He attracted the attention of the Vatican and Pope Paul VI, particularly for his advocacy of the term 'transignification' to communicate in a contemporary way how the bread and wine of the Eucharist represent Christ's body and blood. His choice came under fire from Catholic authorities, including the Pope, who in a 1965 encyclical, *Mysterium fidei*, restated the church's preference for language that retained the objective reality of Eucharistic substance instead of the merely subjective meaning for those elements as Schillebeeckx proposed. This was an early skirmish that was a harbinger of things to come.

Like Tillich, Schillebeeckx promotes the mutually critical correlation of the Christian tradition with church life and cultural experience. What Schillebeeckx adds to the concept of critical correlation is the explicit socio-political dimension that is relatively absent in Tillich. For Schillebeeckx, the hermeneutical task is established not only on the basis of advances made by Gadamer and Ricoeur, but also on the basis of critical theory of the Frankfurt School, especially the contributions of Max Horkheimer and Theodor Adorno. He did not arrive at this theological engagement with political theory lightly, however. In his early years as a theologian, Schillebeeckx had focused on the sacramental dimension and related ecclesiological concerns. By the time he came to write his last large study *Church: The Human Story of God* in 1989, Schillebeeckx had returned to the issue of the structure and authority of the church, but with a totally different perspective than that with which he had initiated his study of sacramental theology back in the 1950s. His own tensions with the Congregation for the Doctrine of the Faith at the Vatican climaxed in 1979 with an interview that led to the eventual conclusion the next year that Schillebeeckx's theology would not receive condemnation for error.

His engagement with critical political theory is not by any means a surrender of theological ground to another discipline. Indeed, the two volumes of his theological systematics develop an alternative formulation of Christology, brought on by his formation under Marie-Dominique Chenu and by his discovery of hermeneutics in 1965. In *Jesus* and then *Christ*, both of which were published in the 1980s, Schillebeeckx shapes a new approach to Jesus Christ. This approach is the retrieval of the historical experience of Jesus by the early church, a reversal of Bultmann's separation of faith and history. It is worth considering the contrarian possibility that it is more plausible to think of Schillebeeckx, not Barth, as the theologian who most forcefully opposes Bultmann's separation of faith and history. For Schillebeeckx, knowledge of the historical context of the gospel helps us understand the gospel and its powerful message.

In his two-volume Christology, which contains a myriad of tangential suggestions informed by biblical exegesis and philosophy alike, Schillebeeckx adopts a distinctively anthropological viewpoint towards salvation by taking the historical accounts of Jesus' ministry on earth most seriously. Unique for blending a doctrinal concern with historical analysis, Schillebeeckx succeeds in writing a theology that sees the methodological criterion of coherence between the universal and the particular, between doctrine and the experiences reported in the Bible. Hampered by occasional lapses in reasoning and accused by many of eclecticism, Schillebeeckx nonetheless performs a feat of immense benefit by bringing into close contact fields of inquiry that usually have nothing to do with one another. Were it not for his resolute focus on the historical experience of the first Christians and modern critical theory, this approach might resemble many other modern Christologies based on the criterion of experience in the construction of theological statements. However, Schillebeeckx moves decisively beyond the late twentieth-century methodological stand-off between biblical exegesis and doctrinal theology by choosing the very particular experience of the historical suffering of Jesus as the basis for thinking about him and believing in him. Taking his cue from critical theorists, Schillebeeckx talks about negative experiences:

> Ideas and expectations of salvation and human happiness are invariably projected from within concrete experience and the pondered fact of calamity, pain, misery and alienation – from within negative experiences accumulated through centuries of affliction, with here and there a fleeting promise of a happier lot, fragmentary experiences of well-being in a story, stretching from generation to generation, of hopes unfulfilled, of guilt and evil – the 'Job's problem' of our human history. Hence there eventually emerges an anthropological projection, a vision of what is held to be the true, good and happy mode of human life. This is why man's craving for happiness and well-being, always being submitted to critical judgment yet again and again surviving every critique, inevitably acquires – in diverse forms – the pregnant nuance of 'release from' or 'deliverance out of' and – at the same time – of entering into a 'completely new world'.[58]

This might be the kind of talk about salvation that Karl Barth could not abide. It would also seem to be vulnerable to Ludwig Feuerbach's famous charge that all of theology is a consequence of anthropological projection. But, in the case of Schillebeeckx, the desire for release from suffering is linked to more than some claim about God or transcendence. It is associated with the very historical reality of the life, passion and death of Jesus. This Christology is a 'narrative practical christology', a Christology that does not begin with the events marked in the church's liturgical calendar during Holy week. Instead, his Christology begins with the life of Jesus, which implies that for Schillebeeckx, 'in one sense, we are saved despite the death of Jesus'.[59] This is an extraordinary claim, but it is made utterly possible by Schillebeeckx's radically anthropocentric theological method. For him, the anthropological starting point leads to a consideration of Jesus' human life in which God's revelation is evident as Jesus resists sin and evil. This methodological choice contrasts starkly with much of the traditional Christology, with its focus on the atonement wrought through Jesus' death, not to mention the formulations of Jesus' personhood at the Councils of Nicaea and Chalcedon. Nevertheless, echoing the concerns of political theologians, Schillebeeckx deals with Jesus' death too as the 'ultimate negative contrast experience', language borrowed freely from critical theory but expressing precisely where God is to be found.

For Schillebeeckx, the climax of his position, and therefore the climax of his theological method, is his reflection on the critical value of suffering for doing theology. Suffering unites the two most basic forms of human knowledge: the active and the contemplative. Since suffering can prompt us to reflect and to take action, it is a form of experience that becomes a privileged locus of revelation. He clarifies that the kind of suffering that he validates is the suffering borne in relation to a cause, a suffering that is for the other. Schillebeeckx is not validating random or meaningless suffering. But what does this mean? For Schillebeeckx, the suffering Christ becomes the privileged locus of God's revelation. In Christ, there is no straightforward answer to the human question. Correlation for Schillebeeckx does not suggest a correlation between some human question and some other divine answer.

In the man Jesus, man's question about himself and the human answer to this question are translated into a divine question put to man and the divine answer to this question: Jesus is the Son of God, expressed in terms of humanity. He *is* the question-answer correlation.[60]

We need to stand back for a moment to appreciate the move that Schillebeeckx makes with regards to his narrative practical Christology. At first glance, we are dealing with an anthropologically sensitive theological method that begins where most twentieth-century Western theology begins: with an aspect of human inquiry, structured in this case according to socio-political priorities. But where we end up is frankly not that far from a Barthian approach. By identifying the experience of Jesus in such stark, ultimate terms, Schillebeeckx has almost travelled full circle as he takes the negative dialectics of the Frankfurt School to what he feels is its logical conclusion: a universal pre-understanding of positive views of human beings which is captured in the life, suffering, death and resurrection of Jesus. Now, admittedly, with the resurrection, we begin to see radical discontinuities between him and more traditional theologians – for instance, Schillebeeckx echoes the theology of correlationists by speaking of the resurrection strongly in terms of the rise of faith in the disciples and among the early Christians.

The most revolutionary aspect of Schillebeeckx's theology may not be the role he assigns to human experience, however. If it were, Schillebeeckx would be justifiably categorized in terms similar to those of Bultmann. But, Schillebeeckx is engaging in something noticeably different from Bultmann's methodical framework. He is not a 'Catholic Bultmannian'. Indeed, even on a subject as fraught as the resurrection, he questions the extent to which New Testament exegetes like Bultmann have fallen into the trap of equating the resurrection and belief in the resurrection as 'one and the same thing'.[61]

Schillebeeckx is offering a Christology that avoids both Bultmann's turn to the faith of the subject, on the one hand, and the doctrinal tradition which develops Christology exclusively from the purview of the creed on the other hand. He is offering, instead, a 'third way' in theology, a methodological direction that lies between the historical-critical method and the dogmatic tradition. He does this by stressing the distinction between the Easter experience and its interpreted expression; for instance, regarding the 'empty tomb' narratives. The priority given to the visual aspect of the experience of

Jesus' resurrection shows that the interpretive framework governing any expression of faith is present in the experience. It does not come later. Yet Schillebeeckx retains the distinction in advocating the importance of interpreted experience as the hermeneutical basis for all theology.

By prioritizing experience, Schillebeeckx is not introducing a better way of engaging in biblical exegesis than the standard historical critical treatments necessarily, although that has been how his work was interpreted by some biblical scholars. Rather, he sets himself the very foundational task of relating his account of experience through the prism of the early followers of Jesus to the concept of revelation. Revelation, contrary to so much of Christian tradition, is not a message, but 'an experience that became a message'.[62] Revelation, as Schillebeeckx is anxious to assert, is neither a subjective (Bultmann) nor an objective (literalist) form of divine communication, but is both of these together. Affirming something that is reminiscent of Bonaventure, and even Joseph Ratzinger, Schillebeeckx fosters a theological method that stresses the links between history and experience or foundations. His basic insight is that one cannot historically reconstruct the gospels without forgetting that the distinction between experience and interpretation that is present in the scriptural text is also present in the interpreter.

Schillebeeckx attempts to relate a kind of primary interpretation onto the experience of the early Christians to which the contemporary interpreter might relate, but in practice this is extraordinarily difficult to achieve. Nevertheless, as mentioned already with respect to the theme of suffering, it would seem that Schillebeeckx has achieved some measure of success by following through with his distinction between experience and interpretation and his tying revelation to experience, because, as a consequence, he has articulated a way beyond the simplistic Bultmannian approach to history. For Schillebeeckx, history is not a set of objective facts to which the interpreter stands from the outside. Rather, for Schillebeeckx, it is still possible to discern the revelatory aspect of the original experience not as something merely preached, but also as something encountered from God.

One of the critical insights that Schillebeeckx makes late in his career is the connection between his approach to the biblical accounts of the person of Jesus and the late twentieth-century philosophy of science. Especially key is the thought of Thomas Kuhn who, along with several others, develops the notion of interpreted experience, the idea that there is no such thing as raw or uninterpreted experience.

If there is a criticism that we might make of Schillebeeckx in regards to method, it would be that he is inconsistent in following through with his initial desire to critically assess the interpretive framework of the early Christians. He averts his gaze away from the salvation brought through Christ, especially in the second part of his two volume Christology - and in other works too – by incorporating other, disparate ideas. Schillebeeckx allows a number of disparate elements to accompany the early tight methodological rigour that he wants to apply. Also missing, according to philosopher Louis Dupré, is a critical awareness of some of the modernisms in his own thought, such as the speculations that he takes up about God, captured in such chapter subtitles as 'God Does Not Want Mankind to Suffer'. For a theologian as daring as Schillebeeckx on the relationship between interpretation and revelation, Dupré wonders why 'while discussing the relation between God and the creature, he briefly confronts the issue of pantheism and panentheism, but peremptorily dismisses it'.[63] When Schillebeeckx comes to translate some of the traditional philosophical frameworks into the more 'secular idiom of contemporary culture), Dupré wonders whether this is executed in an imbalanced way: critical with regards to the traditional philosophy but accommodating towards the secular culture of modernity. If one may diagnose Schillebeeckx's ambivalence in any structured way, we might say that he is much more deft with regards to the relationship between the present of foundational theology and the past of historical interpretations of Christ. What he lacks from a methodological perspective, employing Lonergan as our means of a diagnosis , is a systematic account. A full-blown constructive intent seems to elude Schillebeeckx in his critical methodology. This may be seen in his less than adept handling of the issue of panentheism. Nevertheless, it should not obscure what is a significant theological achievement. The vision that Schillebeeckx employs is a root and branch re-aligning of the relationship between a revelation-based theology and historical-critical methodology in biblical studies. Exposed is the philosophically time-bound character of Bultman and the empiricist bias in many historical-critical studies too. He also hints at a more open and experiential

Catholic theology of revelation, which is more biblical and less
laden with the problematic aspects of the phrase 'deposit of faith'.
In conclusion, theology for Schillebeeckx is a dialectical enterprise
that serves the tasks of contemplation and action (praxis). In this
respect, his theology resembles a sophisticated liberation theology
that fuses certain theological tasks while eschewing the systematic
impulse of theology.

Conclusion

In conclusion, we can see that in this diverse sampling of twentieth-
century theologians, methodical themes running in a number of
directions. Even in thinkers with obvious interests in a systematic
theology, such as Barth and Tillich, we can see radically diverse
means of implementing a systematic theology. In this comparison,
we see quite clearly that the descriptive term 'systematic theology'
is inadequate for distinguishing the method, not to mention the
contents, of these respective theologians. The difference between
these theologians is even difficult to boil down to the question
of whether philosophy be admitted to speak for theology. That is
obviously a point which supports the strength of Tillich's systematics
to flourish because of its philosophical flexibility. However, it is also
arguable that Barth may possess greater strength to his 'method'
because of the confidence he has in the doctrinal traditions of
Confessional Reformed orthodoxy, which determine what may and
may not be systematized. Barth's judgements are strong pillars for
a distinctly theological enterprise. Of course Barth's approach is
hampered by a lack of adept handling of philosophical matters,
apart from a limited engagement with Kierkegaard and Kant. Thus,
the portrait of twentieth-century theology is one of mixed strengths
and weaknesses in regards to method. Some theologians are strong
on procedural matters or philosophy, while others are strong on the
coherence of the criteria or the perception of the theological task
which directs the theological inquiry.

Is it possible to construct a philosophically adept theology with
methodical gravitas which, at the same time, contains within it a
respect for the historical judgements elaborated through doctrine
on the basis of theological categories? The twentieth century
seems, if anything, to have provided us with repeated suggestions

that there is a mutually exclusive relationship between methodical awareness and theological identity. Tillich is methodically aware, while Barth is clear about theological identity – and this choice of emphasis re-appears in numerous descriptions of twentieth-century theologians as either liberal (methodical) or conservative (doctrinal and non-methodical). In the final chapter we will consider a few examples of figures and movements on the contemporary theological scene whose work *combines* methodical rigour with a robust theological identity. There are indications that now, in the twenty-first century, we are moving past the methodological divisions of the twentieth century.

CHAPTER EIGHT

Contemporary theological method as wisdom

Whereas the twentieth century is witness to strongly divergent directions in theological method, a glance at the contemporary theological scene reveals much more subtle forces at work in overlapping perspectives on theological method. In this chapter, I will briefly account for some of these fresh subtleties. Naturally, an overview of contemporary developments extends the narrative of Chapter Seven where the division between correlationist and anti-correlationist theological approaches was laid out. As we saw, this division has become a fixed feature of the theological scene from the late nineteenth century onwards. But, contemporary developments are taking on a new hue in distinction to the bold divergences of the recent past.

This chapter will draw on the tendencies of several theological schools of thought and individual figures to make the case that contemporary theology is increasingly wedded to a fusion of methodical concerns with a clearer theological identity. This chapter will examine the causes of post-liberal theology, Radical Orthodoxy and liberation theology, as well as review some of the methodological insights of Joseph Ratzinger (Pope Benedict XVI) in order to explore the possibilities of theological method as wisdom.

German theologian and Catholic Cardinal Walter Kasper has said that 'If the church worries about identity, it risks a loss of relevance; if on the other hand it struggles for relevance, it may forfeit its identity'.[1] This catch-22, which Kasper identified in the 1970s, was a reality that faced the church at that time and is still a dynamic in many Christian churches today. But it is a much less significant dynamic in contemporary theology, where methodical concerns have receded from view to some extent, to be replaced by a more adept range of theological proposals which marry method and theological identity. This marriage or fusion of method with theological identity is being carried out in a pluralistic world of scholarship which is expressed in vastly differing degrees of ecclesial commitments. Nevertheless, a certain awareness of theological reflection as wisdom is evident among contemporary theologies. Such wisdom seeks to overcome earlier naive correlationism and naive traditionalism.

For instance, despite the obvious disjunctions, a certain parallel exists between the tradition-minded post-liberal theologians associated with Yale Divinity School in the United States and the liberationist, feminist and post-colonial theology that has sprouted forth in many geographic regions. Counterintuitive as it may seem, both traditions of theology think about God through an explicit recourse to narrative, including the narrative of biblical text, human experience and, especially, both of these together. Of course, this observation is just a descriptive instance of similar style. It is true that there are more fundamental questions at stake.

What this book has revealed, in summary, are five fundamental questions at issue in theological method. They are:

1 the role of philosophy and related epistemological and metaphysical presuppositions in theology
2 the coherence of individual criteria that serve as theological starting points (e.g. Barth's Word of God)
3 how one emphasizes various sources of theology such as the Bible
4 the nature of the theological task (e.g. Tillich's conception of critical correlation with other disciplines)
5 procedure (e.g. Lonergan's functional specialties).

Each of these five questions includes within it subsidiary issues. For instance, in terms of the emphasis on scripture, as per Question 3, there is the subsidiary question of whether *sola scriptura* should be understood to mean that scripture interprets itself, in the sense that the biblical text provides the means to interpret one passage or book by means of other biblical passages and/or books. The emphasis on scripture and its interpretation was the most compelling issue in theological method for many church fathers and Reformation theologians, as we have already seen. But in raising that issue of a source, another issue of the criteria of its raising is also implicated.

While that issue has never gone away and never will, the history of methodology in Christian theology is a history of one relatively small issue slowly evolving to ensnare other methodological issues. The approach towards scripture, such as the method of allegory, eventually gave way to the issue of hermeneutics as Augustine conceptualized it. The need for a hermeneutic necessitated the establishment of criteria and procedures, something that the medieval theologians, in particular, would come to embody in their work. Such a narrative can be seen as a movement from problems involved in providing a meaning system for the biblical narrative to a problem of making that system of meaning coherent, generally speaking. This involved, as Lonergan would say, moving from questions of understanding the text to questions about how one should judge between different interpretations of the text, as well as the further judgement of how categories and their doctrines might formulate what the historical judgements of interpretation meant. Thus, the engagement with scripture has meant a movement over time from interpretation to history to dialectics, with some eventual returns to interpretation under the guidance of new insights or categories of thought.

Each of the theologians and movements described in this book are involved directly in one methodological problem but implicated either backwards or forwards in other methodological issues. In the twentieth century, individual questions of method tended to be selected for attention and emphasis in purposeful isolation from particular methodological priorities; whether the priority of history was raised to the exclusion of doctrine or vice versa, for instance. In the contemporary period, they tend to arise together; that is, it seems more apparent in recent theological movements and contemporary theologians that theological method is perceived as an important issue in the communication of theological wisdom.

Radical Orthodoxy

According to Radical Orthodoxy (RO), a theological 'movement' that emerged in the United Kingdom, a moribund theological culture has resulted from a close entwinement between theology and the reigning social scientific narrative of human nature, human desire and meaning. Embracing what John Milbank terms a 'postmodern critical Augustinianism',[2] Radical Orthodox theologians are inspired by Neo-Platonism, postmodernism, the *nouvelle théologie* of Henri de Lubac, as well as several other theological currents. It is an ecumenical yet catholic effort to raise up the importance of ontology in theological discourse while chiding theological (correlationist) accommodation to the West's radical secularization. In the words of James K. A. Smith, RO seeks a 'post-secular theology'.[3]

Writing against what he regards as a radical secularization in cultural habits and social expectations, Milbank and other British theologians have articulated the problems that beset the theological mimicking of social scientific methods. While Radical Orthodox theologians strongly validate the role of philosophy at the heart of the theological task, their criterion for theological reflection is not reducible to one category, such as Barth's Word of God. Nor does Radical Orthodoxy subscribe to anything like the critical correlationism that previous theological movements which appropriated philosophy tried to achieve.

More vitally, there is a strong assertion of theology's rightful independence from other disciplines and opposition to a cultural environment that is inimical to the aims of the Christian theologian. For Radical Orthodoxy, theological method is not about procedure. As Milbank's own adoption of the category of gift shows, it is more concerned with criteria for starting theological reflection properly. Milbank's theology has been termed a 'rhetorical method'. I take this to signify a form of foundational theology – in Lonergan's terms – because of its focus on particular categories as ways by which theology needs to articulate a post-Christendom, post-liberal church. Milbank and his colleagues Catherine Pickstock, Graham Ward, Connor Cunningham and others, understand theological criteria and principles as first steps in establishing procedures, not the other way around.

Akin to Barth's doctrinal *loci*, Radical Orthodox theologians prioritize judgements of a particular kind that establish the terms of systematic theology and interdisciplinary inquiry. Coalescing the engagement with philosophy alongside the setting of their theological agenda, Radical Orthodox theologians endorse postmodern philosophical insights and language. For instance, relying on Gilles Deleuze and using the thought of Jacques Derrida as a foil, Milbank shows how the category of gift, for example, can be shown to enlighten the theological horizon from within the most secular of thought habits:

> in local societies, creativity in gift-giving, and (I am arguing) gift *as such*, has a somewhat restricted place. By exactly the same token, spontaneous generosity is subordinate to the priority of debt, or the duty to always return things to their 'proper' places, and maintain the *same* things in circulation . . . in local gift economies, contract characteristically *interrupts* status, but only to bring it as far as possible back within the scope of status, or the identically repeated . . . Without a primary relationality, there can be no gift-exchange, and without the latter, no gift at all . . . But such a primary relationality was already thought by the Hebrews. It is established in the notion of a covenant (*berith*) with God or other humans.[4]

This briefest of quotes explicates the reversal of critical correlationism, something Milbank's entire corpus, beginning with the blockbuster *Theology and Social Theory* (Blackwell, 1990), has endeavoured to do. The success (or notoriety) of the book is as much a matter of theological methodology as any particular material contents which that book and others contain. Milbank shows how philosophical insights depend upon a theologically laden view of things. On the matter of gift exchange, Catherine Pickstock's *After Writing: On the Liturgical Consummation of Philosophy* provides a similar methodological perspective. She argues, among other things, for language's doxological character: 'Language exists primarily, and in the end only has meaning as, the praise of the divine.'[5] The precision of language's true meaning is exemplified in the Roman rite of the Mass. Theology, on this account, does not need a hermeneutical theory, so much as language, hermeneutically and historically situated as it is, needs theology for it to be understood as such.

The constructive intent of this theological movement is unmistakable in two respects. Radical Orthodoxy issues a critical questioning in regards to Enlightenment modernity and its impact on all modern theology, a diagnosis made possible through postmodern theology. But, RO issues a second critique against postmodernism itself, through a retrieval of Christian theology's most traditional sources and doctrinal reference points. In procedural terms, therefore, RO does not engage in the recourse to history that we find in Schleiermacher, Ritschl or Schillebeeckx. Neither is there the straightforward recourse to doctrine, as we find in Newman, Barth or von Balthasar. Radical Orthodox theologians offer a different form of constructive theology. It is foundational theology in Lonergan's sense of the term, a theology that hinges on the opening provided by categories such as gift and sacrifice, categories that relate general philosophical or anthropological meaning in the service of theological meaning. Because of its deep-rooted *ressourcement* or theological retrieval of basic categories of thought, Radical Orthodoxy seeks a comprehensive vision, the basis for the possibility of doctrinal judgements. It weaves a fabric of theological insights that are gleaned from a dialectical struggle with an expansive range of postmodern philosophical thought. Its categories, as foundational, are the criteria that serve to re-think Christian theology.

Post-liberalism

Lauded as a watershed moment in twentieth-century theology when it was published, George Lindbeck's *The Nature of Doctrine* has become a serious counterweight to the otherwise predominant liberal method of critical correlationism practised by Paul Tillich and Chicago theologian David Tracy. Another Yale theologian deeply associated with the post-liberal school is Hans Frei, whose attention to biblical interpretation is an appreciation for the act of narration and a confidence in the ability of human language to disclose the reality of God. Together with David Kelsey and several other theologians, Frei and Lindbeck have opened up a way of thinking about theological method. But, theological priorities are laid out without the Neo-Platonic philosophical categories typical of Radical Orthodox theology.

Focusing instead on the hermeneutics of the tradition *vis-à-vis* the biblical narrative (Frei) and the practical contingencies of the church theologian (Lindbeck), post-liberal theologians have adapted an interpretation of 'Christian grammar', which means, as Paul De Hart comments: 'The doctrinal authority accorded a statement lies in this grammatical function, not in its being a true proposition.'[6] It is claimed that post-liberalism involves an implicit endorsement of a Wittgensteinian philosophy of language in combination with a Kuhnian epistemology. Post-liberals follow Wittgenstein's creed that rationality falls within radically differing frameworks of language games. Likewise, post-liberals endorse philosopher of science Thomas Kuhn's claim that rationality is determined by historically bound paradigms of acceptable knowledge. In addition, post-liberal theologians value Christian particularity though the key of 'generous orthodoxy'.[7]

The label of 'post-liberal' was thrust on Frei and Lindbeck more than they might have wished, but in using the term, we are including the distinct theory of intratextuality in Frei's work and Lindbeck's 'cultural-linguistic' understanding of religion in relation to doctrine. Intratextuality, as we recall from Paul's engagement with the Hebrew Bible, is a term that refers to the re-description of Christian identity in relation to the tradition's texts. The concern for identity is itself rather Barthian, and to a great extent, Barth serves as the inspiration for post-liberal theology. But, partly due to a concern to communicate the plausibility of Christian academic theology for Christians, post-liberals want to deal more forcefully with the issue of language and epistemology, philosophical topics that Barth left largely alone. For Lindbeck, intratextuality refers especially to the work of the Christian theologian whose standing in the Christian 'symbol system' means that the meaning of faith is immanent to the semiotics of Christian reading and practice. Lindbeck suggests that intratextuality works in theology because it is a general theory:

> intratextuality is characteristic of the descriptions of not only religion but also other forms of rule-governed behaviour from carpentry to mathematics to languages and cultures. Hammers and Saws, ordinals and numerals, winks and signs of the cross,

words and sentences are made comprehensible by indicating how they fit into systems of communication or purposeful action, not by reference to outside factors.[8]

Church doctrines function, as a consequence, in regulative terms to tell and 'use' the Christian story. In accordance with his cultural-linguistic theory of religion, Lindbeck proposes that the pragmatic needs of the church community are the most vital priority: 'Church doctrines are communally authoritative teachings regarding beliefs and practices that are considered essential to the identity or welfare of the group in question.'[9] Yet, doctrines themselves are liable to be misunderstood: 'The modern mood is antipathetic to the very notion of communal norms.' And besides, for Lindbeck, doctrines are not to be perceived as propositional truths or expressions of some pre-linguistic experience, although he recognizes the urge to accommodate in contemporary culture: 'doctrines no longer represent objective realities and are instead experienced as expressions of personal preference . . . as long as each person is honest and sincere, it makes no difference which faith they embrace.'[10]

Against this kind of easy accommodationism, Lindbeck advocates a post-liberal theology of narrative Christian community. For example, shifts in Christological affirmations (Lindbeck refers to Bonhoeffer's 'Man for Others'and Barth's 'Humanity of God') do not undo the fact that the underlying 'story of the passion and resurrection' and the 'rules for its [story's] use remain the same'.[11] What this suggests is a significant modification of the concept of doctrine. It implies a modification of theological method, but only in terms of the relative importance that is attached to doctrine *vis-à-vis* biblical interpretation, systematic theology and the communication in the church of the meaning of doctrine. Lindbeck is effectively suggesting that doctrines function like hermeneutical rules and not much more than that. They do not judge, certainly not in the feared sense of being propositional, since he perceives a conflict between propositional statements and the evolution of meaning. If they are not changed into serving an exclusively hermeneutical function, doctrines would be caught between the need to reflect an objective description and an inner experience.

Lindbeck's proposal, while it has attracted a great deal of attention for a period of time, nevertheless leaves many questions unanswered. Other post-liberal theologians are more straightforward in regards to their methodological intent. Yale theologian David Kelsey, for instance, reflecting a basically Barthian form of procedure, has written a two-volume work (*Eccentric Existence: A Theological Anthropology*) in theological anthropology, which argues for the congruence between the post-liberal love of narrative and the Barthian priority of God talk. Breaking from other contemporary efforts to describe human nature with attention to the social sciences, Kelsey instead re-focuses theological attention on the Trinity as the condition of possibility for deciphering human nature. While eschewing an allegiance to any particular method, Kelsey goes on to identify his project as a kind of 'secondary theology', crucially dependent on the public practices of ecclesial communities that comprise 'primary theology'.

Though similar in some ways to historic dogmatic theology, Kelsey freely countenances the analytical, critical and even revisionary nature of secondary theology. Secondary theology, so far as Kelsey is concerned, is far from being exclusively academic. It is oriented, despite the need for theoretical construction and specialized knowledge, to the practice and traditions of the church and especially to the story of the human that arises from canonical scripture.

Deliberately attentive to the 'premodern' portraits of human nature, Kelsey arrives at three general *desiderata* which constitute the groups of questions that contemporary theological anthropology must address. These groups are the thematic (that anthropologies be theocentric and communal), systematic (that anthropologies derive from more basic Christian claims about God's Trinitarian nature and our relations with God rather than rely on comparisons with other creatures) and conceptual (that anthropologies be distinguished from modern psychological claims, scriptural and scientific claims).[12] It is the last *desideratum* which is most intriguing, for Kelsey acknowledges, albeit implicitly, the role of interdisciplinary inquiry in theological concept formation. Obviously, there is much more to be said in relation to Kelsey's project. It is perhaps the most systematic project to date by a post-liberal theologian, despite the fact that Kelsey wants to be 'systematically unsystematic'. But his nod to other disciplines in relation to human nature substantiates the claim I made earlier about growing convergences on the part of theologians with roots in one methodological style for the insights of other styles. In this case, without exaggerating any confluences that have taken place thus far, there is evidence for a greater appreciation of theological method as the necessary element in articulating theological wisdom than we have seen previously among theological post-liberals.

Liberation theology

Never having been confused as a movement centred on the provision of wisdom for its own sake, liberation theology emerged in Latin America in the 1960s as a largely Catholic alliance of theologians, pastors, intellectuals and political figures who adapted various strands of Marxism and a biblical theology in order to affirm God's 'preferential option for the poor'. The pioneer and 'father' of liberation theology is Gustavo Gutierrez, a Catholic priest who joined the Order of Preachers (Dominicans) later in life, an affiliation that has helped him to develop and promote liberation theology in his native Peru as well as internationally. Gutierrez and other liberation theologians take their cues from sociological and historical studies, which detail a history of suffering on the part of the poor and the otherwise vulnerable.

Taking Christian faith's active interest in orthopraxis as the corollary of orthodoxy, liberation theologians are keen to apply social and historical diagnoses in the name of a theological mandate to be in solidarity with the poor, wherein the language of the 'preferential option for the poor', from the 1968 Medellin Conference of Latin American Catholic bishops is the most well-attributed slogan. Methodically, liberation theologians choose to invest a great deal of intellectual energy in the analysis of economic relationships and structural distortions in society that accentuate inequality and social bias against marginalized groups. This choice appears to reinforce a correlationist mindset, in which the needs of the poor and disadvantaged are given pride of place as the starting point for theological reflection. That is, theology does not necessarily appeal to the scriptural text or the Christian tradition from which it then proceeds; and the cursory evidence shows that, sociologically speaking, liberation theologians have received a generous and welcome hearing from churches and academic theologians who are broadly aligned with correlationist thinking.

Yet there are two aspects of liberation theology that should give us pause in associating it too closely with correlationism in the West. The first is the accent placed by a number of liberation theologians on Christ's 'scandal of the cross', a singular focus on the suffering of the person of Jesus. Jesus is Christ the liberator, the one anointed by God to prophetically denounce every sort of optimism and oppressive social regime that arises because of the denial of sin. Sin itself, as expounded by liberation theology is re-defined as social sin. Christ's gift to us is a radical liberation, because in him, 'the all-comprehesiveness of the liberating process reaches its fullest sense'.[13]

Second, liberation theologians typically place much more emphasis on the narratives of biblical material than correlationist theologians, notably the exodus of the Israelites out of Egypt. Jesus' human identity as an outcast and scapegoat is highly relevant to the *modus operandi* of liberation theology. The impulse to reference scriptural passages provides a glimpse into a theology that is markedly different from that of the European/North American academy. In these two respects where scriptural references are infrequent among correlationists. In these two respects, although it seems counterintuitive to suggest it, liberation theology's method is more akin to Barth's approach – for similar reasons as Schillebeeckx's theology is theocentric – in each case, there is great attention paid to biblical sources. Furthermore, inasmuch as liberation theology is a theology of the church, as a living body of believers committed to social change on behalf of the downtrodden, there are certain parallels with post-liberals who also accent the pragmatic, moral nature of Christian claims. Liberation theology and post-liberalism in turn share a thread of theological methodology that goes back to Schleiermacher precisely in this ecclesial respect too.

Gutierrez certainly distinguishes liberation theology in several methodological ways. For example, he cites theology's priority of critical reflection on praxis as opposed to classical theology's focus on theoretical abstraction. He also identifies specific ways that the sources of theology ought to be interpreted; for instance, in the importance of seeing human reason as political reason. He also makes a shift from thinking of experience *per se* to the experience of the poor as the locus for authentic theological reflection. On procedure, liberation theologians are more reticent to articulate a full theological strategy in comparison with their keen interest in the methods of social analysis on which they rely for correlating biblical stories.

Therefore, we can summarize the method of liberation theology in general terms by understanding it to be purposeful, in terms of political philosophy, a criterion by which theology is carried out. Liberation theology is also more certain in terms of the nature of the task it sets for itself; but in terms of actual procedure or measuring how the sources of theology are treated, liberation theologians are less precise. However, procedurally speaking, feminist theology has benefitted from the priorities that liberation theologians have established. They have followed up those benchmarks by articulating more precisely what the functions of theology should be. Thinking of the work of Phyllis Trible or Elizabeth Schüssler-Fiorenza, for instance, we can say that the method of feminist theologians has been far sharper with respect to the biblical narrative and the hermeneutical implications of feminist scriptural analysis than has the method of liberation theologians. Though their theology is contested along with any other school of thought, feminist and liberation theologians integrate interests and styles that could not have been integrated, methodically speaking, even half a century ago. This becomes especially noticeable the more feminist and liberationist thought has become absorbed and accepted by more traditional theologians, whose respect for their insights overcomes the distrust of their political motives.

Joseph Ratzinger

Once the most public and forceful opponent of liberation theology, Joseph Ratzinger has been one of the most esteemed Catholic theologians of the past half-century, emerging to prominence as an advisor to German Cardinal Frings at the Second Vatican Council before eventually becoming Pope in 2005. Ratzinger's theological interests are various and he plumbs the depths of Catholic tradition in ways not well appreciated by either admirers or critics. Drawing especially on the theological orientation to history in Augustine, to Bonaventure's theology of revelation, to the patristic unity of scripture with tradition and to the *nouvelle théologie* movement, Ratzinger's theological contributions have ranged widely from careful biblical exegesis (including his two-volume work on Jesus of Nazareth, published since he was elected Pope) to philosophical theology.

Ratzinger has devoted the bulk of his theological work over his academic and ecclesial career to foundational theology with many forays into systematic theology and doctrine, as well as biblical exegesis. What is somewhat unique is the extent to which he blends his various interests and scholarly expertise into a unified whole. In fact, it may even be possible that because of the responsibilities and burdens that have accompanied his tenure as Pope, rather than despite these things, his theology has become more multi-faceted. His speeches and papal encyclicals are a bit trickier to analyse in terms of his own theology, obviously because of the editing process and wider ecclesial concerns that characterize the theological direction of those documents which are not as directly attached to his thinking.

Of all the suggestions, elements of insight and emphases in Ratzinger's theology, one of the most important is his repeated reflection on the relationship between theology and philosophy. Drawing, to some extent, on the Thomist tradition of the faith-reason relationship, Ratzinger has made the case for rationality in theology and the rationality of God in strong terms. Famously, at a speech at the University of Regensburg in 2006, he precipitated some controversy with remarks that appeared to portray Muslim ideas of God as irrational, in contradistinction to the Platonic rationality of the Christian God. It is more likely, however, as several attentive readers of the speech are aware, that Ratzinger had certain Protestant theologies uppermost in his mind in the speech. It is plausible to read the speech as one which deals, however implicitly, with theological method in light of God's rational nature. Just how far-reaching the problem of method appears for Ratzinger can be seen from his understanding of method in other disciplines. Near the end of the speech he states:

> modern scientific reason with its intrinsically Platonic element bears within itself a question which points beyond itself and beyond the possibilities of its methodology. Modern scientific reason quite simply has to accept the rational structure of matter and the correspondence between our spirit and the prevailing rational structures of nature as a given, on which its methodology has to be based. Yet the question why this has to be so is a real question, and one which has to be remanded by the natural sciences to other modes and planes of thought – to philosophy and theology.[14]

So, how one thinks about method is revelatory of a great deal of things for Ratzinger. The lesson for Christian theology, in this speech, concerns how to relate scripture and reason, the Bible and Greek thought. Against what he sees as the falsehood of 'de-hellenization', Ratzinger advocates, Newman-like, a developmental approach to faith in theology:

> The New Testament was written in Greek and bears the imprint of the Greek spirit, which had already come to maturity as the Old Testament developed. True, there are elements in the evolution of the early Church which do not have to be integrated into all cultures. Nonetheless, the fundamental decisions made about the relationship between faith and the use of human reason are part of the faith itself; they are developments consonant with the nature of faith itself.[15]

With reason understood as a part of faith, Ratzinger can justify a positive mutual relationship between philosophy and theology, which is a constant theme in his early work. In *Principles of Catholic Theology*, Ratzinger writes:

> 1. Theology has to do with God. 2. Theological speculation is linked to philosophical inquiry as its basic methodology. The two themes will seem contradictory if, on the one hand, we include under philosophy a way of thinking that, by its nature, belongs – and must belong – to revelation and if, on the other hand, we adopt the view that God can be known only by way of revelation and that the question of God is actually not a problem of reason as reason. I am convinced that such a position, which in recent times, has become more and more a kind of *sententia communis* for philosophers and theologians, will in the end prove crippling to both philosophy and theology.[16]

As with Barth, theology is not subject to philosophy, since revelation is not something that philosophy can account for. But unlike Barth and akin to the thought of von Balthasar, whom Ratzinger admires greatly, philosophy must be retained to aid theology in making sense of reality, in the light of God's revealing activity in salvation history. To retreat from truth itself to 'mere faith', as he says elsewhere, is to mimic the ancient philosophers' retreat from the *logos*, the retreat 'from nature to politics'.[17]

Ratzinger opposes the development, made explicit since Harnack's programme of de-hellenization, of the division between the God of faith and the God of the philosophers. Perhaps the most widely known book in which this opposition is developed is his *Introduction to Christianity* where he speaks of the 'transformation of the God of the philosophers, not their complete overthrow. The God of eternal mathematics becomes, in Christianity, the God of human history, and also the God of *agape*, the power of creative love.'[18] The God of reason is not replaced but overcome by the God of love.

Ratzinger's foundational theology is further elaborated in reflections on themes and concepts in which philosophy and theology can be said to exercise overlapping jurisdiction. In one place, amid the papal encyclical *Caritas in Veritate*, Ratzinger reflects on the implications for an understanding of personhood in which philosophy needs theology's guidance:

A metaphysical understanding of the relations between persons is . . . a great benefit for their development. In this regard, reason finds inspiration and direction in Christian revelation, according to which the human community does not absorb the individual, annihilating his autonomy, as happens in the various forms of totalitarianism, but rather values him all the more because the relation between individual and community is a relation between one totality and another. (n. 53)

With respect to categories such as personhood, Ratzinger writes with a keen sense of the philosophical anticipation of revealed knowledge. This approach to the discipline of philosophy both indicates its value but also its need for a theological account of philosophy, a two-sided approach that marks Ratzinger's understanding of theological method. It suggests some similarities with Radical Orthodoxy as a consequence.

The other subject to which Ratzinger has devoted much of his energy is biblical criticism. The most cited text in this regards comes from a speech given in New York in 1988 titled 'Biblical Interpretation in Crisis'. In it, Ratzinger opens up a line of attack against historical-critical method, especially in the legacy of German exegetes Martin Dibelius and Rudolf Bultmann. His diagnosis is blunt:

> Modern exegesis . . . completely relegated God to the incomprehensible, the otherworldly, the inexpressible in order to be able to treat the biblical text itself as an entirely worldly reality according to natural-scientific methods.

The application of such methods to a treatment of the Bible is a ruse, for reasons having first of all to do with science and objectivity:

> Now, if the natural science model is to be followed without hesitation, then the importance of the Heisenberg principle should be applied to the historical-critical method as well. Heisenberg has shown that the outcome of a given experiment is heavily influenced by the point of view of the observer. So much so that both the observer's questions and observations continue to change in the natural course of events. When applied to the witness of history, this means that interpretation can never be just a simple reproduction of history's being, 'as it was.' The word *interpretation* gives us a clue to the question itself: every exegesis requires an 'inter' – an entering in and a being 'inter,' or between things; this is the involvement of the interpreter himself. Pure objectivity is an absurd abstraction. It is not the uninvolved who comes to knowledge; rather, interest itself is a requirement for the possibility of coming to know.[19]

Extending this interpretation of interpretation itself, Ratzinger moves to justify a form of theological exegesis, the form of analysis of biblical texts that prioritizes the theological questions of a given text. Theological inquiries into biblical texts are justified by the theological purpose of the biblical authors' intentions and their redaction. In the process, Ratzinger calls upon the patristic style of biblical exegesis, such as his development of a typology between Moses and Jesus in the first volume of his *Jesus of Nazareth* work. Moses speaks with the Lord 'as to a friend', yet he only sees God's back (Exod. 33.23).[20] Moses also acts as a mediator who receives the name of the Lord at the scene of the burning bush, while Jesus reveals the name of the Lord, as 'Father' and in so doing reveals himself to be a mediator, in line with Moses. The typological comparison of Moses and Jesus is not to be missed in Ratzinger's treatment. It is an explicit recourse to a traditional form of biblical interpretation that Ratzinger believes has not been overtaken by historical-critical methods of biblical exegesis.

Conclusion

While it is unwise to attempt a summary of the variety of theological methods treated in this book, it might be helpful to go back to Lonergan's *Method in Theology* by way of revisiting a few themes that serve as common ground for many of the approaches described in these chapters. As I mentioned in Chapter One with regard to Paul, Lonergan's acknowledgement of religious conversion is the key to understanding the structure of theology that he lays out – as a twofold series of four steps each. The apex of the theological task is the theologian's acceptance of God's love and its specific role in going beyond a dialectical consideration of various worldviews so that categories, doctrines and systematic inquiries reflect a set of constructive theological tasks. For Lonergan, the theologian must be converted religiously, but also morally and intellectually too.

What such a criterion means for Lonergan is a notion of revelation, wherein God's communication precedes any knowledge that we might possess and express. This is no small thing. In fact, Lonergan's highlighting of the role of conversion would seem to ally him (improbably, some would say) with Barth or Balthasar, since the systematic task of correlating theological statements with psychological, social and cultural factors is not primary. Lonergan is very much an Augustinian in describing theology as a discipline that flows from God's love 'flooding our hearts' (Rom. 5.5). God communicates, we pay attention, understand, judge and act accordingly. The centrality of love that we saw in Augustine's *DDC* is exactly what Lonergan is proposing. It is also why, for instance, both Augustine and Lonergan hold to a differentiated notion of revelation, as *both* a message *and* a converted believer, not just one or the other.

On the other hand, Lonergan also calls attention to the shift that has taken place from what he terms a 'classical' to a pluralist paradigm. The cultural discontinuity between the hermeneutical perspective of eighteenth-century theological discourse and those which govern theology in the twenty-first century is radical. It is sufficient to warrant Lonergan's judgement that the meaning attributed to doctrinal statements or biblical expressions in the past may not be adequate for the contemporary world. This is what Lonergan refers to as the difference between the classicist and the modern perspective, a difference that pertains to views of culture and revelation alike. Whereas classicist views of culture assume a normative meaning for shared values and formulations of revelation, a modern view of culture sees the control of meaning as a process, containing the distinction between core meanings and changeable formulations. Newman made suggestions on this theme central to his view of doctrine. In regards to pluralism, Lonergan sounds much more like Bultmann and the modern correlationists, whose own perception of the difference between the world of the New Testament and modern scientific culture set the theological agenda for the latter half of the twentieth century.

What Lonergan and the other examples described in this chapter demonstrate is the possibility of moving beyond strict boundaries between correlationist and anti-correlationist factionalism. The sheer complexity of elements in the theological method of Radical Orthodoxy, post-liberals, liberation theologians and Joseph Ratzinger shows a penchant for wisdom. Yet it is certainly true that schools of thought in theological method (e.g. Yale and Chicago) are internally diverse. As these other contemporary examples show, it is also true that individual theologians and smaller groups often diverge when it comes to integrating seemingly different historic trajectories of theological method into a single theological system or portrait.

It is always tempting, therefore, to demarcate methods in theology in accord with certain 'types', 'models' or the degree to which theology tends to resemble the theologians of a school. And perhaps no issue serves to separate theologians like the role of philosophy in theology. As we have already seen from the differences between Barth and Bultmann, this is a critical issue. It is also historically rooted in the intellectual developments of Western society as a whole, reflected in Kant's blockbuster judgement of the *Critique of*

Pure Reason's preface: 'I have therefore found it necessary to deny knowledge, in order to make room for faith.'[21]

It would be possible to characterize contemporary theological methods according to whether they adopt or repel this Kantian division of knowledge and faith, as Hans Frei did in his little book on the five types of theology. But, as we have seen, philosophy is only one issue among several others that reflects the theological method undertaken. If one can generalize on the basis of the contemporary examples described in this chapter alone, it is both commendable and feasible to reject blanket formulas regarding the role of philosophy, culture and sources in the theological task. There is a danger, however, in moving too hastily in the direction of embracing the postmodern ethos of individual expression. While pluralism will be a perennial state of theological reflection, increasingly ad hoc interpretations of method carry the possibility of an inability to communicate. This is especially the case with regards to biblical exegetes and constructive theologians' ability to speak to one another.

In the United States, the methodological outlook between partisans of the Chicago School (e.g. Tillich, Tracy and followers of Bultmann) and the Yale School (e.g. Hans Frei, George Lindbeck and post-liberals thereafter) is a longstanding division. But methodological contentions have faded since the 1980s as exhaustion over the divisions set in. Other 'substantive' issues emerged with much greater prominence, whether it was the relationship between Christianity and society or narrower hermeneutical issues. Outside the United States, contemporary dialectics over method have not been argued so keenly, but nevertheless, they traverse roughly similar conceptual terrain, especially in Britain, Germany and Latin America. However, what Kathryn Tanner, a Yale-trained theologian teaching in the University of Chicago's Divinity School says about the contemporary situation could be applied to many theological locales:

it is misguided to search for a proper theological method with the expectation that it will make clear, all by itself, the proper Christian stance on the contested sociocultural issues of one's day. Search for proper method with that expectation encourages blanket judgments about the wider culture as a whole – it [culture] is to be resisted, or welcomed as the ground floor for the contributions of grace, or transformed as a whole – when what is really necessary is an often more difficult and nuanced discernment about particulars.[22]

Tanner's methodological ambivalence presents a challenge, and as a description, there is much about the contemporary scene to corroborate her reticence. Her reference to 'particulars' alludes to more modest projects and contributions. It suggests less than grand narratives in the spirit of postmodernism. The idea that social and cultural complexity renders the interpretation of Christianity in any given situation more challenging is certainly correct. But does such modesty denude theologians of the proper instinct to affirm how we claim what we claim?

I would respond to Tanner by suggesting that social and ecclesial complexity and attention to particulars does not make theological method redundant. On the contrary, it suggests greater care be sought so that theologians understand the differentiated set of tasks that make up theology. Theological tasks have always been about particulars, and that is as it should be. However, identifying the common ground among those tasks moves us beyond particulars.

It is far better for theologians to know what it is that they are doing, rather than simply 'muddling through' when engaged in tracking the meaning and practice of Christian doctrine and symbols. This is why theological method will always re-emerge as an issue, even if the aims of past efforts seemed overly ambitious. Postliberals have been the most vigorous in denouncing the generalities of theological method, but they should not overlook the genuine questions that point to possibilities of coherence and opportunities for shared purpose across theological fields.

This book began with the question, 'Is there a theological epistemology?' Given the sheer diversity with which theologians over the ages have accounted for how they know what they know, the answer must surely be 'no'. That is, there is clearly not 'a' theological epistemology, since theology involves many insights, judgements and decisions that lead to more insights and judgements. For reasons of theological principle, various theologians would add that there cannot be such a thing as a theological epistemology. And yet, as we have noted in each chapter, theologians tend to perform a set task or set of tasks when making theological claims; and, over time, we are able to correlate these tasks as belonging to one kind or another.

So, as we saw in Origen's *systematic* attempts to marry doctrines with scriptural interpretation, or with Luther's attempt to signify the *dialectics* between one set of historical interpretation over another in light of the justification by faith principle, we see, over time, patterns of theological procedures which can be diagnosed as in accord with one or more of Lonergan's eight functional specialties in procedure. True, Lonergan's eightfold tasks by themselves are only descriptive of what it is that a theologian does procedurally. But once the procedures have been identified, and the analysis of the theologians described in this book have made this clear I think, then one can make sharper claims about the principles and priorities of this or that theologian.

As we saw in Chapter Four, for instance, in the case of Dionysius, there are consequences with starting off with a highly Platonic way of characterizing knowledge. It is bound to affect one's theology in ways that others will not share, because it means that much less is to be expected from scriptural interpretation or a history of interpretation for instance. Dionysius does not engage in scriptural interpretation very much at all, and his theology is the poorer for it, although many contemporary theologians feel quite differently. Claiming that Dionysius' theology does not suffer from the onto-theological tradition's way of conceiving God as essentially a Being above other beings, there are some postmodern and Eastern Orthodox theologians (e.g. C. Yannaras) who look to Dionysius' theological method admiringly.

Does this example not suggest that theology is in thrall to the individual preferences of theologians and that no methodological rigour can really be discerned in the discipline? If we stick with the Dionysius example for a minute, we should want to probe whether and under what conditions a scripturally credible, incarnational theology is feasible, while simultaneously incorporating his apophatic style. It would be the job of a systematic theologian who has both of these potential sympathies to develop some sort of integration, noting the dialectics involved in praising and critiquing Dionysius' contribution. In fact, Radical Orthodoxy, with its twin ecumenical and Neo-Platonic sympathies, is specifically well suited to bringing Dionysian mysticism together with a postmodern Augustinian concern for tangible realities. Likewise, post-liberals like David Kelsey are uniquely situated to bring a Calvinist attention to the connection between doctrine and scripture together with an attention to language and philosophical, interdisciplinary hermeneutics. Liberation theologians and Joseph Ratzinger have also, in their unique ways, made otherwise disparate inquiries their own and championed coherence in theology as a result.

Yes, Christian theology is presently undergoing a time of attention to particulars, but as the functions that these particular inquiries serve, and as contemporary theologians show, the future is not closed to theological wisdom, coherence or system. I believe that there are far too many advances in wisdom made in various historical periods by various figures for theological method to disappear as an urgent matter of attention. The theological relationship to philosophy, the balance afforded to sources, the nature of the theological task and criteria of judgement in theological claims are all up for scrutiny and debate in theology. The problems associated with these elements in theological reflection never really go away. Theological method will return as a major question for Christian theologians, given theology's present state of flux. The current fusing of theological styles is an interesting harbinger of new directions in theological method.

NOTES

Introduction

1 Mark McIntosh, *Mystical Theology* (Malden, Mass.: Blackwell, 1998), p. 10.

2 Janet Martin Soskice, 'Athens and Jerusalem, Alexandria and Edessa: Is there a Metaphysics of Scripture?' *International Journal of Systematic Theology* 8, No. 2 (April 2006), 149–62, 161.

3 Bernard Lonergan, *Method in Theology* (NY: Seabury Press, 1972), p. 4.

4 Aristotle, *Metaphysics* 984b. Quoted by Walter Kasper, *The Methods of Dogmatic Theology* (New York: Paulist Press, 1969), p. 6.

5 Andrew Louth, *Discerning the Mystery* (Oxford: Clarendon Press, 1983), and the various works of Joseph Ratzinger (Pope Benedict XVI).

6 See the volumes published in the *Brazos Theological Interpretation of the Bible series*.

7 Ted Peters, 'Truth in History: Gadamer's Hermeneutics and Pannenberg's Apologetic Method'. *Journal of Religion*, Vol. 55, No. 1 (January 1975), 36–56, 36.

8 Lonergan, *Method in Theology* (New York: Seabury Press, 1972), p. 296.

9 Karl Barth's formulation as cited by Alister E. McGrath, *Christian Theology: An Introduction* (Malden, Mass.: Blackwell, 2007), p. 156.

10 Kevin Vanhoozer, *First Theology: God, Scripture and Hermeneutics* (Downers Grove, Ill.: Intervarsity Press, 2002), Chapter Five.

11 Paul Ricoeur, 'The Task of Hermeneutics', in *From Text to Action: Essays in Hermeneutics*. Translated by Kathleen Blamey and John B. Thomson (Evanston, Ill.: Northwestern University Press, 1991), p. 53.

12 Michael Polanyi, *The Tacit Dimension* (New York: Doubleday, 1967), p. 4.

13   Harold Bloom, *How to Read and Why* (New York: Simon and
     Schuster, 2000), p. 28.
14   Andreas J. Kostenberger and Michael J. Kruger, *The Heresy of
     Orthodoxy: How Contemporary Culture's Fascination with Diversity
     Has Reshaped Our Understanding of Early Christianity* (Wheaton,
     Ill.: Crossway Books, 2010).
15   See Crossan, *Jesus: A Revolutionary Biography* (New York:
     HarperOne, 1995), and Ben Witherington's response in *The Jesus
     Quest: The Third Search for the Jew of Nazareth* (Downers Grove,
     Ill.: Intervarsity Press, 1997), Chapter Three.
16   Werner Jeanrond, *Theological Hermeneutics: Development and
     Significance* (New York: Crossroad, 1991).
17   See Ben F. Meyer, *Critical Realism and the New Testament* (Allison
     Park, PA: Pickwick, 1989), p. 59.
18   Hans Küng, *Does God Exist?* Translated by Edward Quinn (New
     York: Vintage Books, 1981), p. 111.
19   Gadamer, *Truth and Method* 2nd. rev. edn. (New York: Continuum,
     1995), p. 295.
20   Ibid., p. 298.
21   Lonergan, *Method in Theology* (New York: Seabury, 1972), p. 80.
22   Andrew Louth, *Discerning the Mystery: An Essay on the Nature of
     Theology* (Clarendon Press, 1983), p. 83.

Chapter 1

1   See Lucy Beckett's mention of this unattributed quote cited by
    Austin Farrer in her review of books dedicated to Farrer's theology,
    'Not a Theory, but a Life', in *The Times Literary Supplement*
    3 August 2007, 23.
2   F. F. Bruce, 'Pauline theology' in Raymond E. Brown, S. S., Joseph
    Fitzmyer, S. J. and Roland Murphy, O. Carm. (eds). *The Jerome
    Biblical Commentary* (Englewood Cliffs, N.J.: Prentice Hall: 1968),
    803. F. F. Bruce, *Paul and Jesus* (London: SPCK 1974), p. 15.
3   William Wrede, *Paul* (London: Philip Green, 1907), p. 156.
4   See H. Räisänen, *Paul and the Law*, 2nd. edn (Tübingen: Mohr,
    1987).
5   Wrede, p. 179.
6   Freud, *Moses and Monotheism* (New York: Vintage, 1939).
7   Thanks to Daniel J. R. Kirk for this insight.
8   See J. Pelikan, *Jesus through the Centuries: His Place in the History
    of Culture* (New York: Harper and Row, 1985), p. 212.

9 Strabo, *Geography*, 14.5.13, LCL. Cited in Stanley Porter, 'Paul and His Bible: His Education and Access to the Scriptures of Israel', in Stanley Porter and Christopher D. Stanley (eds), *As It is Written: Studying Paul's Use of Scripture* (Society of Biblical Literature, 2008), p. 99.

10 See, for instance, Alain Badiou, *Saint Paul: The Foundation of Universalism* (2003), p. 14: 'Paul's general procedure is the following: if there is an event, and if truth consists in declaring it, then . . . since truth is eventual . . . it is singular . . . there cannot be a law of truth . . . second . . . nothing communitarian or historically established can lend its substance to the process of truth.'

11 Francis Watson, *Paul and the Hermeneutics of Faith* (T&T Clark, 2004), p. 275.

12 Richard Hays, *Echoes of Scripture in the Letters of Paul* (New Haven: Yale University Press, 1989).

13 Albert Schweitzer, *The Mysticism of Paul the Apostle* (London: A.&C. Black, 1931), p. 225.

14 Watson, pp. 47–9.

15 J. R. Daniel Kirk, *Unlocking Romans: Resurrection and the Justification of God* (Eerdmans, 2008), p. 208.

16 See Earl Richard's discussion in *First and Second Thessalonians*, Sacra Pagina Series, Vol. 11 (Liturgical Press, 1995), pp. 186–209.

17 E. P. Sanders, *Paul, the Law and the Jewish People* (SCM, 1983), p. 106.

18 See Francis Watson, 'Is There a Story in these texts?' in Bruce W. Longenecker, ed. *Narrative Dynamics in Paul: A Critical Assessment* (Louisville: Westminster John Knox Press, 2002), pp. 231–9.

19 See *Christology in the Making* (London: SCM Press, 1989), p. 146.

20 Gerald O'Collins, *The Tripersonal God: Understanding and Interpreting the Trinity.* (Paulist, 1999), p. 63.

21 Ibid., p. 58.

22 For a fuller account of Paul's inter-/intratextual hermeneutics, see Hays, pp. 62–5, 86 and 111–14.

23 Ibid., p. 108.

Chapter 2

1 See William Schoedel, 'Philosophy and Rhetoric in the *Adversus Haereses* of Irenaeus', in *Vigilae Christianae*, Vol. 13, No. 1 (April 1959), 22–32, 27–30.

2 See the summary in Anders-Christian Jacobson, 'The Importance of Genesis 1-3 in the Theology of Irenaeus', in *Zeitschrift für Antikes Christentum*, Vol. 8, Issue 2 (2005), 299–316.

3   Osborn, *Irenaeus of Lyons* (Cambridge University Press, 2001), p. 21.
4   See William Schoedel, 'Theological Method in Irenaeus (*Adversus Haereses* 2.25-28)', *Journal of Theological Studies* 35 (1984), 31–49.
5   On which, see Mark S. M. Scott, 'Suffering and Soul-Making: Rethinking John Hick's Theodicy', *Journal of Religion* Vol. 90, No. 3 (2010), 313–34.
6   See Farrow, p. 349. Cf. *AH* 5.5.
7   Richard Norris, 'The Insufficiency of Scripture: *Adversus haereses* and the Role of Scripture in Irenaeus's Anti-Gnostic polemic', in Charles A. Bobetz and David Brakke (eds). *Reading in Christian Communities: Essays on Interpretation in the Early Church* (University of Notre Dame Press, 2002), pp. 63–79, 72.
8   Osborn, p. 172.
9   Irenaeus, Letter to Florinus, in Eusebius, *Ecclesiastical History* 5.20.5-6; cf. *AH* 3.3.4
10 *Demonstration of the Apostolic Preaching* 44–5.
11 Cf. John Behr, *The Formation of Christian Theology vol. 1: The Way to Nicea* (Crestwood, N.Y.: St. Vladimir's Seminary Press, 2001), p. 123. Cf. Quintilian, *Institutio Oratia* 6.1.1.
12 Ibid., p. 132.
13 *AH* II.25.4.
14 Rowan Williams, 'Origen', in G. R. Evans (ed.), *The First Christian Theologians* (Blackwell, 2004), p. 135.
15 Henri de Lubac, *History and Spirit* (San Francisco: Ignatius Press, 2007), p. 104.
16 Ibid., pp. 36, 40.
17 Joseph W. Trigg, *Origen: The Bible and Philosophy in the Third Century* (London: SCM Press, 1983), p. 127.
18 Ibid., p. 129.
19 See Donald Fairburn's discussion in 'Patristic Soteriologies: Three Trajectories', in *The Journal of The Evangelical Theological Society* 50/2 (June 2007), 289–310, 298–300. On the issue of philosophy's relationship to theology in dealing with evil, see Mark S. M. Scott, *Journey Back to God: Origen on the Problem of Evil* (New York: Oxford University Press, 2012).
20 Origen, *On First Principles* III, 1,1. Translated by G. W. Butterworth (Gloucester, Mass: Peter Smith, 1973), p. 157.
21 Origen, *On First Principles*, I, Preface, p. 3.
22 Porphyry, in Eusebius, *History of the Church* 6.19.4-5 and 6-8.
23 Russell Reno, 'Origen and Spiritual Interpretation', in *Pro Ecclesia*, Vol. 15, No.1 (December 2006), 108–26, 116.
24 Origen, *Commentary on the Gospel According to John: Books 1–10* Translated by Ronald E. Heine. The Fathers of the Church (Washington, D.C.: Catholic University of America Press, 1989), p. 168.

25 See de Lubac, *History and Spirit*, 205ff.

26 Quoted from G. W. Butterworth (ed.), *Origen on First Principles* (London: SPCK, 1936), p. 6. Cf. Colin Gunton's discussion of Origen in relation to systematic theology in 'A Rose By Any Other Name? From "Christian Doctrine" to "Systematic Theology"', in *International Journal of Systematic Theology*, Vol.1, No. 1 (1999), 4–23, 7.

27 Frend, *The Rise of Christianity* (Philadelphia: Fortress Press, 1984), p. 524.

28 Andrew Louth, 'The fourth-century Alexandrians: Athanasisus and Didymus', in Frances Young, Lewis Ayres and Andrew Louth (eds), *The Cambridge History of Early Christian Literature* (Cambridge: Cambridge University Press, 2004), pp. 275–82, 278.

29 Athanasius, 'Letter 40: To Adelphius, Bishop and Confessor, Against the Arians', in Khaled Anatolios, *Athanasius* (New York: Routledge, 2004), p. 237.

30 Anatolios, p. 235.

31 *Athanasius, Orations against the Arians* 3.3.

32 Berthold Altaner, *Patrology*. Translated by Hilda Graef (New York: Herder & Herder, 1961), p. 322. Cf. Athanasius, *Orations against the Arians* 1.39.

33 Athanasius, *Orations against the Arians* 2.2.

Chapter 3

1 References to the text (heretofore *DDC*) are to the Oxford World's Classics edition: Saint Augustine, *On Christian Teaching*. Translated by R. P. H. Green (Oxford University Press, 1997).

2 Though James O'Donnell's way of interpreting the title is somewhat unwieldy, it is more accurate than alternatives, such as the laconic *Christian Education*. See O'Donnell, '*Doctrina, Christiana, De*' in Allan D. Fitzgerald, O.S.A., *Augustine Through the Ages: An Encyclopedia* (Grand Rapids, Mich.: Eerdmans, 1999), pp. 278–80, 278.

3 Rowan Williams, 'Language, reality and Desire in Augustine's *De doctrina Christiana*', in *The Journal of Literature and Theology*, Vol. 3, No. 2 (1989), 138–50, 138.

4 See the discussion of William S. Babcock, '*Caritas* and Signification in *De Doctrina Christiana* 1–3', in Duane Arnold and Pamela Bright (eds), *De Doctrina Christiana: A Classic of Western Culture* (Notre Dame, 1995), pp. 145–63.

5 Werner Jeanrond, *Theological Hermeneutics: Development and Significance* (New York: Crossroad, 1991), p. 23.

6 O'Donnell, p. 280.
7 Williams, 'Language, Reality and Desire', 140.
8 Ibid., 142–3: 'A language which indefinitely postpones fulfilment or enjoyment is appropriate to the Christian discipline of spiritual homelessness, to the character of the believing life as pilgrimage.'
9 See John C. Cavadini, 'The Sweetness of the Word: Salvation and Rhetoric in Augustine's *De Doctrina Christiana*', in Duane Arnold and Pamela Bright (eds), *De Doctrina Christiana: A Classic of Western Culture* (Notre Dame, 1995), pp. 164–81, 170.
10 Matthew Lamb, 'Eternity Creates and Redeems Time: A Key to Augustine's *Confessions* within a Theology of History', in Michael Treschow, Willemien Otten and Walter Hannam (eds), *Divine Creation in Ancient, Patristic and Early Modern Thought* (Brill, 2007), p. 137.

Chapter 4

1 Thomas Aquinas, *Super Boetium de Trinitate* q.2, a.3 ad 5. Translated by Rose E. Brennan, S.H.N. (Herder, 1946). Available at: http://dhspriory.org/thomas/BoethiusDeTr.htm (Accessed 7 October 2011).
2 *Luther's Works* [LW], Jaroslav Pelikan and Helmut T. Lehmann (eds) (St Louis, MO: Concordia, and Philadelphia, PA: Fortress Press, 1955–86), Vol. 36, p. 109.
3 Paul Rorem, 'Foreword', in Colm Luibheid, transl. *Pseudo-Dionysius, The Complete Works* (London: SPCK, 1987), p. 3.
4 Dionysius, *The Divine Names* 1.2, in Luibheid, p. 50.
5 Dionysius, *The Mystical Theology* in Luibheid, p. 135.
6 Ibid., 1.3, p. 137.
7 Ibid.
8 Ibid., p. 139.
9 Janet P. Williams, 'Pseudo Dionysius and Maximus the Confessor', in G. R. Evans, *The First Christian Theologians* (Blackwell, 2004), pp. 186–200, p. 189.
10 Vladimir Lossky, *The Mystical Theology of the Eastern Church* (London: J. Clarke, 1957).
11 John D. Jones, '(Mis?)-reading the Divine Names as a Science: Aquinas' Interpretation of the Divine Names of (Pseudo) Dionysius Areopagite' in *St. Vladimir's Theological Quarterly*, 52, 2 (2008), 143–72.
12 Dionysius, Letter 9, in Luibheid, p. 283.
13 *Celestial Hierarchy* 2.2, in Luibheid, p. 149.
14 Ibid., 3.1 in Luibheid, p. 153.
15 Ibid., 2.3 in Luibheid, p. 149.

16 Ian Logan, *Reading Anselm's* Proslogion: *The History of Anselm's Argument and its Significance Today* (Aldershot, UK: Ashgate, 2009), p. 23.

17 See Barth, *Anselm: Fides Quarens Intellectum*. Translated by Ian W. Robertson (London: SCM Press, 1960).

18 I am dependent on Richard Campbell's analysis to a large extent here in 'Anselm's Theological Method', in *Scottish Journal of Theology* 32 (1979), 541–62, 557.

19 Logan, *Reading Anselm's* Proslogion, p. 20.

20 Ibid., 14–17, 125–7.

21 *Reply to Gaunilo*, p. 1. See Brian Davies and G. R. Evans (eds), *Anselm of Canterbury The Major Works* (Oxford University Press, 1998), p. 111.

22 *Proslogion*, p. 18. See Brian Davies and G. R. Evans (eds), *Anselm of Canterbury The Major Works* (Oxford University Press, 1998), p. 97.

23 See David Hogg, *Anselm of Canterbury: The Beauty of Theology* (Ashgate, 2004), p. 168.

24 See the discussion in Hogg, pp. 174–81.

25 See Brad Kallenberg, 'Praying for Understanding: Reading Anselm Through Wittgenstein', in *Modern Theology* 20: 4 (October 2004), 527–46.

26 G. R. Evans, 'Anselm of Canterbury', in G. R. Evans, *The Medieval Theologians* (Blackwell, 2001), pp. 94–101, 100.

27 *Monologion* 68, in Davies and Evans, p. 74.

28 See Thomas Aquinas, *Summa Theologiae* II, II, q. 94, a.1.

29 Ibid., I, 1, a.2. The citation is quoted from Anton Pegis (ed.), *Basic Writings of Thomas Aquinas*, Vol. 1 (New York: Random House, 1945), pp. 6–7.

30 See John I. Jenkins's discussion of this in *Knowledge and Faith in Thomas Aquinas* (Cambridge Univ. Press, 1997), pp. 53–5.

31 Summa Theologiae I, 1, a.7.

32 Ibid., I, 1, a.5.

33 Ibid.

34 See Christopher Kaczor, 'Thomas Aquinas on the Development of Doctrine', in *Theological Studies* 62 (2001), 283–302.

35 Jean-Pierre Torrell O. P., *Aquinas's Summa Background, Structure and Reception* (Catholic University of America Press, 2005), pp. 71–3.

36 *Method in Theology* (New York: Seabury, 1972), pp. 336–7.

37 We cannot know what God is or how God is, only that God is, what God is not and how God is not, a claim that appears in the prologue of the *Summa Theologiae* I, q. 2. Cf. Torrell, p. 22.

38 See Rudi te Velde's discussion of this issue in *Aquinas on God: The 'Divine Science' of the* Summa Theologiae (Aldershot, UK: Ashgate, 2006), pp. 37–9.

Chapter 5

1   Martin Luther, *D. Martin Luthers Werke: Kritische Gesamtausgabe*
    (Weimar: Böhlau, 1883-): Vol. 5, 176, 32–3. The German *Weimarer
    Ausgabe* edition of the Collected Works is cited hereafter in
    abbreviated form as *WA* with its volume, page and line number(s).
2   See B. A. Gerrish, *Grace and Reason: A Study in the Theology of
    Luther* (Oxford: Clarendon Press, 1962), p. 1.
3   See Paul Hacker, *The Ego in Faith: Martin Luther and the Origins of
    Anthropocentric Religion* (Chicago: Franciscan Herald Press, 1970).
4   Roland Bainton, *Here I Stand: A Life of Martin Luther* (Nashville,
    Tenn.: Abingdon Press, 1950), pp. 18–19.
5   Bernhard Lohse, *Martin Luther's Theology: Its Historical and
    Systematic Development* (Edinburgh: T&T Clark, 1999), p. 10.
6   *WA* 5,166, 11; 5, 85, 2f.
7   Ibid., 54, 179–87.
8   Ibid., 39, 1, 205.
9   Oswald Bayer, 'Luther as an Interpreter of Holy Scripture' translated
    by Mark Mattes in Donald McKim (ed.), *The Cambridge Companion
    to Martin Luther* (Cambridge University Press, 2003), pp. 73–85, 76.
10 English translation by Alister E. McGrath in *Luther's Theology of the
    Cross* (Basil Blackwell, 1985), p. 148.
11 Ibid, p. 149.
12 Luther, 'The Freedom of a Christian', re-printed in Denis Janz
    (ed.), *A Reformation Reader: Primary Texts with Introductions*
    (Minneapolis, Minn.: Fortress Press, 1999), pp. 98–106, 100.
13 Quoted by James Arne Nestingen, 'Approaching Luther', in McKim
    (ed.) (2003), p. 249.
14 *WA* 9, 98, 21; 40 III, 63, 17f. See Oswald Bayer, 'Martin Luther
    (1483–546)', in Carter Lindberg (ed.), *The Reformation Theologians:
    An Introduction to Theology in the Early Modern Period* (Blackwell,
    2002), pp. 51–66, 52–3.
15 This is reported by Sachiko Kusukawa in *The Transformation of
    Natural Philosophy: The Case of Philip Melanchthon* (Cambridge
    University Press, 1995), p. 57.
16 Ibid., p. 70
17 See Gerald Strauss, *Luther's House of Learning: Indoctrination of
    the Young in the German Reformation* (Baltimore: Johns Hopkins
    University Press, 1978).
18 *Loci communes Theologici*. Translated by Lowell Satre and Wilhelm
    Pauck in Wilhelm Pauck, (ed.), *Melanchthon and Bucer*, Library of
    Christian Classics, Vol. 19 (Philadelphia: Westminster Press, 1969),
    p. 24.

19 See *Melanchthons Werke in Auswahl: Studienausgabe*, in
    R. Stupperich (ed.) (Gütersloh: Bertelsmann, 1963), Vol. I, 31.Cf.
    Kusukawa, p. 41.

20 Quoted in Kusukawa, p. 66. Cf. *Corpus reformatorum Philippi
    Melanthonis opera quae supersunt omnia*. Edited by C. B.
    Bretschneider and H. E. Bindseil (Halle, 1834–52; Brunswick
    1853–60), XII, p. 692.

21 Ibid., XII, p. 695.

22 Melanchthon, 'Apology of the Augsburg Confession', in Janz (ed.),
    p. 157.

23 Cited in Eberhard Busch, *Karl Barth: His Life from Letters and
    Autobiographical Texts* transl. John Bowden (Philadelphia: Fortress
    Press, 1976), p. 439.

24 Calvin, *Institutes of the Christian Religion*. Translated by Ford
    Lewis Battles in The Library of Christian Classics. Edited by John
    T. McNeill. 2 vols. (London: SCM Press, 1960), I, 1.1, 35.

25 Ibid., I,1.1, 36, n. 3.

26 *Calvin's Institutes*. Abridged and edited by Donald K. McKim.
    (Louisville: Westminster John Knox, 2000), pp. 68–9.

27 Calvin, *Institutes*, I, 3.1, 43; Cf. McKim, p. 4.

28 Ronald Wallace, *Calvin, Geneva and the Reformation: A Study
    of Calvin as Social Reformer, Churchman, Pastor and Theologian*
    (Edinburgh: Scottish Academic Press), pp. 223–4.

29 John T. Thompson, 'Calvin as Biblical Interpreter', in Donald K.
    McKim (ed.), *The Cambridge Companion to Calvin* (Cambridge:
    Cambridge University Press, 2004), pp. 58–73. See pp. 61–2.

30 Calvin, *Institutes*, 1.6.2, 71; Cf. McKim, p. 9.

31 Calvin, *Institutes* 1,7.1, 75. Cf. McKim, p. 10.

32 Calvin, *Institutes* 1.9.1, 94. Cf. McKim, p. 13.

33 Calvin, *Institutes* 1.9.1, 93.

34 Calvin, *Institutes* 3.2.33–4.

35 Calvin, *Institutes* 4.1.9. See. McKim, p. 129.

36 Calvin, *Institutes* 4.1.9. See. McKim, p. 129.

37 See 'Prefatory Address to King Francis I of France', in Calvin,
    Institutes, p. 9.

38 See Dulles, *The Craft of Theology: From Symbol to System*
    (Dublin: Gill and Macmillan, 1992), Chap. 5.

Chapter 6

1 See Brian A. Gerrish in *Continuing the Reformation: Essays on
   Modern Thought* (Chicago: University of Chicago Press, 1993),
   p. 151.

2 F. D. E. Schleiermacher, *On Religion: speeches to its cultured despisers* (New York: Harper Torchbook, 1958), p. 36.

3 B. McCormack, 'What Has Basel to Do with Berlin? Continuities in the Theologies of Barth and Schleiermacher', in *Princeton Seminary Bulletin* 23, 2 (2002), 146–73, 161.

4 F. D. E. Schleiermacher, *The Christian Faith*. Edited by H. R. Mackintosh and J. S. Stewart (Edinburgh: T&T Clark 1999), I, §3, 5, 11

5 Schleiermacher, *The Christian Faith* I, I §4, 13.

6 Ibid., I, III, §11, 56.

7 Hunsinger, *Disruptive Grace: Studies in the Theology of Karl Barth* (Grand Rapids, MI: Eerdmans, 2000), p. 283.

8 Christine Helmer, 'Schleiermacher', in David Fergusson (ed)., *Blackwell Companion to Nineteenth Century Theology* (Wiley Blackwell, 2010), pp. 31–57, 47.

9 Richard Crouter, 'Shaping an Academic Discipline: The *Brief Outline on the Study of Theology*', in Jacqueline Mariña (ed.), *The Cambridge Companion to Friedrich Schleiermacher* (Cambridge University Press, 2005), pp. 111–28, 120.

10 Schleiermacher, *Brief Outline of the Study of Theology*. Translated by Terrence N. Tice (Richmond, Va.: John Knox Press, 1966), §97, 48.

11 See Helmer, p. 40.

12 Schleiermacher, *Brief Outline of the Study of Theology*, §1, 19.

13 Ibid., § 101, 49.

14 Schleiermacher, *The Christian Faith* 62.3. Edited by H. R. Mackintosh and J. S. Stewart (Edinburgh: T&T Clark, 1928), p. 261.

15 Francis Fiorenza's characterization of contemporary dialectics which turn on the interpretation of Schleiermacher strike me as plausible. See Fiorenza, 'The Construction of a Contemporary Roman Catholic Foundational Theology', in *Harvard Theological Review* 89:2 (1996), 175–94 and 'Schleiermacher's Understanding of God as Triune', in Mariña (ed.), *The Cambridge Companion to Friedrich Schleiermacher* (Cambridge University Press, 2005), pp. 171–88.

16 *The Great Dissent: John Henry Newman and the Liberal Heresy* (New York: Oxford University Press, 1991), p. 5.

17 Newman, *Essay on the Development of Christian Doctrine* (London: Sheed & Ward, 1960), p. 6.

18 Ibid., p. 9.

19 Ibid., p. 13.

20 Ibid., pp. 42–3.

21 Newman, *University Sermons* quoted by Brian Daley, 'The Church Fathers', in Ian Ker and Terrence Merrigan (eds), *The Cambridge Companion to John Henry Newman* (Cambridge: Cambridge University Press, 2009), p. 36.

22 Daley, pp. 43–4.

23 See the excellent discussion of this aspect of Newman's thought in Fergus Kerr, 'Tradition and Reason: Two Uses of Reason, Critical and Contemplative', in *International Journal of Systematic Theology*, Vol.6, 1 (January 2004), 37–49, 40–2.

24 Quoted by Sheridan Gilley, 'Life and Writings', in Ian Ker and Terrence Merrigan (eds), *The Cambridge Companion to John Henry Newman* (Cambridge: Cambridge University Press, 2009), pp. 1–28, 23.

25 Quoted in Terrence Merrigan, 'Revelation', in Ker and Merrigan, pp. 47–72, 51.

26 As summarized by Max Reischle in *Ein Wort zur Controverse über die Mystik in der Theologie* (Freiburg im Breisgau: J. C. B. Mohr [Paul Siebeck], 1886), 5. Quoted in Christine Helmer, 'Mysticism and Metaphysics: Schleiermacher and a Theological-Historical Trajectory' in *Journal of Religion*, Vol. 83, No. 4 (2003), 517–38.

27 Albrecht Ritschl, *The Christian Doctrine of Justification and Reconciliation III*. Translated by H. R. Mackintosh and A. B. Macaulay (Edinburgh, 1900), pp. 2–3.

28 Ritschl, p. 393.

29 Ibid., p. 9.

30 Harnack, 'Über die Sicherheit und Grenzen geschichtlicher Erkenntnis', in *Redden und Aufsätze*, IV, 7. Cited in Wilhelm Pauck, *The Heritage of the Reformation* (New York: Oxford University Press, 1961), p. 340.

31 *Marcion: Das Evangelium von frenden Gott* 2nd edn. (Leipzig: Hinrichs 1924), p. 217. Cf. Wilhelm Pauck, *The Heritage of the Reformation* (New York: Oxford University Press, 1961), p. 343.

32 Harnack, *What is Christianity?* Translated by T. B. Saunders (London: Williams and Norgate, 1901), p. 51.

33 See Harnack, *What is Christianity?* 5th edn. Translated by Thomas B. Saunders (London: Ernest Benn Ltd., 1958), p. 184.

Chapter 7

1 Paul Tillich, *Systematic Theology*, Vol. 1 (Chicago: University of Chicago Press, 1951), p. 34.

2 Hans Frei, *The Five Types of Theology*. Edited by George Hunsinger and William C. Placher. (New Haven, Conn.: Yale University Press, 1992).

3 Schubert Ogden, 'The Significance of Rudolf Bultmann', in *Perkins Journal of Theology* (Winter, 1962), 5–17, 7.

4 Rudolf Bultmann, 'New Testament and Mythology', in Hans Werner Bartsch (ed.), *Kerygma and Myth* (New York: Harper and Row, 1961), pp. 1–44, 42.

5 Ibid., p. 39.

6   Ibid., p. 10.
7   Rudolf Bultmann, *Essays Philosophical and Theological* (London: SCM Press, 1955), p. 256.
8   'Bultmann Replies to his Critics', in Hans-Werner Bartsch (ed.), *Kerygma and Myth*, (New York: Harper and Row, 1961), pp. 191–211, 210–11.
9   Thomas Torrance, *Theological Science* (Oxford: Oxford University Press, 1969), pp. 327, 329–30. Cf. Benjamin Myers' helpful, counterintuitive article 'Faith as Self-Understanding: Towards a Post-Barthian Appreciation of Rudolf Bultmann', in *International Journal of Systematic Theology*, Vol. 10, No. 1 (January 2008), 21–35.
10 Bultmann quoted in Joseph Ratzinger, *Jesus of Nazareth* (New York: Doubleday, 2007); and Bultmann, *The Gospel of John: A Commentary*, translated by G. Beasley-Murray. (Philadelphia: The Westminster Press, 1955), p. 26.
11 Bultmann, *Primitive Christianity in its Contemporary Setting*. Translated by Rev. R. H. Fuller (Cleveland: World Pub. Co., 1956), p. 188.
12 Bultmann, 'New Testament and Mythology', p. 4.
13 Bultmann, *Theology of the New Testament*, Vol. 2 (Waco, TX: Baylor University Press, 2007), p. 237.
14 Karl Barth, *Church Dogmatics*, III/2 (Edinburgh: T & T Clark, 1975), 6.
15 Ibid., I/2, 820.
16 Ibid., 1/1, 16.
17 Ibid., 1/1, 463.
18 Ibid., I/2, 458.
19 Ibid., I/1, 39.
20 Ibid., I,1, 41.
21 Ibid., I,1, xiii. Barth's comment is cited most frequently with respect to his averring that such a formula of natural theology prevents him from becoming a Catholic. A more extensive reading of the preface to the first volume in the *Church Dogmatics* reveals that Barth makes this dramatic statement in order to answer the charge made that he is becoming a scholastic.
22 See *Church Dogmatics*, I/2, 866. Cf. Stephen Sykes (ed.), *Karl Barth: Studies of his Theological Method* (Oxford: Clarendon Press, 1979), p. 33.
23 Rudolf Bultmann, 'New Testament and Mythology', p. 9.
24 *Church Dogmatics*, I,1, 11.
25 Karl Barth, *Church Dogmatics*, I,1, 4–5.
26 Ibid., I,1, 5.
27 Bultmann, Letter to Karl Barth, 8 June 1928. See Bernd Jasper (ed.), *Karl Barth ~ Rudolf Bultmann Letters 1922–66*. Translated by Geoffrey W. Bromiley. (Grand Rapids, Mich.: Eerdmans, 1991), p. 39.

28 See Sykes, *Karl Barth*, p. 31.
29 Cited in H. Martin Rumscheidt, *Revelation and Theology. An Analysis of the Barth-Harnack Correspondence of 1923* (Cambridge: Cambridge University Press, 1972). Cf Sykes, pp. 27–8.
30 Barth, *The Theology of Schleiermacher*. Edited by Dietrich Ritschl, translated by Geoffrey W. Bromiley (Edinburgh: T&T Clark, 1982), p. 264.
31 Barth, The Theology of Friedrich Schleiermacher, p. 190.
32 Ibid., p. 210.
33 Tillich, 'The Problem of Theological Method', reprinted in Mark Kline Taylor (ed.), *Paul Tillich: Theologian of the Boundaries* (London: Collins, 1987), pp. 126–41, 128.
34 Tillich, *Systematic Theology*, Vol. 1 (University of Chicago Press, 1951), p. 61.
35 Ibid., Vol. 1, 3.
36 Ibid., Vol. 1, 60–1.
37 Ibid., Vol. 1, 62–3.
38 Ibid., Vol. 1, 65.
39 From Tillich, *The Courage to Be* (New Haven, Conn.: Yale University Press, 1952), pp. 187–8.
40 *Systematic Theology*, Vol. 3 (1963), p. 201.
41 Tillich, 'Theology and Symbolism', in F. Ernest Johnson (ed.), *Religious Symbols* (Harper and Row, 1955), p. 108. Cf. David Kelsey, *The Fabric of Paul Tillich's Theology* (New Haven, Conn.: Yale University Press, 1967), p. 3.
42 Tillich, *Systematic Theology*, Vol. 1, p. 242.
43 Ibid., Vol. 1, p. 127.
44 See Kelsey, *The Fabric of Paul Tillich's Theology*, pp. 38–40.
45 See *The Glory of the Lord* V, p. 656. Cf. Fergus Kerr, 'Balthasar and Metaphysics', in Edward T. Oakes, S. J. and David Moss (eds), *The Cambridge Companion to Hans Urs von Balthasar* (Cambridge University Press, 2004), pp. 224–38, 224.
46 'Theology and Philosophy', in Medard Kehl and Werner Löser (eds). *Von Balthasar Reader*. Translated by Robert J. Daly S.J. and Frederick Lawrence (New York: Crossroad, 1997), pp. 362–7, 363.
47 Von Balthasar, 'Theology – A Science?' in Kehl and Löser, pp. 359–62, 361.
48 Balthasar, *The Theology of Karl Barth* (San Francisco: Ignatius Books, 1992), p. 98.
49 Aidan Nichols, *The Word has been Abroad: A Guide through Balthasar's Aesthetics* (Edinburgh: T&T Clark, 1998), p. 92. Cf. Balthasar, *The Glory of the Lord*, Vol. III (Edinburgh: T&T Clark, 1986).
50 Balthasar, *Mysterium Paschale*. Translated by Aidan Nichols, (Edinburgh: T&T Clark, 1990), p. 49.

51 He assumed humanity so that we might become God. See Athanasius, *On the Incarnation of the Word* 54.3, 93.

52 Ben Quash and John Riches, 'Hans Urs von Balthasar', in David Ford (ed). *The Modern Theologians* (Oxford: Blackwell, 1997), pp. 134–51, 147.

53 See Rahner, 'The Future of Theology', in *Theological Investigations* XI (New York: Crossroad, 1960), p. 134. Cited by Francis Schüssler-Fiorenza, 'Method in Theology', in Declan Marmion and Mary E. Hines (eds). *The Cambridge Companion to Karl Rahner* (Cambridge University Press, 2005), pp. 65–82, 78.

54 Paul Imhof and Hubert Biallowons (eds). *Karl Rahner in Dialogue* (Crossroad, 1986), pp. 196–7.

55 Charles Taylor, *Philosophical Arguments* (Cambridge: Cambridge University Press, 1995), p. 21. Cf. J. A. DiNoia OP, 'Karl Rahner', in David Ford (ed.). *The Modern Theologians: An Introduction to Twentieth Century Theology* (Blackwell, 1997), pp. 118–33, 122.

56 Karen Kilby, *Karl Rahner: A Brief Introduction* (New York: Crossroad, 2007), p. 57.

57 Rahner, 'Christ the Mediator: One Person and Two Natures', in Gerald A. McCool, *A Rahner Reader* (New York: Crossroad, 1984), pp. 155–6.

58 Schillebeeckx, *Jesus: An Experiment in Christology*. Translated by Hubert Hoskins (New York: Crossroad, 1989), pp. 19–20.

59 Schillebeeckx, *Christ: The Experience of Jesus as Lord* (New York: Seabury, 1980), p. 729.

60 Schillebeeckx, 'Toward a Full Humanity', in Robert Schreiter (ed.). *The Schillebeeckx Reader* (New York: Crossroad, 1987), p. 63.

61 Schillebeeckx, *Jesus*, p. 644.

62 Schillebeeckx, *Interim Report on the Books* Jesus *and* Christ. (New York: Crossroad, 1981), p. 51.

63 Louis Dupré, 'Experience and Interpretation: A Philosophical Reflection on Schillebeeckx' *Jesus* and *Christ*', in *Theological Studies* 43, 1 (1982), 30–51, 47.

Chapter 8

1 Walter Kasper, *Jesus the Christ* (Mahwah, N.J.: Paulist Press, 1976), p. 15.

2 John Milbank, 'Postmodern Critical Augustinianism: A Short *Summa* in Forty-two Responses to Unasked Questions', in Graham Ward (ed.), *The Postmodern God: A Theological Reader* (Oxford: Blackwell, 1997), pp. 265–78.

3 See his accessible *Introducing Radical Orthodoxy: Mapping a Post-Secular Theology* (Grand Rapids, Mich.: Baker Academic, 2004).

4 John Milbank, 'Can a Gift be Given?', in L. G. Jones and S. E. Fowl (eds), *Rethinking Metaphysics* (Oxford: Blackwell, 1995), pp. 119–61, 145.

5 Pickstock, *After Writing*, xiii.

6 Paul De Hart, *The Trial of the Witnesses: The Rise and Decline of Postliberal Theology* (Oxford: Blackwell, 2006), p. 85.

7 See David Ford, 'Hans Frei and the Future of Theology', in *Modern Theology* 8, 2 (1992), 203–14, 207.

8 George Lindbeck, *The Nature of Doctrine: Religion and Theology in a Postliberal Age* (Philadelphia: Westminster Press, 1984), p. 114.

9 Ibid., p. 74.

10 Ibid., p. 77.

11 Ibid., pp. 82–3.

12 David Kelsey, *Eccentric Existence: A Theological Anthropology*, Vol. 1 (Louisville, Ky.: Westminster John Knox Press, 2009), p. 41.

13 Gustavo Gutierrez, *A Theology of Liberation: History, Politics and Salvation* Rev. edn. (Maryknoll, N.Y.: Orbis Books, 1988), p. 104.

14 Joseph Ratzinger (Pope Benedict XVI), *Faith, Reason and the University: Memories and Reflections* (*Aula magna* of the University of Regensburg, 12 September 2006). http://www.vatican.va/holy_father/benedict_xvi/speeches/2006/september/documents/hf_ben-xvi_spe_20060912_university-regensburg_en.html (accessed 15 December 2010)

15 Ratzinger, *Faith, Reason and the University*. http://www.vatican.va/holy_father/benedict_xvi/speeches/2006/september/documents/hf_ben-xvi_spe_20060912_university-regensburg_en.html

16 Ratzinger, *Principles of Catholic Theology* (San Francisco: Ignatius Press, 1987), p. 316.

17 Ratzinger, *Introduction to Christianity* (New York: Continuum, 1986), p. 98.

18 Ibid., p. 99.

19 Ratzinger, 'Biblical Interpretation in Crisis', in John F. Thornton and Susan B. Varenne (eds), *The Essential Pope Benedict XVI: His Essential Writings and Speeches* (New York: HarperCollins, 2007), pp. 254, 247.

20 Ratzinger, *Jesus of Nazareth* (New York: Doubleday, 2007), pp. 4–8, 236.

21 Kant, *Critique of Pure Reason*, B. Translated by N. Kemp Smith (New York: St Martin's Press, 1965), preface.

22 Kathryn Tanner, 'How I changed My Mind', in Darren C. Marks (ed.), *Shaping a Theological Mind: Theological Context and methodology* (Aldershot, UK: Ashgate, 2002), pp. 115–22, 119–20.

BIBLIOGRAPHY

Allen, Diogenes. *Philosophy for Understanding Theology*, 2nd edition. Nashville, TN: Westminster John Knox Press, 2007.

Altaner, B., *Patrology*. Translated by Hilda Graef. New York, NY: Herder & Herder, 1961.

Anselm, 'Monologion', 'Proslogion' and 'Reply to Gaunilo'. In *Anselm of Canterbury: The Major Works*. Edited by Brian Davies and G. R. Evans. Oxford: Oxford University Press, 1998, pp. 5–81, 82–104 and 111–22.

Aquinas, T., *Summa Theologiae*. Blackfriars edition in 60 vols. Cambridge: Blackfriars/New York: McGraw Hill, 1964–73.

—*Super Boetium de Trinitate*. Translated by Rose E. Brennan, S. H. N. New York, NY: Herder, 1946.

Aristotle, *The Metaphysics*. Translated by Hugh Tredennick. Cambridge, MA: Harvard University Press, 1974.

Athanasius, *On the Incarnation of the Word*. Crestwood, NY: St. Vladimir's Seminary Press, 1993.

— 'Letter 40: To Adelphius, Bishop and Confessor, Against the Arians'. In *Athanasius*. Edited by Khaled Anatolios. New York, NY: Routledge, 2004, pp. 234–42.

—*Orations against the Arians*. Edited by William Bright. Oxford: Clarendon Press, 1873.

Augustine, *On Christian Teaching*. Translated by R. P. H. Green. Oxford: Oxford University Press, 1997.

Babcock, W. S., '*Caritas* and Signification in *De doctrina Christiana* 1–3'. In *De Doctrina Christiana: A Classic of Western Culture*. Edited by Duane Arnold and Pamela Bright. Notre Dame, IN: University of Notre Dame Press, 1995, pp. 145–63.

Badiou, A., *Saint Paul: The Foundation of Universalism*. Stanford, CA: Stanford University Press, 2003.

Bainton, R., *Here I Stand: A Life of Martin Luther*. Nashville, TN: Abingdon Press, 1950.

Balthasar, H. U. von., *The Glory of the Lord: A Theological Aesthetics*, Vols I–VII. Edited by Joseph Fessio and John Riches. Translated by Erasmo Leiva-Merikakis. Edinburgh: T&T Clark, 1982.

— *Mysterium Paschale*. Translated by Aidan Nichols. Edinburgh: T&T Clark, 1990.

— *The Theology of Karl Barth*. San Francisco, CA: Ignatius Books, 1992.

— 'Theology – A Science?' and 'Theology and Philosophy'. In *The Von Balthasar Reader*. Edited by Medard Kehl and Werner Löser. Translated by Robert J. Daly S. J. and Frederick Lawrence. New York, NY: Crossroad, 1997, pp. 359–67.

Barth, K., *Anselm: Fides Quarens Intellectum*. Translated by Ian W. Robertson. London: SCM Press, 1960.

— *Church Dogmatics*, Vols I–V. Translated by G. W. Bromiley. Edinburgh: T&T Clark, 1936.

— *The Theology of Schleiermacher*. Edited by Dietrich Ritschl. Translated by Geoffrey W. Bromiley. Edinburgh: T&T Clark, 1982.

Bayer, O., 'Luther as an Interpreter of Holy Scripture'. In *The Cambridge Companion to Martin Luther*. Edited by Donald McKim and translated by Mark Mattes. Cambridge: Cambridge University Press, 2003, pp. 73–85.

— 'Martin Luther (1483–1546)'. In *The Reformation Theologians: An Introduction to Theology in the Early Modern Period*. Edited by Carter Lindberg. Oxford: Blackwell, 2002.

Beckett, L., 'Not a Theory, but a Life'. In *The Times Literary Supplement*, 3 August 2007, 23–4.

Behr, J., *The Formation of Christian Theology Vol. 1: The Way to Nicea*. Crestwood, NY: St. Vladimir's Seminary Press, 2001.

Beker, J. C. *Paul the Apostle: the Triumph of God in Life and Thought*. Philadelphia, PA: Fortress Press, 1980.

Bloom, H., *How to Read and Why*. New York, NY: Simon and Schuster, 2000.

Brown, R. E., J. A. Fitzmyer and R. E. Murphy (eds.) *The New Jerome Biblical Commentary*. London: Geoffrey Champman, 1989.

Bruce, F. F., *Paul and Jesus*. London: SPCK, 1974.

— 'Pauline Theology'. In *The Jerome Biblical Commentary*. Edited by Raymond E. Brown, (S.S.), Joseph Fitzmyer, (S.J.) and Roland Murphy, (O.Carm). Englewood Cliffs, NJ: Prentice Hall, 1968.

Bultmann, R., 'Bultmann Replies to his Critics'. In *Kerygma and Myth*. Edited by Hans Werner Bartsch. New York, NY: Harper and Row, 1961, pp. 191–211.

— *Essays Philosophical and Theological*. London: SCM Press, 1955.

— *The Gospel of John: A Commentary*. Translated by George Beasley-Murray. Philadelphia, PA: The Westminster Press, 1955.

— 'Letter to Karl Barth, June 8, 1928'. In *Karl Barth ~ Rudolf Bultmann Letters 1922–66*. Edited by Bernd Jasper and translated by Geoffrey W. Bromiley. Grand Rapids, MI: Eerdmans, 1991.

—'New Testament and Mythology'. In *Kerygma and Myth*. Edited by Hans Werner Bartsch. New York, NY: Harper and Row, 1961, pp. 1–44.

—*Primitive Christianity in its Contemporary Setting*. Translated by Rev. Reginald H. Fuller. Cleveland, OH: World Publishing Company, 1956.

—*Theology of the New Testament*, Vol. 2. Translated by Kendrick Grobel. Waco, TX: Baylor University Press, 2007.

Busch, E., *Karl Barth: His Life from Letters and Autobiographical Texts*. Translated by John Bowden. Philadelphia, PA: Fortress Press, 1976.

Butterworth, G. W. (ed.), *Origen on First Principles*. London: SPCK, 1936.

Calvin, J., *Institutes of the Christian Religion*. Edited by John T. McNeill. Translated by Ford Lewis Battles. 2 vols. The Library of Christian Classics 20–1. Philadelphia, PA: Westminster, 1960.

Campbell, R., 'Anselm's Theological Method'. *Scottish Journal of Theology*, 32 (1979), 541–62.

Cavadini, J. C., 'The Sweetness of the Word: Salvation and Rhetoric in Augustine's *De Doctrina Christiana*'. In *De Doctrina Christiana: A Classic of Western Culture*. Edited by Duane Arnold and Pamela Bright. Notre Dame, IN: University of Notre Dame Press, 1995, pp. 164–81.

Crossan, J. D., *Jesus: A Revolutionary Biography*. New York, NY: HarperOne, 1995.

Crouter, R., 'Shaping an Academic Discipline: The *Brief Outline on the Study of Theology*'. In *The Cambridge Companion to Friedrich Schleiermacher*. Edited by Jacqueline Mariña. Cambridge: Cambridge University Press, 2005, pp. 111–28.

Daley, B., 'The Church Fathers'. In *The Cambridge Companion to John Henry Newman*. Edited by Ian Ker and Terrence Merrigan. Cambridge: Cambridge University Press, 2009, pp. 29–46.

De Lubac, H., *History and Spirit*. San Francisco, CA: Ignatius Press, 2007.

De Hart, P., *The Trial of the Witnesses: The Rise and Decline of Postliberal Theology*. Oxford: Blackwell, 2006.

DiNoia OP, J. A., 'Karl Rahner'. In *The Modern Theologians: An Introduction to Twentieth Century Theology*. Edited by David Ford. Oxford: Blackwell, 1997, pp. 118–33.

Dionysius, 'The Celestial Hierarchy', 'The Divine Names', 'The Mystical Theology' and 'The Letters'. In *Pseudo-Dionysius, The Complete Works*. Edited and translated by Colm Luibheid. London: SPCK, 1987, pp. 143–92, 47–132, 133–42 and 261–90.

Dulles, A., *The Craft of Theology: From Symbol to System*. Dublin: Gill and Macmillan, 1992.

Dunn, J., *Christology in the Making*. London: SCM Press, 1989.

Dupré, L., 'Experience and Interpretation: A Philosophical Reflection on Schillebeeckx' *Jesus* and *Christ*'. *Theological Studies*, 43, 1 (1982), 30–51.

Eusebius of Caesarea, *The History of the Church from Christ to Constantine* (*Ecclesiastical History*). Edited by Andrew Louth. London: Penguin, 1989.

Evans, G. R., 'Anselm of Canterbury'. In *The Medieval Theologians*. Edited by G. R. Evans. Oxford: Blackwell, 2001, pp. 94–101.

Fairburn, D., 'Patristic Soteriologies: Three Trajectories'. *The Journal of The Evangelical Theological Society*, 50, 2 (2007), 289–310.

Farrow, D., 'St. Irenaeus of Lyons: The Church and the World'. *Pro Ecclesia*, 4, 3 (1995), 333–55.

Fiorenza, F. S., 'The Construction of a Contemporary Roman Catholic Foundational Theology'. *Harvard Theological Review*, 89, 2 (1996), 175–94.

—'Method in Theology'. In *The Cambridge Companion to Karl Rahner*. Edited by Declan Marmion and Mary E. Hines. Cambridge: Cambridge University Press, 2005, pp. 65–82.

—'Schleiermacher's Understanding of God as Triune'. In *The Cambridge Companion to Friedrich Schleiermacher*. Edited by Jacqueline Mariña. Cambridge: Cambridge University Press, 2005, pp. 171–88.

Ford, D., 'Hans Frei and the Future of Theology'. *Modern Theology*, 8, 2 (1992), 203–14.

Frei, H., *The Five Types of Theology*. Edited by George Hunsinger and William C. Placher. New Haven, CT: Yale University Press, 1992.

Frend, W. H. C., *The Rise of Christianity*. Philadelphia, PA: Fortress Press, 1984.

Freud, S., *Moses and Monotheism*. New York, NY: Vintage, 1939.

Gadamer, H.-G., *Truth and Method* 2nd rev. edn. Translated by Joel Weinsheimer and Donald G. Marshall. New York, NY: Continuum, 1995.

Gerrish, B. A., *Continuing the Reformation: Essays on Modern Thought*. Chicago, IL: University of Chicago Press, 1993.

—*Grace and Reason: A Study in the Theology of Luther*. Oxford: Clarendon Press, 1962.

Gilley, S., 'Life and Writings'. In *The Cambridge Companion to John Henry Newman*. Edited by Ian Ker and Terrence Merrigan. Cambridge: Cambridge University Press, 2009, pp. 1–28

Gunton, C., 'A Rose By Any Other Name? From "Christian Doctrine" to "Systematic Theology"'. *International Journal of Systematic Theology*, 1, 1 (1999), 4–23.

Gutierrez, G., *A Theology of Liberation: History, Politics and Salvation*. Rev. edn. Maryknoll, NY: Orbis Books, 1988.

Hacker, P., *The Ego in Faith: Martin Luther and the Origins of Anthropocentric Religion*. Chicago, IL: Franciscan Herald Press, 1970.

Harnack, A. von., *Marcion: Das Evangelium von Frenden Gott*. 2nd edn. Leipzig: Hinrichs, 1924.

— *What is Christianity?* Translated by Thomas Bailey Saunders. London: Williams and Norgate, 1901. 5th edn. London: Ernest Benn Ltd., 1958.

Hays, R., *Echoes of Scripture in the Letters of Paul*. New Haven, CT: Yale University Press, 1989.

Helmer, C., 'Schleiermacher'. In *Blackwell Companion to Nineteenth Century Theology*. Edited by David Fergusson. Oxford: Wiley Blackwell, 2010, pp. 31–57.

— 'Mysticism and Metaphysics: Schleiermacher and a Theological-Historical Trajectory'. *Journal of Religion*, 83, 4 (2003), 517–38.

Hogg, D., *Anselm of Canterbury: The Beauty of Theology*. Aldershot, UK: Ashgate, 2004.

Hunsinger, G., *Disruptive Grace: Studies in the Theology of Karl Barth*. Grand Rapids, MI: Eerdmans, 2000.

Imhof, P. and H. Biallowons (eds), *Karl Rahner in Dialogue*. New York, NY: Crossroad, 1986.

Irenaeus. *Adversus Haereses*. Translated by Dominic J. Unger. New York, NY: Paulist Press, 1992.

— *Demonstration of the Apostolic Preaching*. Edited by John A. Robinson. London: SPCK, 1920.

Jacobson, A.-C., 'The Importance of Genesis 1–3 in the Theology of Irenaeus'. *Zeitschrift für Antikes Christentum*, 8, 2 (2005), 299–316.

Jasper, B. (ed),. *Karl Barth ~ Rudolf Bultmann Letters 1922–66*. Translated by Geoffrey W. Bromiley. Grand Rapids, MI: Eerdmans, 1991.

Jeanrond, W., *Theological Hermeneutics: Development and Significance*. New York, NY: Crossroad, 1991.

Jenkins, J., *Knowledge and Faith in Thomas Aquinas*. Cambridge: Cambridge University Press, 1997.

Jones, J. D. '(Mis?)-reading the Divine Names as a Science: Aquinas' Interpretation of the Divine Names of (Pseudo) Dionysius Areopagite'. *St. Vladimir's Theological Quarterly*, 52, 2 (2008), 143–72.

Kaczor, C., 'Thomas Aquinas on the Development of Doctrine'. *Theological Studies*, 62, (2001), 283–302.

Kallenberg, B., 'Praying for Understanding: Reading Anselm Through Wittgenstein'. *Modern Theology*, 20, 4 (2004), 527–46.

Kant, I., *Critique of Pure Reason*, B. Translated by N. Kemp Smith. New York, NY: St Martin's Press, 1965.

Kasper, W., *Jesus the Christ*. Mahwah, NJ: Paulist Press, 1976.

— *The Methods of Dogmatic Theology*. New York, NY: Paulist Press, 1969.

Kelsey, D., *Eccentric Existence: A Theological Anthropology*, Vols 1–2. Louisville, KY: Westminster John Knox Press, 2009.
— *The Fabric of Paul Tillich's Theology*. New Haven, CT: Yale University Press, 1967.
Kerr, F., 'Balthasar and Metaphysics'. In *The Cambridge Companion to Hans Urs von Balthasar*. Edited by Edward T. Oakes, S. J. and David Moss. Cambridge: Cambridge University Press, 2004, pp. 224–38.
— 'Tradition and Reason: Two Uses of Reason, Critical and Contemplative'. *International Journal of Systematic Theology*, 6, 1 (2004), 37–49.
Kilby, K., *Karl Rahner: A Brief Introduction*. New York, NY: Crossroad, 2007.
Kirk, J. R. D., *Unlocking Romans: Resurrection and the Justification of God*. Grand Rapids, MI: Eerdmans, 2008.
Kostenberger, A. J. and M. J. Kruger, *The Heresy of Orthodoxy: How Contemporary Culture's Fascination with Diversity Has Reshaped Our Understanding of Early Christianity*. Wheaton, IL: Crossway Books, 2010.
Kuhn, T. S., *The Structure of Scientific Revolutions*. Chicago, IL: Chicago Univ. of Chicago Press, 1970.
Küng, H., *Does God Exist?* Translated by Edward Quinn. New York, NY: Vintage Books, 1981.
Kusukawa, S., *The Transformation of Natural Philosophy: The Case of Philip Melanchthon*. Cambridge: Cambridge University Press, 1995.
Lamb, M., 'Eternity Creates and Redeems Time: A Key to Augustine's *Confessions* within a Theology of History'. In *Divine Creation in Ancient, Patristic and Early Modern Thought*. Edited by Michael Treschow, Willemien Otten and Walter Hannam. Leiden: Brill, 2007, pp. 117–40.
Lindbeck, G., *The Nature of Doctrine: Religion and Theology in a Postliberal Age*. Philadelphia, PA: Westminster Press, 1984.
Logan, I., *Reading Anselm's Proslogion: The History of Anselm's Argument and its Significance Today*. Aldershot, UK: Ashgate, 2009.
Lohse, B., *Martin Luther's Theology: Its Historical and Systematic Development*. Edinburgh: T&T Clark, 1999.
Lonergan, B., *Method in Theology*. New York, NY: Seabury Press, 1972.
Lossky, V., *The Mystical Theology of the Eastern Church*. London: J. Clarke, 1957.
Louth, A., *Discerning the Mystery: An Essay on the Nature of Theology*. Oxford: Clarendon Press, 1983.
— 'The fourth-century Alexandrians: Athanasisus and Didymus'. In *The Cambridge History of Early Christian Literature*. Edited by Frances Young, Lewis Ayres and Andrew Louth, 275–82. Cambridge: Cambridge University Press, 2004.

Luther, M., 'The Freedom of a Christian'. In *A Reformation Reader: Primary Texts with Introductions*. 1st edn. Edited by Denis Janz. Minneapolis, MN: Fortress Press, 1999, pp. 98–106.

— D. *Martin Luthers Werke: Kritische Gesamtausgabe*. Weimar: Böhlau, 1883.

McCool, G. A., *A Rahner Reader*. New York, NY: Crossroad, 1984.

McCormack, B., 'What Has Basel to Do with Berlin? Continuities in the Theologies of Barth and Schleiermacher'. *Princeton Seminary Bulletin*, 23, 2 (2002), 146–73.

McGrath, A. E., *Christian Theology: An Introduction*. Malden, MA: Blackwell, 2007.

— *Luther's Theology of the Cross*. Oxford: Basil Blackwell, 1985.

McIntosh, M., *Mystical Theology*. Malden, MA: Blackwell, 1998.

McKim, D. (ed.), *Calvin's Institutes*. Abridged edition. Louisville, KY: Westminster John Knox, 2000.

Melanchthon, P., 'Apology of the Augsburg Confession'. In *A Reformation Reader: Primary Texts with Introductions*. 2nd edn. Edited by Denis Janz. Minneapolis, MN: Fortress Press, 1999, pp. 150–7.

— *Corpus reformatorum Philippi Melanthonis opera quae supersunt omnia*. Edited by C. B. Bretschneider and H. E. Bindseil. Halle: C.A. Schwetschke und Sohn, 1834–52 and Brunswick 1853–60.

— *Loci communes Theologici* In *Melanchthon and Bucer*, Library of Christian Classics, Vol. 19. Edited by Wilhelm Pauck. Translated by Lowell Satre and Wilhelm Pauck. Philadelphia, PA: Westminster Press, 1969.

— *Melanchthons Werke in Auswahl: Studienausgabe*. Edited by R. Stupperich. Gütersloh: Bertelsmann, 1963.

Merrigan, T., 'Revelation'. In *The Cambridge Companion to John Henry Newman*. Edited by Ian Ker and Terrence Merrigan. Cambridge: Cambridge University Press, 2009, pp. 47–72.

Meyer, B. F., *Critical Realism and the New Testament*. Allison Park, PA: Pickwick, 1989.

Milbank, J., *Theology and Social Theory: Beyond Secular Reason*. Oxford: Blackwell, 1990.

— 'Can a Gift be Given?' In *Rethinking Metaphysics*. Edited by Lg G. Jones and Stephen E. Fowl. Oxford: Blackwell, 1995, pp. 119–61.

— 'Postmodern Critical Augustinianism: A Short *Summa* in Forty-two Responses to Unasked Questions'. In *The Postmodern God: A Theological Reader*. Edited by Graham Ward. Oxford: Blackwell, 1997, pp. 265–78.

Myers, B., 'Faith as Self-Understanding: Towards a Post-Barthian Appreciation of Rudolf Bultmann'. *International Journal of Systematic Theology*, 10, 1 (2008), 21–35.

Nestingen, J. A., 'Approaching Luther'. In *The Cambridge Companion to Martin Luther*. Edited by Donald McKim and translated by Mark Mattes. Cambridge: Cambridge University Press, 2003, pp. 240–56.

Newman, J. H., *Essay on the Development of Christian Doctrine*. London: Sheed & Ward, 1960.

Nichols, A., *The Word has been Abroad: A Guide through Balthasar's Aesthetics*. Edinburgh: T&T Clark, 1998.

Norris, R., 'The Insufficiency of Scripture: *Adversus haereses* and the Role of Scripture in Irenaeus's Anti-Gnostic polemic'. In *Reading in Christian Communities: Essays on Interpretation in the Early Church: Essays on Interpretation in the Early Church*. Edited by Charles A. Bobetz and David Brakke. Notre Dame, IN: University of Notre Dame Press, 2002, pp. 63–79.

O'Collins, G., *The Tripersonal God: Understanding and Interpreting the Trinity*. Mahwah, NJ: Paulist, 1999.

O'Donnell, J., '*Doctrina, Christiana, De*'. In *Augustine Through the Ages: An Encyclopedia*. Edited by Allan D. Fitzgerald, O.S.A. Grand Rapids, MI: Eerdmans, 1999, pp. 278–80.

Ogden, S., 'The Significance of Rudolf Bultmann'. *Perkins Journal of Theology*, 15 (Winter 1962), 5–17.

Origen, *Against Celsus*. Edited by Henry Chadwick. Cambridge: Cambridge University Press, 1980.

— *Commentary on the Gospel According to John: Books 1–10*. Translated by Ronald E. Heine. The Fathers of the Church. Washington, DC: Catholic University of America Press, 1989.

— *Homily on Luke, Fragments on Luke*. Translated by Joseph T. Lienhard. Washington, DC: Catholic University Press of America, 1996.

— *On First Principles*. Translated by George W. Butterworth. Gloucester, MA: Peter Smith, 1973.

Osborn, E., *Irenaeus of Lyons*. Cambridge: Cambridge University Press, 2001.

Pattison, R., *The Great Dissent: John Henry Newman and the Liberal Heresy*. New York, NY: Oxford University Press, 1991.

Pauck, W., *The Heritage of the Reformation*. New York, NY: Oxford University Press, 1961.

Pegis, A. (ed.), *Basic Writings of Thomas Aquinas*, Vol. 1. New York, NY: Random House, 1945.

Pelikan, J., *Jesus through the Centuries: His Place in the History of Culture*. New York, NY: Harper and Row, 1985.

Pelikan, J. and Helmut T. Lehmann (eds). *Luther's Works*. St. Louis, MO: Concordia Publishing Co., and Philadelphia, PA: Fortress Press, 1955–86.

Peters, T., 'Truth in History: Gadamer's Hermeneutics and Pannenberg's Apologetic Method'. *Journal of Religion*, 55, 1 (1975), 36–56.

Pickstock, C., *After Writing: On the Liturgical Consummation of Philosophy*. Oxford: Blackwell, 1998.

Polanyi, M., *The Tacit Dimension*. New York, NY: Doubleday, 1967.

Porter, S., 'Paul and His Bible: His Education and Access to the Scriptures of Israel'. In *As It is Written: Studying Paul's Use of Scripture*. Edited by Stanley Porter and Christopher D. Stanley. Atlanta, GA: Society of Biblical Literature, 2008, pp. 97–124.

Quash, B. and J. Riches, 'Hans Urs von Balthasar'. In *The Modern Theologians*. Edited by David Ford. Oxford: Blackwell, 1997, pp. 134–51.

Rahner, K., *Theological Investigations* XI. New York, NY: Crossroad, 1960.

Räisänen, H., *Paul and the Law*. 2nd edn. Tübingen: Mohr, 1987.

Ratzinger, J., *Faith, Reason and the University: Memories and Reflections*. Aula magna of the University of Regensburg, 12 September 2006. Vatican Website. http://www.vatican.va/holy_father/benedict_xvi/speeches/2006/september/documents/hf_ben-xvi_spe_20060912_university-regensburg_en.html (accessed 15 December 2010).

—*Introduction to Christianity*. Translated by J. R. Foster. New York, NY: Continuum, 1986.

—*Jesus of Nazareth*. Translated by Adrian J. Walker. New York, NY: Doubleday, 2007.

—*Principles of Catholic Theology*. Translated by Sr Mary Frances McCarthy, S.N.D. San Francisco, CA: Ignatius Press, 1987.

Reischle, M., *Ein Wort zur Controverse über die Mystik in der Theologie*. Freiburg im Breisgau: J.C.B. Mohr [Paul Siebeck], 1886.

Reno, R., 'Origen and Spiritual Interpretation'. *Pro Ecclesia*, 15, 1 (2006), 108–26.

Richard, E., *First and Second Thessalonians*, Sacra Pagina Series, Vol. 11. Collegeville, MN: Liturgical Press, 1995.

Ricoeur, P., *From Text to Action: Essays in Hermeneutics*. Translated by Kathleen Blamey and John B. Thomson. Evanston, IL: Northwestern University Press, 1991.

Ritschl, A., *The Christian Doctrine of Justification and Reconciliation III*. Translated by H. R. Mackintosh and A. B. Macaulay. Edinburgh: T&T Clark, 1900.

Rumscheidt, H. M., *Revelation and Theology: An Analysis of the Barth-Harnack Correspondence of 1923*. Cambridge: Cambridge University Press, 1972.

Sanders, E. P., *Paul, the Law and the Jewish People*. London: SCM, 1983.

Schillebeeckx, E., *Christ: The Experience of Jesus as Lord*. Translated by John Bowden. New York, NY: Seabury, 1980.

—*Interim Report on the Books* Jesus *and* Christ. New York, NY: Crossroad, 1981.

—*Jesus: An Experiment in Christology*. Translated by Hubert Hoskins. New York, NY: Crossroad, 1989.

Schleiermacher, F. D. E., *Brief Outline of the Study of Theology*. Translated by Terrence N. Tice. Richmond, VA: John Knox Press, 1966.

— *The Christian Faith*. Edited by Hugh R. Mackintosh and James S. Stewart. Edinburgh: T&T Clark, 1999.

Schleiermacher, F. *On Religion: speeches to its cultured despisers*. New York, NY: Harper Torchbook, 1958.

Schoedel, W., 'Philosophy and Rhetoric in the Adversus Haereses of Irenaeus'. *Vigilae Christianae*, 13, 1 (1959), 22–32.

— 'Theological Method in Irenaeus (*Adversus haereses* 2.25–8)'. *Journal of Theological Studies* 35 (1984), 31–49.

Schreiter, R. (ed.), *The Schillebeeckx Reader*. New York, NY: Crossroad, 1987.

Schweitzer, A., *The Mysticism of Paul the Apostle*. London: A&C. Black, 1931.

Scott, M. S. M., *Journey Back to God: Origen on the Problem of Evil*. New York, NY: Oxford University Press, 2012.

— 'Suffering and Soul-Making: Rethinking John Hick's Theodicy'. *Journal of Religion*, 90, 3 (2010), 313–34.

Smith, J. K. A., *Introducing Radical Orthodoxy: Mapping a Post-Secular Theology*. Grand Rapids, MI: Baker Academic, 2004.

Soskice, J. M., 'Athens and Jerusalem, Alexandria and Edessa: Is there a Metaphysics of Scripture?' *International Journal of Systematic Theology*, 8, 2 (2006), 149–62.

Strabo, *The Geography*, Loeb Classical Library. 8 vols. Translated by Horace L. Jones after John R. S. Sterrett. Cambridge, MA: Harvard University Press, 1960–70.

Strauss, G., *Luther's House of Learning: Indoctrination of the Young in the German Reformation*. Baltimore, MD: Johns Hopkins University Press, 1978.

Sykes, S. (ed.), *Karl Barth: Studies of his Theological Method*. Oxford: Clarendon Press, 1979.

Tanner, K., 'How I changed My Mind'. In *Shaping a Theological Mind: Theological Context and Methodology*. Edited by Darren C. Marks. Aldershot, UK: Ashgate, 2002, pp. 115–22.

Taylor, C., *Philosophical Arguments*. Cambridge: Cambridge University Press, 1995.

te Velde, R., *Aquinas on God: The 'Divine Science' of the* Summa Theologiae. Aldershot, UK: Ashgate, 2006.

Thompson, J. T., 'Calvin as Biblical Interpreter'. In *The Cambridge Companion to Calvin*. Edited by Donald K. McKim. Cambridge: Cambridge University Press, 2004, pp. 58–73.

Thornton, J. F. and S. B. Varenne (eds), *The Essential Pope Benedict XVI: His Essential Writings and Speeches*. New York, NY: HarperCollins, 2007.

Tillich, P., *The Courage to Be*. New Haven, CT: Yale University Press, 1952.

—'The Problem of Theological Method'. In *Paul Tillich: Theologian of the Boundaries*. Edited by Mark Kline Taylor. London: Collins, 1987, pp. 126–41.

—*Systematic Theology*, Vols 1–3. Chicago, IL: University of Chicago Press, 1951–63.

—'Theology and Symbolism'. In *Religious Symbols*. Edited by F. Ernest Johnson. New York, NY: Harper and Row, 1955.

Torrance, T., *Theological Science*. Oxford: Oxford University Press, 1969.

Torrell, J.-P., *Aquinas's Summa Background, Structure and Reception*. Washington, DC: Catholic University of America Press, 2005.

Trigg, J. W., *Origen: The Bible and Philosophy in the Third Century*. London: SCM Press, 1983.

Vanhoozer, K., *First Theology: God, Scripture and Hermeneutics*. Downers Grove, IL: Intervarsity Press, 2002.

Wallace, R., *Calvin, Geneva and the Reformation: A Study of Calvin as Social Reformer, Churchman, Pastor and Theologian*. Edinburgh: Scottish Academic Press, 1988.

Watson, F., 'Is There a Story in these texts?' In *Narrative Dynamics in Paul: A Critical Assessment*. Edited by Bruce W. Longenecker. Louisville, KY: Westminster John Knox Press, 2002, pp. 231–9.

—*Paul and the Hermeneutics of Faith*. London: T&T Clark, 2004.

Williams, J. P., 'Pseudo Dionysius and Maximus the Confessor'. In *The First Christian Theologians*. Edited by Gillian R. Evans, pp. 196–200. Oxford: Blackwell, 2004.

Williams, R. 'Language, Reality and Desire in Augustine's *De doctrina Christiana*'. *The Journal of Literature and Theology*, 3, 2 (1989), 138–50.

—'Origen'. In *The First Christian Theologians*. Edited by Gillian R. Evans. Oxford: Blackwell, 2004, pp. 132–42.

Witherington, B., *The Jesus Quest: The Third Search for the Jew of Nazareth*. Downers Grove, IL: Intervarsity Press, 1997.

Wrede, W., *Paul*. London: Philip Green, 1907.

INDEX